A NEW HEARTLAND

A NEW HEARTLAND

Women, Modernity, and the Agrarian Ideal in America

Janet Galligani Casey

2009

OXFORD
UNIVERSITY PRESS

Oxford University Press, Inc., publishes works that further
Oxford University's objective of excellence
in research, scholarship, and education.

Oxford New York
Auckland Cape Town Dar es Salaam Hong Kong Karachi
Kuala Lumpur Madrid Melbourne Mexico City Nairobi
New Delhi Shanghai Taipei Toronto

With offices in
Argentina Austria Brazil Chile Czech Republic France Greece
Guatemala Hungary Italy Japan Poland Portugal Singapore
South Korea Switzerland Thailand Turkey Ukraine Vietnam

Published by Oxford University Press, Inc.
198 Madison Avenue, New York, New York 10016

www.oup.com

Library of Congress Cataloging-in-Publication Data
Casey, Janet Galligani.
A new heartland : women, modernity, and the agrarian ideal in America / Janet Galligani Casey.
p. cm.
Includes bibliographical references and index.
ISBN 978-0-19-533895-9
1. American fiction—20th century—History and criticism. 2. Pastoral fiction, American—History and criticism.
3. Women in literature. 4. Farm life in literature. 5. Rural conditions in literature. 6. Literature and society—
United States—History—20th century. I. Title.
PS223.C36 2009
810'.9'0052—dc22 2008030331

1 3 5 7 9 8 6 4 2

Printed in the United States of America
on acid-free paper

For

Francis J. Galligani

and in memory of

Neil A. Malmquist

ACKNOWLEDGMENTS

I HAVE INCURRED many debts in researching and writing this book. Not least of these is to the numerous and varied scholars and writers—rural historians, literary critics, social and aesthetic theorists—who are freely referenced here, and whose work has enabled and enlightened mine. I have also benefited enormously from those rural women of the early twentieth century who are quoted throughout chapters 1 and 2: collectively they generated a spirited body of inquiry and opinion that allowed me to better understand my subject, especially the nuances of the artistic texts that first sparked my interest in women, rurality, and modernity.

Special thanks go to those directly involved in my archival work. Patty Dean and Debbie Miller of the Minnesota Historical Society offered invaluable on-site assistance at an early stage and continued to tender encouragement and advice from a distance as the project unfolded. Chatham Ewing of the Washington University Library and John Fleischmann, literary executor of the Josephine Johnson Estate, were quite helpful and encouraging regarding my work on Johnson. Jane Aldrich of the South Carolina Historical Society helped me to unravel the tangled web of rights and permissions related to the photographs of Doris Ulmann. Professor Faye Hammill of the University of Strathclyde generously discussed her work on Martha Ostenso, initiating an ongoing and valuable collegial relationship. And I was privileged to spend a most delightful evening in the company of Sarah Carroll Watson (daughter of Gladys Hasty Carroll), who shared with me a vast collection of historical materials, including, to my great pleasure, treasured films of her mother's Depression-era folk play, *As the Earth Turns.*

The trips necessary to visit particular people and places naturally required funding, which took the form of research grants from the College of the Holy Cross, the National Coalition of Independent Scholars, and the Maine Women Writers' Collection, all of which furthered my primary research considerably. I am especially grateful to the National Endowment for the Humanities: when I was ready for serious writing, an NEH fellowship provided the time to commit to paper the bulk of the manuscript. I am also indebted to the various conference attendees—at meetings of the Modern Language Association, the Rural Women's Studies Association, the American Literature Association, the American Culture and Popular Culture Associations, and the Newberry Seminar in Rural History—who helped me to launch my ideas, as well as to the anonymous Oxford University Press reviewers who stimulated me, at the very end, to refine them.

Permission to quote from correspondence and/or reproduce images has been granted by the following: the Special Collections Research Center, Morris Library, Southern Illinois University, Carbondale; the Lilly Library, Indiana University, Bloomington; the Rare and Manuscript Collections, Cornell University Library, including the College of Human Ecology Historical Photographs; the Maine Women Writers Collection, University of New England; the Miguel Covarrubias Estate; the Maine Historical Society; the Special Collections and University Archives, University of Oregon Libraries; the University of Kentucky Archives; and the South Carolina Historical Society. In addition, portions of chapter 2 and chapter 4 have appeared previously, in different form, as "'This Is YOUR Magazine': Domesticity, Agrarianism, and *The Farmer's Wife*" (*American Periodicals* 14.2 [2004]), and "Agrarian Landscapes, the Depression, and Women's Progressive Fiction" (*The Novel and the American Left: Critical Essays on Depression-Era Fiction* [Iowa UP, 2004]); the publishers of these works have kindly consented to their use herein.

Since arriving at Skidmore College in 2001, I have enjoyed the conviviality and good humor of a warm and lively group of colleagues whose interest and support have been integral to my work; I wish especially to thank Terry Diggory, Susan Kress, Linda Simon, Mason Stokes, and, in particular, Adrienne Zuerner. Susannah Mintz has been that rarest of friends, a comradely scholar and a scholarly comrade. Beyond the Skidmore circle, Maria Frawley and Richard Carson offered material assistance (in the form of reading grant applications), as well as intellectual energy and abiding friendship, all of which are much appreciated. Andrea Lachance and Bruce Lauber hosted me during a key research venture, and have given me, for decades now, a great deal more besides. Thanks, too, to Patricia Grisafi and Katherine Marantz, my former students, who served as able and enthusiastic research assistants, and to Shannon McLachlan, Christina Gibson, and Heather Hartman of Oxford University Press, who saw the book through production.

Not surprisingly, I owe my greatest debt to my family members, who have lived cheerfully with this and other projects over the course of many years. My husband, Michael Casey, remains my first reader and most respected and intelligent critic; our children, Liam and Fiona, challenge and sustain us in all the ways that matter.

Finally, this book is dedicated to my father and to the memory of my uncle, who taught me, by example, to do what I love and love what I do.

CONTENTS

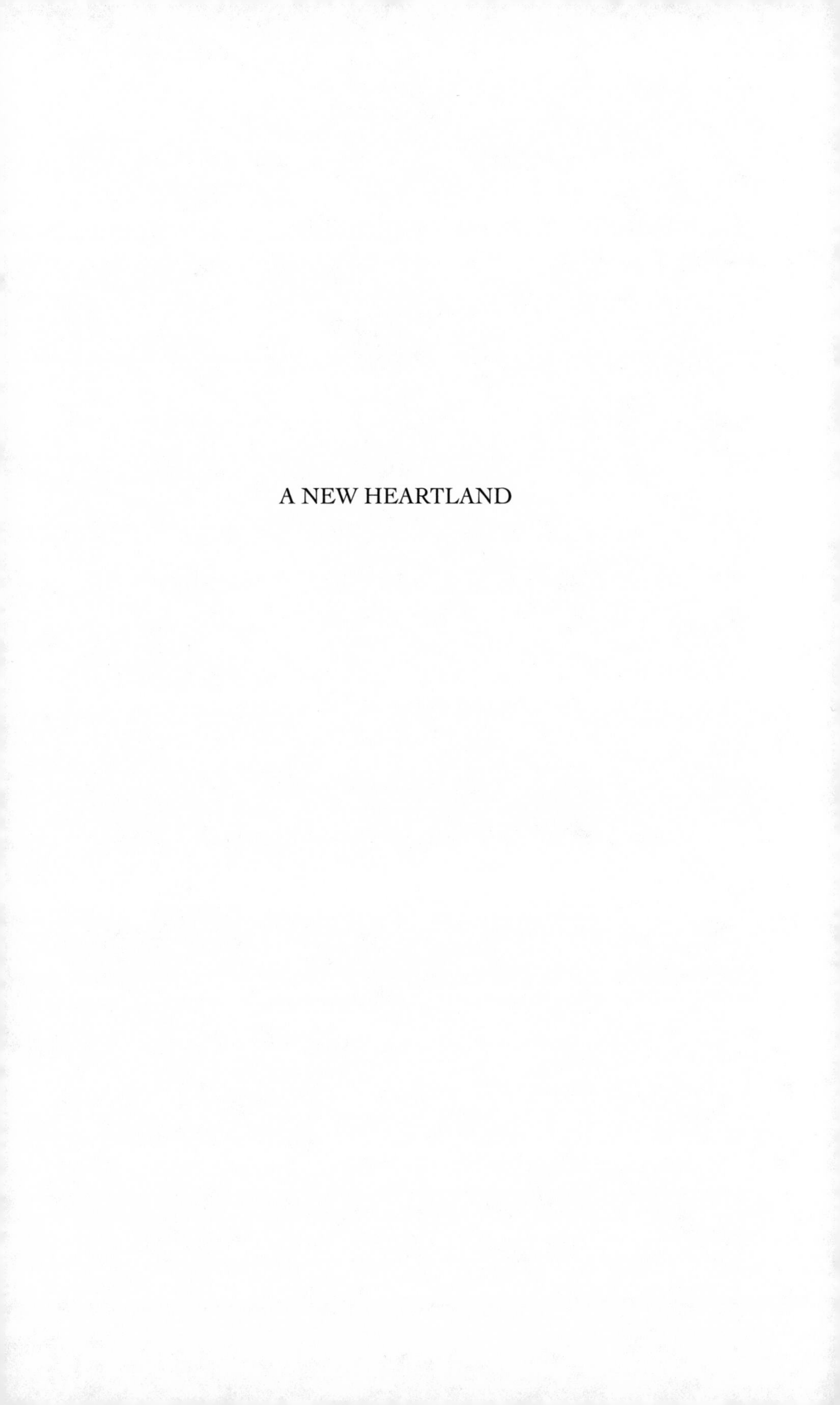

A NEW HEARTLAND

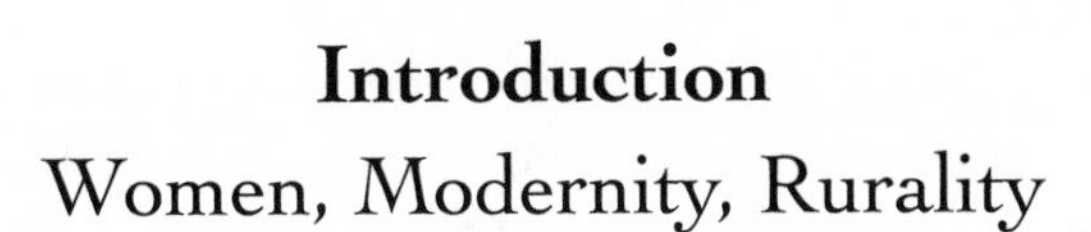

Introduction
Women, Modernity, Rurality

A New Heartland reconceptualizes modernity by focusing on rurality and women. It challenges the notion of the city as the privileged site of modern experience, arguing that rurality—urbanity's opposite, frequently associated with nostalgia and feminine sentimentality—was a fruitful geographic and psychic location for registering women's perceptions of the modern. This is partly due to the recognition that actual rural women, enmeshed in the newly textured ideologies of agrarianism, Americanism, domesticity, and progress, were forced to contend with a modern ethos that radically redefined them and their work, and that exposed the fault lines in the rhetorical construction of a "classless" society. More important, however, is that the twentieth-century American farm served as an especially potent signifier of gendered and nativist values that were being rapidly reconfigured, offering a convenient and compelling point of convergence for protean discourses of inclusion and exclusion, freedom and containment, advancement and tradition. This book, then, investigates the relations between a precisely situated social group negotiating the claims of modernity and the discursive realms and representational aesthetics that drew on that group to re/imagine class, race, and gender in modern America.

Yet, as its title implies, this project is less about the empirical facts of farm life than about its abstractions. It is primarily about the *idea* of rurality, and the ways in which women were positioned, by themselves and others, in reference to it. Of course, since abstractions are related, however obliquely, to real-life circumstances, I explore some of the intersections between the conceptual and the actual, notably in terms of rural women's occasional responses to those discourses and theories by which others attempted to define or appropriate them. First and foremost, though, this project attends to language, to images, and to figurative connections. It demonstrates the theoretical importance of rurality to the imaginative construction of American modernity and modernism, and it asserts that women had a special stake in that relation. In the process, it breaks new ground, since the affiliation between rurality and modernity has been largely overlooked.

Indeed, assumptions about the mutually constitutive relations between modernity and urbanity have obscured, and continue to obscure, rurality's conspicuousness in American culture from the earliest years of the century through the Great Depression. Studies of modernity and the city proliferate, in both broadly cultural and more specifically literary manifestations.[1] Yet rurality was never far from the center of consideration in this period, even if it was most frequently posited as a counterexample to the values of the modern urban imaginary. And, significantly, the articulation of rurality's difference was often noticeably gendered. On one hand, rurality could be linked to a hardiness and virility that countered the effeteness and overcivilization of the city, as Theodore Roosevelt argued. On the other hand, the association of the rural with a bygone America marked it as passive and conventional, an essentially feminine arena in need of masculinist reforms. Of course, this gendering of rurality was a thing apart from the actual experiences of rural citizens, though the two were hardly unconnected. For both rural and urban *women,* the relations between a revered or regressive agrarianism—depending on one's point of view—and ideas about female roles and behaviors reverberated powerfully within a modern culture preoccupied with both gender and work.

This was true even in the realm of the literary. As Michael North has observed, for instance, Willa Cather's fame was at its peak at the very moment when *Ulysses* and *The Waste Land* were published; the "massive condescension of the younger male [modernists]" toward Cather in the early 1920s had as much to do with her supposedly sentimental content as with her comparatively conventional form, both of which were coded derisively as feminine. That her books continued to sell briskly and that she has always been accommodated within more liberal accounts of modernist literary history has not made up entirely for this imposition of a second-rate status. The much-ballyhooed "modern spirit" allegedly embodied by male, city-oriented writers such as Joyce and Eliot made Cather's rural narratives, universally hailed to that point, seem abruptly obsolete, a judgment that she deeply resented but that has nonetheless lingered throughout the twentieth century.[2]

My objection to a version of modernist literature that could bracket a writer of Cather's force and stature largely motivates this project, as it has motivated others before me.[3] Yet my argument—perhaps surprisingly—is not really about Cather at all but, rather, about attitudes toward rurality and women more generally: that is, the cultural climate within which work such as Cather's was created and received. Prevailing critical wisdom long posited Cather as something of an anomaly in the modern literary canon; her association with realism and midwestern rurality, as opposed to the formal experimentation and urban preoccupation of Eliot, Joyce, and others, is key to comprehending her equivocal status as an acclaimed, best-selling, but somehow "backward" modern writer.[4] (Not until the 1930s would William Faulkner legitimate American rurality as a setting for high art, largely by linking it to avant-garde narrative techniques.) But Cather's relevance shifts substantially depending on the lens through which we view her achievement. A broader understanding of the centrality of rural-agrarian concerns to early twentieth-century American culture, and especially to women's culture, implicitly places Cather at the center of a series of rhetorical debates and aesthetic enterprises that exploited notions of rurality and womanhood to interrogate modernity. And while a great deal has been written about Cather and her oeuvre, very little consideration has been given to this larger modern-rural context—a context that deserves and rewards attention in its own right.

That context includes, among other things, a rather large body of farm fiction that was quite popular. If urbanity seemed to be the territory of the avant-garde, rurality was aligned firmly with more accessible structures and images, and hence with broader audiences. This may have hindered its acceptance in the most exalted aesthetic circles, as Cather's case suggests, but it nonetheless reflected and reinforced the fascination that rurality still held for a swiftly urbanizing nation. And this preoccupation with the country was hardly confined to fiction; on the contrary, rurality's visibility was indisputable across a wide range of imagistic and discursive domains, making it quite relevant, even essential, to a consideration of the meanings and manifestations of modernity. This book explores that heretofore unexplored terrain, demonstrating that, without a doubt, rurality as both lived experience and iconographic sign occupied a solid position in modern perspectives. This was especially true in the United States, where the rural approached mythic status in its perceived importance to the nation's founding and development.

In fact, rurality was everywhere, sometimes in places that seem, in retrospect, quite remarkable. For example, the self-consciously bourgeois *Ladies' Home Journal* carried a long-running editorial feature penned by the Country Contributor (a.k.a. Juliet Virginia Strauss) that regularly considered women and modernity through the prism of rurality. The Country Contributor is of interest not only because she raises questions pertinent to this study—what varied shapes might modernity take for rural women, and how does a centering of rurality and its concerns allow us to reframe notions of modernity as well as gender?—but also due to the very vehicle of her discussion. Her column was published monthly between 1905 and 1918, and its title, "Ideas of a Plain Country Woman," suggests its positioning relative to the presumed audience of *Ladies' Home Journal.* That the writer was both *plain* and from the *country* situated her in opposition to the middle-class, sub/urban readers who presumably devoured the magazine's sentimental stories and combed its pages of glossy advertisements: to be sure, the Country Contributor regularly railed against reading contemporary fiction (claiming that it advanced "morbid" and immoral models for women) and lamented women's excessive attention to appearances. A champion of motherhood and the old-fashioned domestic circle, she proclaimed that "Country Folk Have Life's Real Luxuries" and that "the gadding habit" of city dwellers had created "a race of practically homeless people" searching restlessly for new amusements and permanently unmoored from the "anchorage" of home. She professed not to understand those women who harbor "social longings" or who "try to imitate the false Bourgeoisie"—in other words, the very women who constituted the magazine's target audience.[5]

If we are to believe the editor of *Ladies' Home Journal,* the Country Contributor's column was among its most popular departments (a point regularly mentioned in an accompanying editorial note), raising the question of just how its deployment of liminality functioned within a publication deliberately catering to a homogeneous, consumerist, contrivedly *modern* female ideal. In the 1890s, owner Cyrus Curtis had gone to great lengths to associate *Ladies' Home Journal* with a cosmopolitan audience, deliberately distancing it from its origins as a farm magazine; by 1900, it was clearly identified as a middle-class periodical targeted at women with sufficient discretionary income to support its advertisers. In 1910, Curtis oversaw construction in downtown Philadelphia of a state-of-the-art building, including a lavish ballroom, to house the magazine's offices, thereby monumentalizing the link between the *Journal* and a style-conscious readership. Evidence suggests, however, that the publication continued to be read by farm women, who could only aspire to its urban-oriented standards, demonstrating the growing prescriptive influence of magazines as vehicles of mainstream culture.[6] But if it is relatively easy to understand farm women's attraction to the *Journal,* it is not so clear why the *Journal* made room for the Country Contributor—an inclusion that reveals less about the country, it appears, than about the *Journal*'s careful mediation of modernity.

That the Country Contributor was less antagonistic to contemporary shifts in values than she claimed to be is, from our vantage point, rather obvious: despite her repeated refusal to endorse suffrage for women, for instance, she was relatively outspoken about such issues as sex education and hinted that women needed ways to define themselves outside of the marital relation. One recent historian of *Ladies' Home Journal* points out that the Country Contributor even evinced within her columns, and through the very act of writing them, some uncertainty regarding the supposed superiority of country life and domestic avocations, a subtext that betrays her ambivalence about women's paid work and that effectively extends, rather than counters, the magazine's general irresolution regarding women's proper sphere.[7] Of essential importance here, however, is that her projection of these attitudes through the lens of rurality mobilized a host of unspoken assumptions about what modernity itself might *mean.* Rurality, that is, suggestively located this columnist within a romantic past rather than an unstable present, aligning her with a life of production rather than consumption and with a homespun, plainspoken "wisdom" that appeared to set at bay the proliferating specialized discourses clamoring for the attention of the modern reader. (This despite the saturation of rural culture itself by agricultural reform rhetorics and the emerging idiom of agribusiness.) Above all, a stable rural *womanhood* was explicitly contraposed in her columns to an array of confusing and contradictory roles for women that seemed rooted in, and even promoted by, a modernity equated with urbanity.[8]

My point is not only that the Country Contributor fails to reify a simplistic connection between reactionary perspectives and rurality, but also that her engagement with contemporary women's issues was fruitfully situated within the context of a rurality that she promoted as nonmodern or even antimodern. Indeed, the construction of modernity in *Ladies' Home Journal* was in some way dependent on the trenchant cultural significations that were put into play, at least in part, by the Country Contributor.[9] On the surface, of course, rural culture might seem something of an embarrassment to a society, and a magazine, in the throes of a self-conscious modernity; at the very least, rurality's presumed provincialism would appear to render it irrelevant to the energy, innovation, and forward-mindedness perceived as characteristic of a progressive modern world. And yet the popularity of the Country Contributor suggests the importance of keeping rurality visible, both as an ideological foil for modernity's anxieties and instabilities and as a nationalist legacy that needed to be accommodated within the matrix of experience and representation understood as modern. (Not to mention the need to avoid alienating completely the rural female audience, hence selling more magazines.) In the pages of *Ladies' Home Journal,* then, where occasional suggestions about appropriately economical attire for the country woman appeared beside slick advertisements for lacy corsets and fancy layettes, and where the Country Contributor held sway for some thirteen years, rurality was enfolded into the modernist positioning of the magazine as much as it was set up as a contrast to it.

This complex interrelation reflected the altered dynamics of social space in the United States. Population shifts and an influx of immigrants to urban centers meant that, by the 1920s, the American populace was more than half urban. Mass culture media—magazines, newspapers, radio—helped to erode distinctions between the rural and the urban consciousness, while railroads and the automobile made travel between the country and the city more convenient than ever. For some, rurality seemed in danger of being subsumed by urbanity. Yet the newly teeming cities introduced a host of social problems, even as the "city-drift" (as some rural commentators called rural out-migration) precipitated a crisis in the country. The sense that agrarianism must be preserved, not merely because of its centrality to American history and identity but also as a social alternative to urban upheavals, notably racial and ethnic ones, was pronounced, even—perhaps especially—among urban social institutions. For example, a "sisterhood" pageant promoted by the Young Women's Christian Association around 1915 dramatized earlier episodes from American history as failed moments of redemption and clearly privileged the rural as the salvation of modern urban culture. In the pageant's Puritan episode, for instance, white girls are not yet ready to extend fellowship to Indian girls, nor to "colored girls" in the Civil War scene. In the "modern" episode, however, robust, laughing young women emerge from a field of wildflowers to succor successfully a group of "tired and wan" female factory workers; all are presumably white.[10] Against such a backdrop, the Country Contributor's presence in *Ladies' Home Journal* seems less odd, for she, too, reminded urbanites of the restorative power of a "natural" lifestyle that, not coincidentally, seemed removed from racial tensions. And nature helped to sell consumer products beyond magazines and pageants: since "natural" goodness was more and more prominently featured in advertisements for factory-made commodities, it was part and parcel of the acquisitive lifestyle that *Ladies' Home Journal* promoted.

To be sure, the notion of modernity adopted and distilled by mainstream women's publications such as *Ladies' Home Journal,* centered on consumption and "up-to-date-ness," differed from the literary-critical notion of modernism as a "high" aesthetic enterprise, and differed yet again from the concept of social progressivism, or even revolution, that inheres in more broadly cultural notions of the modern. That this study seeks to engage with all these aspects of modern life underscores its investment in a geosocial space rather than a particular cultural posture—a "real" ground, so to speak, rather than an epistemological one. I am interested in rurality as both a conceptual and a literal site that was poised in contradistinction to notions of the modern on virtually all cultural fronts, even as it was itself deeply engaged with modernity. Furthermore, I will argue that rurality called forth especially complicated commentary on the part of women. It is my contention that this has a great deal to do with the special status of rurality in American life, not merely in terms of its alignment with nationalist values but also because of its dual importance to figurative projections and actual circumstances. That is, rural life in the United States resonates historically both with the spatial metaphors of a masculinist aesthetic imagination (captured in such pithy phrases as "Go West, Young Man" or "the lay of the land") and with the gendered ideologies of constructed space that shape the material lives of real women. Inherited modes of representation and inherited models of gendered labor were equally threatened in the early twentieth century; the farm, always iconically potent as the legatee of a pioneering past but nevertheless undergoing vast structural changes, brought these issues to the fore. The result, I suggest, is that rurality in the modernist period presented itself as a provocative cultural setting for nuanced critiques of both invented and lived female experience.

Consequently, this book considers the interpenetration of imaginative and "real-life" realms, treating rural texts by women as literary-historical artifacts that are elucidated equally by considerations of imagistic traditions in literature and art, and by sociopolitical agendas that dictated agricultural and gender reforms. It considers idea(l)s of women and rurality across a field of discourses and representational arenas, including social theory, periodical literature, literary criticism, photography, and, most especially, women's rural fiction. At the heart of this book is a reconsideration of several key novels by and about agrarian women, nearly all of which were critically acclaimed but now remain canonically marginalized. I maintain that these novels collectively challenged prevalent ideologies of American agrarianism at a historical moment marked by agricultural crisis, thus engaging with both conceptual and actual paradigms of rural life, and intersecting with notions of the modern—ideational as well as experiential—in key ways. Read in conjunction with other representations and discussions of farm women in varied media (including the discourses of the New Agriculture premised on the assumption that American agrarianism was in need of modernization), these works reframe both rurality and modernity by positioning the former within the concerns of the latter. In the most extreme cases, the rural landscape is postulated as a setting for radical revisionings of class, gender, and American identity. At minimum, however, women's representations of rurality emerge not as marginal to, but as a coherent idiom of, American modernism, wrestling with many of the same issues—technology, reproductive choice, shifting gender relations, commodification—that we associate with more celebrated versions of modernist cultural production, and offering profoundly different possibilities for the relations between rurality and modern "progress" as compared with those put forth by men.

As a case in point, we might consider what is surely the most famous fictional representation of rurality and social radicalism in the period under consideration here: John Steinbeck's *Grapes of Wrath*. Although not modernist in the high literary sense of that word—an issue I will address momentarily—Steinbeck's novel nonetheless takes up an aspect of modernity, namely, the industrialization of agriculture, and explores in provocative ways the accompanying tensions between stasis and change, both in the literal terms of the battle between "old" and "new" visions of farming and in the range of possible aesthetic responses to that reality.[11] Moreover, the relative dignity with which Steinbeck treats rural people and his unironic presentation of their potential for progressive action accommodate rurality within the experiential context of a reflective modernity—as opposed, say, to the work of Faulkner, in which rural people are often grotesques playing out the alienating effects of a modernity that is beyond their own understanding. Yet despite its apparent progressivism, Steinbeck's novel also draws on traditional figurations of rurality that implicitly do violence to women. Specifically, in premising its ideals of collective, reformist action on the fundamentally conservative values of the yeoman farmer, *Grapes* draws upon an interlocking set of assumptions and images through which, as various scholars have shown, the open landscape, a patriarchal social system, and the notion of "Americanness" have been compellingly conflated.[12] By the 1930s, the farmer had long been established as the virtual embodiment of the American way, ensuring that the displacement of the Okies would carry a symbolic weight that could not be approached by parallel Depression narratives of urban impoverishment. And if the farmer epitomized Jeffersonian ideals of autonomy, nobility, virtue, and thrift, then his wife became the ground upon which such ideals were realized. Nowhere is this more powerfully clear than in Steinbeck's final scene, in which the young Rose of Sharon offers her breast and its milk as fortification for an emaciated man, thereby reframing the maternal body as a means of ideological propagation, making visible the (rural) female's assumed role as nurturer for a body politic that is inheritably male.

The example of Steinbeck contrasts sharply, as we shall see, with certain texts by women that radically reconfigure the relations among female bodies, agriculture, and social imperatives. Yet Steinbeck is useful as a reminder of the hegemony of classic masculinist paradigms of agrarianism (even within a text perceived as insurrectionary in its anticapitalism) and points, again, to the expressive impact of rural tropes within disparate modes of modernist discourse. If Steinbeck shares anything with the Country Contributor, or indeed with a high modernist such as Faulkner, it is a deployment of rurality that helps to shape a conception of the modern, whether in terms of leftist political ideals, shifting notions of gender roles relayed by popular culture media, or aesthetic formulations of dislocation and crisis. This is not to deny or minimize the very real differences among these writers, but rather to suggest the influence and prominence of rurality across a range of versions of the modern. And it is here that a few words about those versions, those *modernities,* are in order.

This project inserts itself into the new work on modernity not by seeking to establish an overriding definition that accommodates the various texts addressed herein but by attempting to float multiple notions of the modern simultaneously, a tactic that reflects recent theoretical perspectives of modernity as culturally and textually variegated, and that remains faithful to the range of uses the term enjoyed in the first forty years of the twentieth century. While our understanding of modernity, especially in reference to gender, has been altered in irrevocable ways by sweeping studies such as those by Alice Jardine, Sandra Gilbert and Susan Gubar, and Andreas Huyssen, this project is particularly indebted to more recent theoretical stances that resist reducing the modern to a single explanatory narrative or historical logic, or even to a particular disciplinary perspective.[13] Modernity has become a newly invigorated category resonating with acknowledged disruptions in virtually all areas of lived and represented experience in the years between 1900 and 1940; I employ the rubric here as a means of periodizing that sense of disruption (acknowledging, of course, that we might draw lines at other temporal points)[14] and, more specifically, as a signifier of a self-conscious break with the past—its methods, its ideas, its cultural authorities, its presumed hierarchies. The search for and/or negotiation of fresh modes of behavior, understanding, and expression, which seemed to be emerging at an accelerated rate, is thus characteristic of modernity as I define it here. However, I reject the notion, often perpetuated by classic literary-critical studies of the period, that these new modes were always, or necessarily, liberating. One of the premises of this study is that the writers and social critics I discuss had clear, if different, ideas of what constituted the modern, and that they viewed its alleged promises as deeply unsettling as well as potentially exhilarating.

This was not unrelated to their choice of rurality as a signifying cultural setting: rural culture, like most subcultures in the United States, was undergoing enormous changes in the first few decades of the twentieth century and was deeply affected by claims that it was ill adapted to the exigencies of modern life. It is not often noted that the rapid industrialization of agriculture in this period—accompanied, as William Conlogue points out, by the development of the farm novel genre[15]—corresponded to the emergence of other aspects of modernity that have enjoyed more critical attention, including the perceived crisis over modes of representation in the aesthetic realm, the increasing popularity of magazines and newspapers as mediators of cultural values, the growing instability of traditional gender roles, and the rising influence of the organized Left. But when we position rurality within the concerns of such cultural currents, as I attempt to do here, we stand to gain a deeper understanding of how a lived experience of the modern was constituted for a particular social group in the United States. Even more important, I hope that we may also acquire a usefully complicated and more carefully situated appreciation of aesthetic works that draw on rurality as a means of responding to modernity.

With this in mind, I have found Rita Felski's study of modernity especially useful in shaping my perspectives, as it raises issues pertinent to a consideration of rurality, modernity, and representation. In *The Gender of Modernity,* Felski argues that sociology and literature were "mutually determining" discourses at the beginning of the century, and that the rise of sociology "affected the ways in which all of us envision the modern"—an especially relevant point, since rural sociology, in particular, became a legitimate branch of study in the late teens and early 1920s, and since its masculinist focus shaped ideologies of the modern farm woman, as I discuss in chapter 1. Further, Felski focuses on the tradition/modernity distinction at the heart of sociological thought and addresses the tendency by intellectuals to construct the nostalgic impulse (a "destructive desire to regress" due to the "dislocations of the modern age") as reactionary. Felski insists that such theorizations overlook the possibility that nostalgia can function as a valid means of critique: "While on the one hand nostalgic desire glosses over the oppressive dimensions of the past for which it yearns, on the other hand it may mobilize a powerful condemnation of the present for its failure to correspond to the imagined harmony of a prelapsarian condition. The yearning for the past may engender active attempts to construct an alternative future, so that nostalgia comes to serve a critical rather than a simply conservative purpose."[16] Felski's perspective has important implications for an exploration of rurality and modernity. Rural society in the United States was often simplistically associated with a premodern idyll, yet nostalgia for that falsely unproblematic past also drove a host of agricultural reforms designed to modernize farming both to increase its imagistic appeal and to make it economically feasible for Americans to return to it or remain with it. Moreover, as we can see with the Country Contributor, recourse to nostalgia offered a context of presumed stability that focalized in acceptable ways critiques of both the present and the past, helping to contain their threatening qualities. In their precarious attempts to mediate nostalgia and critique, then, analyses of rural culture in the early twentieth century constituted an *instance* of modernity even as rurality as an (oppositional) ideological construct helped to further refine notions of an urban-modern hegemony. Rurality thus offers multiple entry points for a consideration of the modern and its various conceptualizations, which can only deepen our understanding of its role in the period's representational texts.

By necessity, and in line with Felski's approach, this study addresses "high" and "low" forms of cultural production and considers political, economic, and social contexts as well as artistic ones. Like Felski, Thomas Strychacz, Ann Ardis, and others, I acknowledge the pressures imposed by the variety of professional rhetorics, epistemological practices, and aesthetic forms newly competing in the modernist period for a piece of the cultural pie. This plurality of interests in manifestations of the modern, however, does not mean that I reject the association of modern*ism* with a particularized aesthetic tradition. On the contrary, despite the many revisionist studies that have demonstrated that the aesthetic enterprise termed "modernism" is only one of many forms of modernist cultural production, the term retains its usefulness as a signifier of a predominantly masculinist group of philosophical attitudes, professional poses, and, especially, formalist experiments against which other aesthetic enterprises of the period have been and continue to be read. (Indeed, it is especially significant as a foil for virtually everything that rurality is not.)[17] These include emphases on the artwork's self-referentiality and an apparent disengagement from the specifics of the contemporary sociopolitical landscape, as well as a pronounced rejection of inherited methods of representation. I find it essential, however, to adopt the now widespread practice of referring to this aesthetic tradition, perhaps best represented in American literature by Eliot, Pound, and Faulkner, as "high modernism," thereby distinguishing it from the broader term "modernism, which includes alternative modes of artistic production in the period as well, notably those with which women have more frequently engaged. ("Modernization" will refer to the perceived improvement of material circumstances through technological and methodological advances, including, notably, the drive for efficiency and increased productivity in both domestic work and field labor. "Modernity" and the "modern" are inclusive terms that embrace any or all of the preceding, and that circumscribe a historical period. The coterminous designation "Progressive Era," also used in this study, invokes the centrality of legislative reform to perceived progressive efforts and is commonly used in rural sociology, among other disciplines; it remains useful due to its special relevance to farming.)[18]

Of key significance is that the recent, capacious definition of literary modernism makes room for the inclusion of realism, long understood as high modernism's opposite. It is now a critical commonplace to note that realism was especially efficacious for many women and minority writers in the period, for whom an accessible representational aesthetic was crucial. In 1988, in *The Social Construction of American Realism,* Amy Kaplan offered a new vision of how realist novels function, positing them as less concerned with mimesis than with "actively creat[ing] and criticiz[ing] the meanings, representations, and ideologies of [their] own changing culture." Kaplan's reframing of realism as an argument, an intervention, a dialectical effort to contend with the threats of social disruptions, has helped to reconceptualize notions of modernist production: the realistic novel, no longer critically viable as a static record of a world outside of itself, must be seen as "an attempt to mediate and negotiate competing claims to social reality by making alternative realities visible while managing their explosive qualities." Her assertion that the realist novel must grapple with "emergent forms of mass media" is especially relevant here, since I am interested in a network of social, economic, and representational discourses that do not privilege the self-consciously literary.[19] In short, Kaplan's study has allowed us to position realism within, rather than against, the grain of a modernism understood, at least in part, as an ontological effort to locate and explore increasingly fluid cultural imperatives. Such attitudes have broadened the validated range of aesthetic responses to modern life, making room for a style and approach that was used effectively and variously by women.

Just as modernism is broadly defined here, so too is rurality. If "heartland" in American parlance has tended to connote the Midwest (and was perhaps first used in this way by Des Moines farm journalist Edwin T. Meredith, who drew a diagram around his magazine's target region that ended up looking like a heart), the term has nonetheless eluded absolutely stable boundaries, and its more powerful connotations have emerged from the notion that farming and rural-village culture constitute the "heart" of America.[20] (For my purposes, the image of a heart also plays on the sentimentality that has been frequently ascribed to women.) While farming subcultures have continued to cohere around relatively narrow regional dynamics predicated on similarities among weather conditions, soils, and crops, farmers in the United States have also ascribed to a national level of agrarian identity first articulated by Thomas Jefferson. As this book reveals, broadly Jeffersonian attitudes about the nobility of agricultural life united farmers from all regions and often trumped local identity politics, especially in the early twentieth century, when distinctions between rurality and urbanity came to seem much more significant than distinctions among regional farming cultures. Indeed, the emphasis on rurality's difference from what was fast becoming the modern-urban mainstream was so pronounced that it even allowed for the occasional conflation of farming culture and more vaguely defined "pioneer" cultures, such as ranching—an elision facilitated by the late nineteenth-century rhetoric of Frederick Jackson Turner, whose classic statements about frontier "traits" suggestively aligned the hardy, independent frontiersman with Jefferson's yeoman farmer.[21]

My use of the terms "rurality" and "agrarianism" acknowledges this tendency of period commentators to lump together country "types" and also points to my ultimate effort in this study to deregionalize the rural. I seek to extricate rurality from more parochial categories, such as southern or midwestern studies—within which rural novels, for instance, have been generally confined[22]—and put it back into play with nationalist mythographies, considering it as a space mapped over, within, and against notions of the modern. This is not to deny regionalist associations; on the contrary, recent scholarship on regionalism stresses its historic role in authorizing the voices of the marginal, a point that is obviously relevant to this study. Nor do I wish to reinvoke the romance thesis of American exceptionalism, which privileges an American literary hero navigating a symbolic universe rather than a textured world of social relations (resulting, as Kaplan and Nina Baym have shown, in a severely limited American canon).[23] Rather, I want to think about rurality as a figurative space *as well as* a particularized place, and consider why that space/place might be especially compelling for women writers and commentators in the early twentieth century. Given our long-standing association of rurality with social, if not political, conservatism,[24] it seems odd indeed that those with a liberal or radical social agenda would choose it as a signifying cultural location: one would hardly link farm culture to the assertion of, for instance, subversive ideologies of gender, much less—as with some of the texts discussed here—a radical theorization of women's bodies. That some women artists effected such a relationship allows us to see anew, and differently, not only rurality but also the varied forms that the period's feminism and leftism could take.

Hence in bringing modernity into relation with *rurality*—as opposed, say, to *nature* or *landscape*, as in other studies of American women and environmental representation[25]—I am both carefully inscribing a specific cultural arena and deliberately invoking an apparent conceptual binary. This allows me to trace a coherent strain of precisely situated social critique while probing its relation to broad societal attitudes and trends. We might consider, for instance, that the generated opposition between modernity and rurality foregrounds class formations in a manner that the less culturally contingent couplings of modernity and landscape, or modernity and nature, do not. And if rural representation in the years between 1900 and 1940 too often meant depictions of a *white* rural class (whether "poor white trash" or an aspirant bourgeois farming culture), rurality nonetheless posits the context for particular kinds of race commentary not only in terms of the African American history of agricultural labor through slavery and tenancy but also through a construction of whiteness that, as David Roediger has observed, takes on particular urgency among the white laboring classes:[26] farm culture in the modernist era, often through its very absence of open discussions of race as well as its invocation of a patrician agrarian ancestry, is a highly racialized culture. Further, radical ideas of sexuality, maternity, and domestic labor in rural-centered texts highlight a particularized working female body, one that challenges feminist and Marxist ideas by problematically, and viscerally, joining production and reproduction. Then, too, a consideration of modernity and rurality necessitates a differently inflected social history, one that draws attention to aspects of American culture—the Country Life Movement and the back-to-the-land movement, the growth of agribusiness, and so on—that intersect with but have eluded aesthetic histories, and that deserve attention outside of the narrow confines of rural history. Of course, none of these specific contexts precludes consideration of more far-reaching figurations of *nature* and *landscape* that remain operative within the qualified category of rurality; indeed, rurality as a concept is useful and elastic precisely because it pinpoints a concrete setting that is nonetheless heavily (in)formed by symbolic land-languages of abiding national significance. Rurality, in short, is a powerful category because it resonates with broad American traditions but also carries specific, highly situated implications for the "patterning of mental and technical possibilities"[27] that maps modernity—including patterns of social relations, modes of expression, habits of consumption, and responses to technology.

Naturally, the breadth of my interests here, ranging across historical, cultural, and geographic horizons, necessitates drawing on a diverse field of previous scholarship. This project would not be possible without important recent work by rural historians of women and farming in the Progressive Era. Though later portions of this book will reference specific studies, it is important here to record my indebtedness to Katherine Jellison, Mary Neth, Melissa Walker, and Deborah Fink, among others, who have facilitated a new terrain of critical inquiry by redressing the long-standing imbalance between studies of farm culture generally (read: male) and studies of farm women.[28] Their work, sophisticated in its investigation of the rhetorical contexts, such as Extension Service publications, that shaped farm womanhood in this period, provides a crucial basis for considering how rurality as a discursive arena figures in texts by modernist women. Perhaps most important is the way these studies foreground farm women's laboring bodies as recognized sites of contention in debates by and about farm women within agricultural reform circles, setting the stage for the hypercorporeality so central to the representational works I discuss. Also significant are their observations about how the New Agriculture, as the reform discourses called it, constructed and promoted a hypothetical farm culture that was white and middle class; this imagistic standard throws into relief alternative cultural conceptions by women that, as I will demonstrate, recapture and critique both class and race tensions as endemic to agrarian experience and to modernity.

Some recent literary-critical studies have also proved influential by opening up provocative new ways of thinking about modernism, radical social critique, and landscape in the United States. Dorothee Kocks's *Dream a Little: Land and Social Justice in Modern America* calls on us to rethink the relations between social reform and symbolic discourses of land, which tend to submerge underlying political imperatives. She reminds us that the New Deal's welfare program had an important precedent in the Homestead Act of 1862 and suggests that our tendency *not* to equate land grants with other charitable programs underscores the special status of the landscape in the United States, which too often appears to transcend social relations altogether. Kocks's linkage of reform ("social justice") to discourses of environmentalism in the modernist period intersects in important ways with my own perspectives. And while Patricia Yaeger's work is delimited by regional, racial, and temporal considerations that distinguish it sharply from mine, her bold insistence that we need to shake up traditional literary and cultural categories in order to revitalize women's writings, which simply refuse alignment with proscriptive models, clearly informs this project.

In *Dirt and Desire: Reconstructing Southern Women's Writing, 1930–1990,* Yaeger's emphasis on excessive, "throwaway" bodies and the refusal of certain women's texts to contain them or manage their refractory qualities, thereby revealing what traditional versions of southern culture "don't want us to say," resonates with some of the texts I discuss here and valorizes a rereading of culture from its supposed margins.[29] In my discussion of rurality, modernity, and women's social critique, especially as it relates to female corporeality, I might be seen as joining Yaeger's perspective in *Dirt and Desire* with that of Paula Rabinowitz in *Labor and Desire: Women's Revolutionary Fiction in Depression America,* suggesting that the insights specific to criticism of women's southern-rural texts and those specific to criticism of women's proletarian texts might be profitably united to map a space of rural-inflected radical-reformism heretofore unrecognized.

Such linkages will remain largely implicit, however, as this book focuses primarily on specific readings of texts within the parameters of the language sets and imagistic concerns of rurality in the modernist period. Because it situates imaginative re/creations of farm women's culture within the actual shaping discourses of both rurality and ideas of the modern, this project is fundamentally interdisciplinary, assuming that literature is one facet of history even as it weighs the impact of history on literature, considering both as constructed realms in which the "ideal" and the "real" are inextricably entwined. To that end, I am particularly interested in related materials that register both aesthetic and documentary impulses, notably the agricultural press, with its rich combination of short stories, advertising, and reform-minded editorial features, and the period's rural photography, which exploited through a new, "modern" medium the tensions between perspective and evidence. These materials contribute, I argue, to a body of representation that both intercedes in the agricultural and feminist reform discourses of the "long" Progressive Era and delineates an underrecognized but nonetheless coherent mode of modernist expression.

The book consists of five major chapters. Chapter 1, "Critical Cartographies: Plotting Farm Women on the Cultural Map," establishes the social, political, and artistic parameters of my study by first situating my primary materials within a largely reactionary set of agrarian-related social movements in the United States prior to World War II, all of which were engaged, implicitly or explicitly, in articulating roles for rural women. The chapter then considers the theoretical challenges posed by the farm woman's laboring body in light of these agrarian debates, and in light of the broader ideological concerns of modernity. For example, I consider the farm woman's cultural positioning in relation to attitudes about domesticity, women's paid work, consumption, and reproduction and eugenics—all of which attest to her symbolic power in a newly urban nation struggling to accommodate its agrarian roots and to adapt itself to the contingencies of a swiftly changing society. The iconic figure of the Farm Woman, I demonstrate, was readily appropriated for a variety of cultural purposes, even if the experiences of real farm women were not so comfortably contained.

Chapter 2 extends and complicates these issues through its reading of a popular monthly periodical, now largely forgotten, called *The Farmer's Wife* (1906–1939). The single national publication dedicated to farm women in the modernist era (or, for that matter, at any point in American history), this journal dramatizes the contradictions within and between the period's agrarian and domestic ideologies, variously working out the ever-shifting relations between rurality and a modern domestic ideal, and documenting the interests and perspectives of actual farm women, whose letters and other contributions were published in large numbers on a monthly basis. Thus *The Farmer's Wife* not only recaptures the complexity of the farm woman's cultural positioning in the years between 1900 and 1940 but also traces the ways that some farm women negotiated the web of reform discourses that sought to (re)define them and their work. Its short fiction, too, as I discuss in detail, establishes parameters for a symbolic deployment of rurality in reference to the concerns of modernity.

Together, these chapters set the stage for my readings of women's rural novels. These include not only best-selling rural romances and antiromances—the popularity of which substantiates the appeal of rurality for a modern reading audience—but also several critically acclaimed but commercially less successful (and now largely forgotten) texts by leftist women who were active in various reform movements, including agricultural reform. Chapter 3, "Women, the Farm, and the Best-seller," opens the discussion by considering popular farm novels by women and their placement within cultural conversations about gender, aesthetics, and the reading public. As prominent entries on the best-seller lists that had recently emerged as important marketing tools for the bookselling industry, these texts were heavily implicated in public debates about the perceived encroachment of middlebrow culture. Ironically, they were also frequent recipients of literary prizes, including the Pulitzer Prize, which demonstrated their straddling of popular and "serious" realms while also embroiling them further in conflicts about literary standards. This chapter considers not only how literary-cultural dynamics situated best-selling rural fiction by women but also how the receptions of four such novels—by Edna Ferber, Martha Ostenso, Elizabeth Madox Roberts, and Gladys Hasty Carroll—exemplify those processes. Through close readings, I also show how these texts, despite their sentimental elements, employ rural themes and settings to offer serious social critiques of modernity.

Chapter 4, "Radical Ruralities," takes up a quite different set of rural novels by women—those that, surprisingly, use the farm as a setting for consciously subversive revisionings of the relations between gender and culture. Edith Summers

Kelley, Josephine Johnson, and Fielding Bourke (née Olive Tilford Dargan) were all writers on the Left whose personal circumstances and/or political involvements drew them to rural settings. But rather than exploiting the farm for nostalgic purposes, as more popular women novelists often did, I show how these writers exploded the American mythography that romanticized and validated rural life, challenging its usual significations and using it as a space from which to launch new ideas about, for instance, women and re/production. Their texts disallow facile equations of social constructs with natural processes and systems, and they posit the farm as a contested ground on which to assert competing ideologies. Hence these novels may be understood as participating rather differently in a cultural appropriation of rurality for the purposes of exploring the pressures of modernity.

These readings will, I hope, initiate recovery of the many modernist women's texts animated by rural settings and concerns, and redress the imbalance predicated by literary and cultural histories that have obscured this body of work.[30] But written texts are not the only locations for rural engagements by women. Chapter 5, "Rural Camera Work: Women and/in Photography," addresses the role of the camera—a quintessentially modern instrument—in interpreting rurality for a modern audience. It explores how the medium of photography helped to define female practitioners as modern, especially when their work embraced a preindustrial rural other. In particular, the chapter considers two photographers, Doris Ulmann and Marion Post, whose penetrating, though quite distinct, visions of the rural refute its often presumed status as an insipid visual setting. Moreover, both Ulmann, who took an old-fashioned pictorialist approach, and Post, with her sharply critical documentary style, enacted through their rural photography their own engagements with contemporary questions of aesthetics and social power. Their very differences reveal, once again, the various ways in which rurality yielded to modernist interpretations and agendas, especially for women.

Indeed, the texts and contexts I explore here are deliberately chosen to suggest this broad range of deployments of the rural, although they necessarily represent, too, my own sense of what is especially provocative. As the reader will perceive, I make no claims to theorize modernity or rurality in absolute terms, but rather seek to explore touchpoints between actual circumstances of farm women in modernity and idealizations and theorizations of farm culture within discourses of social science, popular media, and aesthetics.[31] My perspective, then, is both materialist and feminist, even as I weigh with special care the role of language systems in re/shaping perceived realities. It is perhaps only at this critical-historical moment, when it is possible to harness the tools and perspectives of poststructuralism, cultural studies, and feminism, and when the modern has become again, as it once was, a contested terrain, that the particular group of women's texts I am concerned with here—conventional in form, unapologetically quotidian in subject—can emerge as a cohesive modern, and perhaps even radical, tradition.

Rurality has often been constituted as a set of knee-jerk significations, an unexamined and perpetually flat backdrop for ideologically charged alternatives, rather than a historically investigated "reality" that informs representational texts in precise ways. Twentieth-century rural culture has remained in the shadows of a modern urbanity that has somehow always seemed more compelling, more complex, more progressive. Yet Felski has argued that "the history of the modern needs to be rethought in terms of the various subaltern groups that have contributed to its formation."[32] Women, as commentators on and participants in rural life, as characters in the real and fictional dramas of rurality, have much to offer us in thinking through the implications of both rurality and modernity. In considering these lived and represented rural experiences, this book contributes, I hope, to a remapping of modernity itself.

Chapter 1

Critical Cartographies
Plotting Farm Women on the Cultural Map

IN 1924, MARY Meek Atkeson, Ph.D., the daughter of a prominent professor of agriculture, published a treatise entitled *The Woman on the Farm.* Claiming the modest purpose of merely "introduc[ing] [to the reader] the woman on the farm—her work, her problems, her point of view on life," Atkeson based her study on personal experience and on letters written by farm women to the Department of Agriculture and to two major farm periodicals. Her account of farm womanhood was optimistic, a bias she herself acknowledged, as she wished both to portray what she saw as the genuine resilience of farm women and to offer such women "the inspiration of a bright outlook toward the future."[1] Yet her book, which covered such topics as "The Farm Home," "The Grounds and Gardens," "The Farm Boy and Girl," and "The [Farm] Woman Herself," was derided by her single major reviewer, Rexford G. Tugwell, for precisely this optimism, which Tugwell saw as "incorrigible effusiveness about the minor beauties of country life." In Tugwell's opinion, Atkeson betrayed herself and her work as "trivial," for "The twittering birds and dewy grass in this book show that its author has not learned to discipline a somewhat romantic temperament; they are a little out of place when addressed to plain women who are used to sinks and woodsheds and husbands with a certain stablish smell."

Tugwell's criticism, however, fails to mask his own flatly sentimental view of farm women[2] and overlooks Atkeson's careful efforts to position both her book and its subject within national conversations. Published two years before Kenyon

Butterfield, as president of the American Country Life Association, would proclaim publicly that farm women's interests were still largely unrepresented, Atkeson's book attempts to enter into an agricultural reform discourse that had begun in the early years of the century and that Butterfield admitted was, as late as 1926, almost exclusively masculine.[3] But Atkeson goes further than to imply that women deserve a voice in agricultural matters. In her chapter "Politics and National Organizations," Atkeson laments the absence of the rural woman's perspective from conventions and "general meetings for the advancement of women," thereby staking for rural women a legitimate claim within broader discussions about women's rights. "[T]he present assumption of leadership by so-called national groups of women which are not really national," she asserts, "has its dangers for the nation as well as for the women's cause" (293). Her insistence not only that rural women participate more fully in progressive movements, agricultural and otherwise, but also that city and town women acknowledge the necessity of accommodating the rural woman's perspective, clearly indicates that her audience extends beyond the rural community, a point that Tugwell apparently misses. It also demonstrates that her views are not as simplistically romantic as they may at first appear, since she promotes farm women's participation in reform, even if that is rather vaguely, and conservatively, defined. Among other things, for instance, she urges farm women not only to vote but even to accept public office when necessary, in order to "secur[e] better local conditions" (287).

Significantly, Atkeson also reveals a keen awareness of the pressures of modernity on the farm woman:

> Of course conditions have changed greatly in America in the last hundred years. . . . Our country life is in a state of rapid change, and many an inefficient family is being ground beneath the wheels of its progress. For the good old days of the early American frontier, with their crude methods and open-handed hospitality, are passing, by successive stages, into an organization of forces and a cultured ease and refinement similar to that prevailing in the cities. And the woman on the farm to-day, with her husband and her children, stands somewhere midway, alternately torn by influences toward the old and toward the new.
>
> It is a most difficult position to hold with stability and common sense. (5)

Atkeson's imagery further reinforces this idea of the farm woman's in-between status. She conjures up a farmer's wife who must balance the poles represented by her two nearest neighbors, one of whom lives by old-fashioned rural means and values while the other enacts a citified version of rusticity adopted merely "for health or pleasure" (5–6); later she recalls from her childhood those moments, on her family's farm homestead, when she imagined fantastic destinies for the passengers riding in a train on the horizon, and also wondered what those passengers might think of her, "the little girl in the blue gingham dress" (16–17). Conscious of the permeability of boundaries between old and new, and between city and country, Atkeson's book, despite its obvious investment in rural living as a preferred way of life, nonetheless probes the precariousness of the new farm woman's cultural positioning between the "primitive" and the "modern" (6) even as it appears to present an unproblematic portrait of her as combining the best of both worlds.[4]

If, as Atkeson declares in her opening paragraph, the new farm woman was both progressive and "as typical as Lincoln is of the true American spirit" (3), then she walked a careful line indeed. To be sure, farm men were hardly removed from the tensions between, for instance, traditional agrarian values and the exhilarating, but also threatening, potential of agricultural industrialization; yet it seems that, conceptually speaking, the farm woman troubled the intersection of rurality and modernity in more deep-seated ways. Both Atkeson and Tugwell, in stressing the female's childbearing and homemaking roles, inadvertently suggested how and why the farm woman's figure was more densely signifying than the male farmer's, and more complexly situated in respect to the period's reform discourses—which included, of course, new ideas about not only agriculture but also women and their work, both productive and reproductive. Theoretically, that is, farm women not only were enmeshed in the struggle for an American identity that was prominently imagined in terms of the dichotomy between agrarian and industrial orders; they also were implicated in the ideologies of gender that redefined notions of domestic work as well as relations between re/production and consumption.

On one hand, for instance, for women both on and off the farm, domestic tasks could be recuperated as "real" labor through the era's emphasis on home economics, including the application of management principles to housework and child care and the elevation of efficiency in the home as an ideal. (The infiltration of this mind-set into rural arenas is evidenced, for instance, in agrarian leader Charles Josiah Galpin's treatise *Rural Social Problems,* in which he instructed farm women to create colored charts to better organize their work and visualize their time expenditures.)[5] On the other hand, such emphases generally reasserted the gendered division of labor typical of the middle classes and widely portrayed as normative: in the words of Mrs. Julian Heath, purveyor of the new science of housekeeping and proponent of women's educated consumerism, "You [the wife] must make time to spend wisely just as your husband makes time to earn wisely."[6] But farm women, who self-identified as producers as well as consumers and who often worked in the barn or the fields as well as the kitchen, were marginalized by this bourgeois investment in separate spheres, which persisted imagistically despite women's advances in education and the professions. The figure of the farm woman, then, potentially poised to represent the epitome of efficiency and effective management through, for example, her simultaneous work inside and outside the home, was instead positioned as a problematic exception to mainstream images—more so since traditional agrarian values frequently discouraged the increased consumption, culturally assigned to women, that was celebrated as the happy result of "progress."

Thus to be both appealingly modern and approvingly traditional was, for farm women, an even more layered and complicated proposition than for farm men, a point betrayed by the inconsistencies in Atkeson's discussion, which reveal her attempts to align farm women with new values as well as old ones. For example, quoting Emerson Hough, Atkeson admiringly situates the farm woman within the pioneer tradition, making her part of "the great romance of all America" (4); yet later she asserts that "[h]ousekeeping is a business as practical as farming and with no romance in it" (30). Similarly, she uses prevailing terminology to claim separate spheres for the farm wife and her spouse ("she is interested primarily in the problems of consumption, just as her husband is concerned primarily in the problems of production" [29]), but almost immediately equivocates: "It is true that in some instances too much of the work of the farm takes place in the home, and this is very undesirable, but the home and the farm can never be entirely divorced as are the city home and the city man's business" (35). Later still, she asserts that the farm woman is proud to move beyond the concerns of homemaking, for she "do[es] not lose caste by working outside, for outdoor work to one with courage and strength is uplifting, not degrading" (128). Such apparent shifts in argument might be understood less as rhetorical or conceptual weaknesses on Atkeson's part than as indications of the pressures imposed on farm women by the often incompatible ideologies of domesticity, agrarianism, and gender more generally, each one further inflected by the cultural dictate to "modernize." (This is to say nothing of the more fundamental economic pressures that, for members of the working classes, preclude considerations of preference, or of *identity* in an abstract sense.) To rein in the unwieldy figure of the farm woman so that it might be accommodated within contemporary discussions about womanhood (so often theorized in bourgeois terms) and labor (in the specific and, as we shall see, oddly overlapping contexts of agriculture and reproduction) was no easy task.

Atkeson's text, while hardly influential or even especially compelling, is thus nonetheless provocative in considering the farm woman's relation to the concerns of the time. It also points to the relative absence of rural women from official discussions about agrarianism in the period, as well as from subsequent historical and theoretical studies that treat women more broadly. Rural sociologists have lamented, and rightly so, the erasure of farm women from rural history,[7] and the farm woman, conceptually at least, could not seem further removed from many of the progressive tendencies associated with women and American modernity. The development of urban social services, the fight for woman suffrage, the birth control movement, the drive to limit child labor—all have been major topics of interest for feminist histories, but all revolved around the reformist energies of women who were primarily from a city-based middle class. This does not mean, however, that farm women were culturally negligible, or that their imagined distance from the modern translated into a failure to feel its impact, or indeed, to contribute to its re/formative impulses. On the contrary, many farm women had things to say, especially about the intersections of modernity and rurality, but their unique circumstances meant that they viewed issues such as women's work for wages or commodity consumption through a highly particular lens. And if their perspectives attracted less attention than they (or we) might wish, it is largely because not only urban-based feminist perspectives, but also institutionalized (male) agrarian perspectives, systematically preempted theirs. A consideration of how and why this happened contributes to ongoing discussions about the emerging professional discourses that shaped modernity[8]; it also points to the incommensurability of farm women even within the period's ongoing re/negotiations of ideas about labor, gender, class, and American identity.

Rurality and Men

In the early twentieth century reformist attention turned to farming and rural life in a manner unprecedented in American history. A conflation of circumstances conspired to make the American countryside a site of scrutiny in both positive and negative terms. Among these were advances in technology that promised to revolutionize farming and that contributed to a growing interpenetration of urban and rural cultures; a more intense awareness of the interdependence of urban and rural economies; widespread interest in "improving" societal structures, especially those that affected the social welfare of citizens deemed impoverished; and the increasing legitimacy of social science. Also important was the influx of immigrants in the early years of the century, which, combined with the perceived out-migration of farmers, prompted many observers to reinvest farming with the Jeffersonian prestige of a nativist nobility. "[T]he future farmers of America must truly be a superior race," argued Liberty Hyde Bailey, dean of agriculture at Cornell University and a leading agrarian reformer; hence farm culture was linked not only to an "authentic" American past but also to a eugenics-inspired, racially sanitized future.[9]

It is hardly surprising that Progressive Era discourses centering on agriculture, including those aimed at improving circumstances for and within agrarian communities and attendant attempts to revivify an agrarian ideal, were predominantly masculinist. The reasons have much to do, of course, with turn-of-the-century gender practices generally, which still tended to cordon women off from higher education, professional positions of authority, and public forums. Regarding agriculture, as with most areas of American economic and social life, men had the floor, and attention therefore was focused more on the farmer than on his wife and daughters. Yet farm women were even less likely to have their interests represented in local or national conversations than women in other social categories. Despite a history of agricultural dissent and despite such farming organizations as the Grange, which had always extended equal voice and representation to both sexes, farm women in the early twentieth century—relatively isolated from one another, often burdened with heavy workloads, and frequently of a lower educational level than their urban counterparts—had neither the means nor the opportunity to organize effectively for their own benefit. (Those women who managed to make their voices heard, then—some of whom are discussed in this chapter—necessarily constituted a minority.) And since, as Atkeson argued, rural women were largely external to the web of reform-minded women's organizations in the period, they were widely disregarded even within feminist frameworks.[10]

What is surprising, though, is that farm men were not the driving force behind the century's earliest agrarian-oriented reform efforts; rather, such efforts were organized by men *outside* of farming, a manifestation of an even deeper irony: the great period of agricultural reform discussion in the United States was instigated at a moment of relative bounty for farmers. The years between 1900 and World War I, often referred to as the golden age of American agriculture, witnessed rising prices for farm products, allowing farm families to live in comfort as compared with the dire years of the late nineteenth century. Of course, it was still widely acknowledged that American farmers represented an underclass, making considerably less money on the whole than those in other occupations and subject to unpredictable market fluctuations. And in the 1920s a true agricultural depression set in, anticipating the Great Depression by about nine years.[11] Yet the crystallizing moment of organized attention to rural issues, the appointment in 1908 of President Theodore Roosevelt's Commission on Country Life, was the result of a perceived "need" not by farmers themselves, who were relatively content with present circumstances, but by men outside of farm communities, men in business, politics, and the clergy, as well as teachers in the agricultural colleges and practitioners of the emerging science of rural sociology. Often they were perceived as overwhelming the farmer, as a 1913 cartoon suggests (fig. 1.1). Throughout the twenties, as agricultural conditions indeed worsened, these professionals came to be increasingly valued as arbiters of the so-called rural problem, and a premium was placed on education and theory rather than practical experience. This enmeshment of agrarianism in the growth of institutional and disciplinary conversations, together with the location of such conversations mainly outside of farm communities rather than within them, suggests that the national debate about farmers and their needs and roles was not really about farmers at all. Joining this debate were men who

The Latest Fad: Everybody Wants to Uplift Agriculture

Figure 1.1 Cartoon from *Rural Manhood* 4.3 (Mar. 1913): 85. (Image courtesy of Skidmore College.)

thoroughly idealized rurality and urged a mass return to it, though they too tended to be located outside of working-class farm culture and problematically assumed the attainability of a bucolic rural life, one that would be unaffected by the harsh social and economic realities to which longtime farm families had been subject.

Historian David Danbom has argued that the unprecedented attention paid to farmers and farming in the period between 1900 and 1930, "at a time when urban society was achieving overwhelming dominance in every facet of life," marked a cultural awareness of the enormity of urban-industrial forces.[12] Whether idealizing the country as an antidote to modernity's disruptions, or decrying rural primitiveness and degeneracy as in need of the ameliorative influence of modern, urban-based social and political institutions, agrarian analysts tended to perceive the country from what was essentially an urban perspective. The image of the farmer was repeatedly and variously adapted to serve the ends of more far-reaching cultural commentary. Agrarian idealists, for instance, tended to gloss over the history of Populism—which, historians agree, combined progressive and reactionary impulses[13]—in order to present the farmer as a bulwark of conservative social values, or overlooked the necessarily interdependent nature of the farm family as an economic unit so as to stress the American farmer's mythic yeoman status; for their part, antiagrarian reformers overemphasized the "backward" farming practices and aberrant social behaviors allegedly engendered by rural isolation. These perspectives allowed their authors respectively to make larger points about the shifting social patterns of American society and were united, as Danbom shows, by their essential concern with *urban* culture as a prevailing societal influence, whether for good or ill.[14] The primary documents of the era make this emphasis abundantly clear, as is evidenced, for instance, by a special 1912 edition of the *Annals of the American Academy of Political and Social Science* devoted to "Country Life," in which the "industrial aspect of the farm question" is a constant touchstone.[15]

This is not to say that agrarian commentators were not genuinely interested in, on the one hand, improving material and social conditions for rural people, or, on the other hand, convincing urbanites of the superiority of the agrarian way; it is merely to emphasize that rurality was an important conceptual site for considerations of the growing hegemony of modern urban industrialism. It was also a site of male debate. In another context, Danbom has suggested that the absence of prominent women from this discussion, and especially from the camp that extolled agrarian life for its promise of a recaptured innocence and freedom, may be ascribed to the female's more positive experience of industrialization: the "dehumanizing loss of efficacy" identified by some male observers as intrinsic to the new technologically oriented society might have translated, instead, to a "liberating" experience for women.[16] It is certainly the case that the most vigorously antimodern agrarians were also the most sexist, a link that is not coincidental. A celebration of old-fashioned agrarian values and practices and the moral, civic, and spiritual benefits to be gained therefrom—what Danbom calls "romantic agrarianism"—constituted a chauvinistic brand of nostalgia that, while perhaps effectively critiquing the perceived ills of modernity, also sidestepped consideration of how the purported bounties of country life fell disproportionately to men.

The most virulently sexist versions of romantic agrarianism emerged in the 1920s. Ralph Borsodi, for instance, a prominent member of the back-to-the-land movement, which urged urbanites to reject the social perils of the city by taking up farming, made a name for himself through published treatises that railed against the domination of the factory and its ethic of consumption. In *This Ugly Civilization* (1929), one of his best-known works (a later one was entitled *Flight from the City* [1933]), Borsodi argued that the factory had destroyed the integrity of the family as both a moral force and an interdependent and self-sufficient economic unit; only a return to subsistence agriculture and an emphasis on home crafts would counteract the deleterious effects of urbanity and commercialism. Much of Borsodi's wrath is targeted at "careerist" women who have "turn[ed] their backs on homemaking." Such women are not only fueling the capitalist economy, he argued, but "are almost certain to be poor judges both of values and of merchandise"; they also tend, not incidentally, to lead "abnormal sex lives." According to Borsodi, the last bastion of serious homemaking, and hence the saving grace of society, is the farm, where women still bake their own bread, make their own clothes, can their own food, and raise appropriately sized families. That women may have other ambitions is of course unexamined, and Borsodi seems unaware that the country's "bucolic delights" may be less freely enjoyed by domestic laborers largely confined to the house by sewing, laundry, meal preparation, and children's needs.[17] Such problems did not escape female reviewers, however, one of whom noted that Mr. Borsodi's "'way out' looks very much like the way further in. It reads suspiciously like the time-honored utterance of the outraged male—'What better would any woman want than to make a home for some good man!'" Identifying herself as a country woman, this reviewer suggested that Borsodi understood neither women nor their labor in rural settings.[18]

Similarly, the cultural critics known as the Nashville Agrarians were largely indifferent to the sexist implications of their pro-South manifesto, *I'll Take My Stand* (1930), the very title of which links their rejection of northern, urban-based commerce and consumption to a sentimental idealization of Dixie. More intellectual in their orientation than Borsodi, and certainly better known to today's historians and cultural critics,[19] the Nashville Agrarians nonetheless shared Borsodi's tendency to skim over the complex race, class, and gender tensions of both modern society and earlier periods in American history by reducing cultural conflicts to the simplistic dichotomy of industrialism versus agrarianism. Though more willing to engage in race, and racist, commentary than in commentary specifically about gender, the twelve essayists in the volume betray their sexism through their very lack of attention to women's situations in the southern-agrarian cultural economy, an emphasis that has been perpetuated in the numerous studies of the group. One recent critic points out, for example, that John Crowe Ransom, Allen Tate, and their cohorts persistently sublimated the exploitation of slave and tenant labor in order to cast the South, in contrast to the North, as "the model of a nonmarket social economy"[20]; largely unnoticed, however, are the related ways in which these writers advanced a southern paradigm of gracious hospitality without accounting for the domestic labor of women.

Ransom, the first of the twelve essayists in *I'll Take My Stand,* claimed that "look[ing] backward rather than forward" is "out of fashion" in modern America, yet both *I'll Take My Stand* and the work of Ralph Borsodi tapped into a prominent vein of cultural criticism that posited "lost" agrarian lifestyles as an alternative to the social fragmentation and economic instability reputedly engendered by modernity.[21] To be sure, Borsodi and the Nashville Agrarians were extreme in their reactionism and occupied different outposts of a pro-country stance that, in its earlier and more typical manifestations, was considerably more moderate than theirs, especially in its attitudes toward urban industrialism. Yet even the comparatively temperate Country

Life Movement—which brought together under a large umbrella a wide range of reform efforts in rural sociology, state and federal legislation, and even home economics; which harbored antiagrarianists as well as romantic agrarians; and which tended to see country and city as interdependent rather than oppositional—was a masculinist enterprise that frequently disregarded gender as a valid category of analysis. Popular throughout the teens and 1920s, the Country Life Movement had been a logical outgrowth of Roosevelt's Commission on Country Life, which was, significantly, an exclusively male body: though carefully chosen to muster the cooperation of business, education, and the farm press, its members included no women. In inviting Liberty Hyde Bailey to chair the commission, Roosevelt mentioned, among other things, that "[t]here is no more important person, measured in influence upon the life of the nation, than the farmer's wife, no more important home than the country home"; nonetheless, the weight of Roosevelt's missive concerned the perceived needs of the male farmer and a "farm culture" void of references to women,[22] an emphasis that was reflected in the report of the commission's work and in the more broadly based reform efforts that came out of it.

Roosevelt was a renowned sportsman who associated the outdoors with the development of a racial virility that would counteract the "softening and relaxation of fibre that tends to accompany civilization"; he convened the commission in order to "strengthen" farm life, which would result, he argued, in "the strengthening of the whole nation." "We were founded as a nation of farmers," he wrote in an introduction to the commission's report, "and in spite of the great growth of our industrial life it remains true that our whole system rests upon the farm, that the welfare of the whole community depends upon the welfare of the farmer."[23] The report that followed detailed the commission's survey- and forum-based methodology, its findings concerning the "Special Deficiencies in Country Life," and its suggestions for corrective measures, which included increased outreach through extension services, further data-gathering procedures, and legislative initiatives. To Roosevelt's disappointment, the commission was not backed financially by Congress, which refused even to pay for the printing and dissemination of its findings; yet ultimately its report, eventually published in 1911, provided the impetus for reform efforts on the federal, state, and local levels through general agitation in the agricultural and mainstream presses and the resulting formation of, among other organizations, the American Country Life Association, the USDA Extension Service, and the Farm Bureau. This often diffuse range of efforts, however, reflects what historians have seen as a fundamental vagueness in the commission's recommendations, which were united only by a general sense of the need to uplift the farmer.[24] Especially thin were the fewer than 4 pages of the commission's report (out of a total 150) devoted to "Woman's Work on the Farm," which, while acknowledging that rural hardships such as "poverty, isolation,

[and] lack of labor-saving devices" affect the farmer's wife more seriously than the farmer, merely asserted that "relief to farm women" would have to come through "a general elevation of country living."[25]

Even before the publication of the report, Charlotte Perkins Gilman, writing in *Good Housekeeping* magazine in 1909, had the temerity to stress first, that farm men rightfully resented the intrusion of Roosevelt's commission, and second, that its lack of female representation constituted a grievous oversight. Calling for a series of church- and school-based meetings through which farm women's direct testimonies might be acquired, and insisting that the commission confer with such organizations as the State Federation of Women's Clubs and the National Council of Women, Gilman called on commission members at least to be consistent in considering women's voices where the "business of women" was concerned—that is, regarding the country home. She also made it clear, in more precise terms than those of the commission, that the "problems" of rurality were gendered:

> Presently we shall find out that the women who work on farms are the hardest worked and least paid of any class we have. There is no sweatshop that fails to pay something to its hard-driven slaves; but the sweatshop called a kitchen gives no wages. The work of the farmer's wife begins earlier than his, for she gets his breakfast; lasts longer than his, for she has the supper dishes to clean up, and mending to do in the evening; is more wearing than his because it is carried on together with the cares and labors of child-rearing; and is far more dangerous than his, as is shown by the death rate.
>
> The man works out-of-doors, the woman [mostly] in the house—a great disadvantage to her health. The man's work has some social outlook: he markets his crops, he has his political interests, he gossips with his friends at the store or postoffice—he is in some touch with the world's life. The woman has nothing beyond her house and family except the church.

Gilman's contention that farm women must not be "studied into and recommended about as if they were part of the live stock" resulted in *Good Housekeeping's* decision to inaugurate its own survey of rural women, which generated more than 1,000 replies and substantially corroborated Gilman's assertions about conditions for females.[26] Indeed, whenever farm women were questioned directly about their circumstances, many of them reinforced Gilman's basic position. Only recently, however, have such surveys—of which there were several—been recuperated as a means of studying farm women in the Progressive Era. Some, like the *Good Housekeeping* example, were undertaken by female cultural vehicles (women's periodicals, for example, or home economics units) with limited visibility and influence within the agricultural reform movement, ensuring that the resulting bodies of information remained subsidiary to dominant, masculine agrarian discourses and interests. Others, initiated by male-led institutions, made women a second thought and defined their target groups in ways that hinged on men, as when, for example, the Cornell University extension program, which educated farmers in new scientific methods, developed an ancillary program for the men's wives, or when David Houston, secretary of agriculture under Woodrow Wilson and a "skeptical observer of feminist politics," surveyed the wives of established USDA volunteer crop correspondents. (Responses in the first instance were never intended for publication; those in the second instance were carefully edited, predictably, "to best represent . . . the [USDA's] own position.")[27] Katherine Jellison has shown that, in general, USDA documents on farm womanhood—even, oddly enough, those compiled by a woman (namely, Emily Hoag, a USDA associate economist who wrote a series of reports published in the early 1920s)—fostered a positive, "forward-looking" image of farm women that served the larger purposes of the USDA's push for a mechanized New Agriculture and that deflected attention from farm women's complaints.[28]

Yet charges that farm women's labors were excessive, unappreciated, and unrewarded appeared with great regularity in both public and private forums through the teens and early 1920s, including on the women's pages of male agricultural newspapers and magazines: specifically, farm women noted again and again that their husbands tended to overlook domestic needs, including their wives' health, in favor of pouring their energies and resources into animals and crops. Typical was one wife's letter on the "Household" page of the *Farm Journal*, which suggested that, while farm men were not deliberately cruel, their women were nonetheless worked to death, never managing even to garner the attention lavished on the barnyard creatures: "If [a farmer] would look his wife over with the same judgment and discrimination that he does his stock, he might mend his ways, for most men are more thoughtless than really unkind. If a horse goes off his feed, loses flesh and drags along, he is laid off work a while and his food attended to,—a good policy to pursue with the wife. In one well-to-do farm community an investigator found scarcely a home without a stepmother in it."[29] Bitter recriminations by country women against country life circulated widely enough to gain considerable currency. By 1921, the *Nation* went so far as to argue that the meaning of the word "feminism" was specially inflected for rural women, who were by necessity far less interested in the symbolic "short hair and knickerbockers" assumed by their urban counterparts, or so the editorialist claimed, than in the more substantive gains to be made by demanding more humane living and working conditions, which would radically improve their physical and mental health. The popular press frequently suggested that farm women had made few such gains between the earliest years of the century and the 1920s.[30]

This perspective was challenged by male agrarian leaders and even by alternative survey pools of rural women, who, as Ronald Kline has shown, denied the harshest allegations concerning the average farm wife's circumstances.[31] Yet the idea that farm women endured suffering disproportionate to that of their husbands and other women did not disappear. On the contrary, it maintained a strong cultural hold. Especially telling was the prominence of comic images depicting the farm woman as abused—including advertisements such as those for Fels-Naptha soap, which, as early as 1908, featured an overworked farmer's wife named "Anty Drudge." Assumptions of female oppression even provided fodder for jokes at the male farmer's expense. Another contributor to the *Farm Journal*, for example, wrote in with a playful anecdote describing a bullheaded farmer who refused to spend money on domestic improvements. One night he had a nightmare in which his cultivator and other machines were denied him for a year, forcing him to make do with the methods of his grandfather. Upon awaking in a cold sweat, we are told, the farmer came to the conclusion that perhaps it is not best "for Betsy his wife to do her work with just the conveniences grandmother had."[32]

The image of the ill-treated farm wife on which such humor was predicated surely had some basis in fact, as indicated by Gilman's survey and by many published and unpublished letters of rural women. Yet the very visibility of the trope may have helped to neutralize farm women's critiques of their circumstances, since their stories, which aligned them with familiar caricatures, could potentially be dismissed as popular exaggeration. In any case, serious, sustained attention to the farm woman and her problems was not forthcoming. Instead, her image itself became a site of contention, with the result that a great deal of journalistic and reform-minded energy was expended in attempting to determine whether or not she was happy, or whether she was *really* more likely than urban women to die young, or to go insane (a commonplace assertion that, eventually, was statistically disproved).[33] The "truth" of the farm woman's experiences notwithstanding, back-and-forth accusations of her misrepresentation served to divert attention from material issues, specifically the need to assist those farm women who *were* demoralized and physically spent. It also enabled the continuance of reform efforts that were masculinist in focus and content. Thus while the farm woman's potential disadvantages were much discussed, her criticisms of the gender-based injustices of farm life were, despite their currency, ironically muted.

Of course, if we consider that the Country Life Movement was spearheaded by "agrarian leaders" such as Bailey who were not practicing farmers, then it is true that the voices of farm *men* were muted as well; indeed, many farmers, as Gilman claimed, resented assumptions that rural America was in need of fixing and that those in urban centers knew how to do it.[34] But the specific needs of farm men, especially in terms of education in superior farming methods, were constantly at the forefront of inquiry: it was the economic and social position of the farmer, not his wife, that was at stake, an emphasis that historical studies of agricultural reform in the period have, until very recently, sustained.[35] Significantly, the development of rural sociology, coterminous with the unfolding of the Country Life Movement, virtually depended on male practitioners distancing themselves from women and women's concerns in order to establish professional legitimacy. The charge that rurality itself was a "feminine" subject matter based more in outreach and reform than in scientific scrutiny had to be overcome, resulting in a gendered division of labor that relegated women in the discipline to less remunerative and less influential work as statisticians or field contacts. This meant, too, that within institutional contexts women's interests were represented with less vigor than those of men: not surprisingly, home economics programs, which had long served farm women, were largely separated from rural sociology departments by the early 1920s.[36] Hence if the "real" farmer often seemed external to discussions about agriculture, the farm woman was only more so; as mere adjunct of the farmer, she was doubly removed from the center of genuine investigation, and her concerns were presumed to follow along the same fundamental lines as those of her father, husband, and sons. Indeed, her particular hardships were generally understood as necessary and even "natural" aspects of the farm enterprise as a whole, part of a way of life that was taken to be superior economically, socially, and spiritually.

As an uplift program, the Country Life Movement was largely about class; as an effort to reassert the value of farming in Jeffersonian terms, it was nationalistic and constituted, as we shall see, a validation of whiteness. But gender was not, implicitly or explicitly, a salient category of analysis, and women qua women were given relatively little consideration. As Deborah Fink argues, one oddity of the rural "crisis" to which the Country Life Movement responded was that it served "to deepen the agrarian myth rather than to prompt a rethinking of it. Even as the material promise of agrarian life dissolved, the mainstream of public (male) discourse reemphasized farming as the soul of the country and identified women's sacrifices as critical to the survival of farm life."[37] Just as in the more extreme versions of agrarian-inspired reform such as those of Ralph Borsodi and the Nashville Agrarians—wherein sexism was less a product of attention to women than of its lack—Country Lifers downplayed distinctions between rural women and rural men, focusing instead on rurality in light of its imagined opposite, urban industrialism. And the dominant conception of farming as a male concern was deeply entrenched, further buttressed by cultural organizations that foregrounded the link between rustic vigor and masculinity. These included the Boy Scouts of America, which, at its inception in 1910, was envisioned as an outdoors movement that would toughen boys up mentally and physically, as well as the "village town and country" journal of the Young Men's Christian Association, entitled *Rural Manhood*.[38]

But this hardly means that farm women were felt to be insignificant. On the contrary, like the land itself, the farmer's wife was understood as an essential, if often unacknowledged, component of the farm, a cornerstone of its culture and economy, so much so that her labor and her roles could be merely assumed rather than considered. (One farm press editor quipped that a farmer's success depends first, on his choice of land, and second, on his choice of a wife.)[39] Moreover, her absent presence was clearly manifested within the dynamics of both race and class that undergirded discussions about agrarianism. As a mother, the farm woman was the key to perpetuating a traditional agrarian ethic and identity, as well as literally manufacturing the farm's labor pool; furthermore, as overseer of the household's consumption practices, it was on *her* labors that the family's perceived class status often seemed to hinge. Yet typically she also had a hand in the farm's profit ventures. Both her cultural roles and her very body, then, condensed and refracted the realms of production and reproduction, and production and consumption, that were still presumed mutually exclusive in the broader, middle-class culture. Embodying problematic intersections of rurality and modernity, and often resisting the simplistic model of rural uplift that threatened to subsume her differences both from rural men and from urban women, the farm wife was, theoretically speaking, a volatile figure indeed. It was she, rather than the farmer, who evidenced the tensions between the rural and the modern most richly and provocatively.

The Farm Woman and Modernity

Rita Felski has pointed out the prominence of certain female figures—the prostitute, the actress, the mechanical woman—as cultural emblems of modernity's "ambivalent responses to capitalism and technology" and to shifting notions of gender. Such figures capture in graphic terms the dynamics of commodification and specularity that were such disturbing, but also titillating, preoccupations of modernity, simultaneously revealing how apprehensions surrounding women, especially in relation to power, were articulated through modern concepts.[40] While the farm woman, often stereotyped as a victimized drudge or a glorified earth mother, seemed unexciting in contrast, she, too, was a figure upon whom important modern anxieties converged. In particular, the tension between the artificial and the "natural" that helped to structure modernity, and that obviously informed emblematic deployments of the prostitute, the actress, and the machine-woman, as well as the lesbian,[41] was also played out over and through the body of the farm woman, whose apparent distance from the modern, and from its potential decadence, oddly reinforced her value to ideologies of progress. Furthermore, as an explicitly American mother figure, insistently represented as white in the social imaginary, she brought to the fore the Progressive Era's obsession with perpetuating an unassailable nativism that would consolidate national identity.

Hence the Farm Woman in public discourse was, like other symbolic female figures, fundamentally an abstraction. Ideally imagined as the helpmate of the mythical American yeoman farmer, she was, by popular definition, neither a member of an ethnic or racial minority nor a tenant—categories that compromised the conception of farming as socially and economically stable. Rather, as the wife of a resident-owner, her labor was poured back into the farm enterprise, and she did not leave the farmhome for other employment opportunities, as, for instance, many women of color did.[42] Nor did she substantially challenge the patriarchal structure of farm culture: in theoretical, if not always actual, terms, she accepted her subordinate role, even as she was typically represented as a separate but equal partner. Most important, if she was in need of social or financial assistance, it was not because she failed to work hard but because larger economic circumstances were temporarily disadvantageous to farmers. Indeed, her identity, like that of the male farmer, was premised on the notion that, even if she did not currently enjoy a high standard of living, she was richly deserving of such a standard. But while she appeared to reinforce certain orthodox cultural values and was often seen, for instance, as an antidote to the unconventional Modern Woman, her cultural positioning was more complex than we might expect, and efforts to contain her within codified social categories met with mixed results.

Such efforts were, of course, a response to the shifting social realities of the early twentieth century. The increasing interpenetration of public and private realms characterizing modernity had eroded the nineteenth-century ideology of separate spheres that dichotomized masculinity and femininity. In addition to larger numbers of women entering the workforce, emerging locales of commodity culture such as the department store and the modern women's magazine seemed especially instrumental in blurring the boundaries between public, "male" spaces and private, "female" ones, as scholars have shown.[43] Not surprisingly, this massive redistribution of social roles and sites called forth in more conservative contexts a reactionary reassertion of inherited models, albeit while also accommodating certain modern realities. So, for example, advertising endowed women with new significance as the highly informed arbiters of their families' health and social needs, while what was touted as the New Housekeeping—the application of management principles to domestic labor—elevated the housewife to a level of pseudoprofessionalism that stressed her efficiency and thrift, shown in part by her expert navigation of the world of factory-made goods. Both trends, of course, largely repackaged in more up-to-date terms the middle-class female's domestic role, as did home economics, which responded to women's desire for education in ways that nonetheless reinscribed gender boundaries.[44]

On the surface, the re/affirmation of a gendered division of labor would seem to accommodate farm families: Barbara Melosh has shown, for instance, that publicly funded representations of agrarianism during the 1930s solidified the long-standing popular conception of a white farmer and his wife in "comradely," but separate, work.[45] In reality, though, farm women were unlikely to fit such an image, as their labor was rarely circumscribed entirely by house and children. ("I have known [farm] women who could teach children History, Poetry, Mythology, Arithmetic while taking care of a flock of chickens," wrote one extension correspondent in admiration.)[46] On the other hand, neither did farm women fit neatly into the more liberal "interpenetration" model(s) whereby women increasingly entered into public spheres associated with men and modernity—for instance, as part of the new contingent of women seeking college degrees, as their families' mediators in the vast consumer marketplace, or as full-blown workers themselves in factories or stores. Such models suggested firm class identities, and it was the farm woman's more fragmented class status that problematized her relations both to traditional gender paradigms and to more modern ones. Not strictly a housekeeper but hardly a New Woman, neither a stay-at-home mother nor a factory hireling nor again a bourgeois shopper, the farmer's wife confounded both orthodox and emerging social categories for women. Of course, like the pioneer woman before her, the farm woman had always been something of an exception to both working-class and middle-class gender norms; what was new was the significance of her exceptionalism within a culture freshly concerned with proliferating social roles and categories, and bombarded by the rhetorics of feminism and nativism.

The period's urgent recuperation of Jeffersonian ideals of agriculture effectively framed farm families as a special kind of working class: the noble kind, the nativist kind, the *right* kind. Public rhetoric exalting the farmer implicitly separated him from the new, and less desirable, working classes consisting largely of poorly paid urban-industrial workers, many of whom were immigrants. (Notably, early suggestions that immigrants should be dispersed throughout the countryside were resisted and eventually abandoned.)[47] In contrast, the farmer was imagined as representing an authentic American (i.e., white) synthesis of physical labor and civic pride and autonomy, of working-class experiences and middle-class social sensibilities—an ideal, if unrealistic, model for a country in social and economic flux. The ideology of uplift so central to the Country Life Movement played into these assumptions by striving to link farmers to middle-class markers, especially of consumption, despite the average farm family's inability or refusal to conform fully to bourgeois standards and expectations.[48] Perhaps not surprisingly, women were essential to this linkage. Since some of the more prominent distinctions between working-class and middle-class standing hinged on *women's* roles and behaviors—as workers, as mothers, as shoppers—the (white) farm woman's identity was of necessity a site of scrutiny, her body, literally and symbolically, a contested terrain. This is not to say that farm women themselves were given careful attention, but merely that certain operative assumptions about the Farm Woman as a cultural trope, some of which were incompatible, rippled beneath the surface of male-dominated and male-focused public discourses. Occasionally, farm women themselves entered into discussions about their class and gender identities, revealing the gaps between this masculine rhetoric and a more complicated reality.

The farm woman's fundamental working-class status resided in a body marked doubly by labor, productive as well as reproductive. For starters, it was assumed that farm women of the period were wives and mothers; as Deborah Fink points out, arguments that farm life was more egalitarian, and thus advantageous, for women tended to overlook the fact that marriage was a virtual prerequisite for women's participation. (It is worth noting that the marital relation—the husband's economic condition as well as his attitudes toward women and work—was generally crucial in defining the range of a farm woman's labor.)[49] But it was the extent of their productive work that most acutely distinguished farm women from their bourgeois counterparts. Even *inside* the home, farm women's work was far more physically demanding than that of sub/urban middle-class women, who purchased, rather than made, most of the necessary domestic items. A letter from a farm woman to Martha Van Rensselaer, coordinator of the Cornell Reading Club for Farmers' Wives and a Cornell teacher of home economics from 1900 to 1920, illustrates: "I have always done my own washing and weaving of carpets as I have a large house and it is furnished with rag carpets. . . . [W]e made our own table linen and toweling, spinning and weaving it, and our flannel dresses. I did not find much time to gossip with neighbors." Of course, it was the possibility of farm women doing field work, *men's* work, that even more sharply defined them as external to middle-class models of gendered behavior. This same letter writer adds, "I make my own garden and have helped rake hay and husk corn. One fall alone I husked between five and six hundred bushels. . . . One summer I piled up one hundred cords of wood and did my own housework."[50] Among other things, such labor appeared to violate the cult of motherhood that sentimentalized woman's duties at home (every state observed a Mother's Day by 1911, with a federal mandate following in 1914); it also threatened to perpetuate notions of farming as onerous, possibly contributing to out-migration and further compromising the privileged status of farming in American culture.

Yet primary source materials such as the letter quoted here consistently suggest that most farm women performed field labor, at least at the busiest times of year. More important is that many farm women apparently *desired* to perform such work, despite efforts by official organs of the new, mechanized agriculture to redistribute the emphases of farm women's labors so as to establish farm families more firmly within middle-class parameters. As Jellison shows, attempts by agrarian policymakers to establish an artificial dichotomy between farm work and domestic work largely failed; prescriptive depictions of the farm woman as akin to the urban homemaker, whose purchase of advanced domestic equipment allowed for more leisure, were frequently resisted by farm women themselves, who used time shaved from domestic chores to contribute further to farmwork. Sarah Elbert suggests, moreover, that many farm women were unwilling to relinquish their roles in production activities precisely because those roles ensured their equality in the farm enterprise: they recognized that the farm's efficiency, as well as their own self-interest, was better served by an integration of productive and reproductive work than by an enforced gender separation.[51] This is one way in which broad assumptions about the positive effects of urban-styled "progress" failed to account for the unique social patterns inherent to farming and were especially unreflective in relation to women. It also reveals an arena, only recently addressed by rural historians, in which farm women rejected official attempts to co-opt their identities and images.

Furthermore, even when farm women did not necessarily seek such an integration of housework and field work, they could still seize upon their labor realities as evidence of their equality with men and sometimes positioned themselves in interesting ways within the period's discourses about women, work, and money. The question of whether "nice" women should work for wages, a controversial issue in the public consciousness, could be particularly vexed for farm women, who frequently shared the work of the hired hands as well as doing all the work in the home. Since farm women often perceived themselves as partners with their husbands in the farm enterprise, they sometimes agitated for their rights in allocating and using the farm's money. As one correspondent to *Woman's Home Companion* argued,

> When a woman does her work of caring for the home and children, and the thousand other things she has to do, I think she does her part. But I have done all these, and worked in the fields besides. Last year my son and I hoed fifteen acres of cotton over three times. . . . I have had to do that ever since I was married, thirteen years ago. . . .
>
> It wouldn't be so hard if [my husband] would show his appreciation of my work, and give me a little recreation and money. . . . He says a woman does not need money. . . .
>
> We own our farm of twenty-five acres, and I have helped pay for it in more ways than one and think I am entitled to my part of the income.[52]

That farm women could make such claims distinguished them sharply from middle-class women, who asserted their financial rights, if they did so at all, on the basis of domestic work as an unrecognized but essential piece of the family economy.

Overall, then, the farm woman's lifestyle was not easily superimposed onto the middle-class model of womanhood most frequently invoked in public debates about women's rights and roles—yet the vigorous promotion of the successful farm woman as a bourgeois housewife continued, ironically, throughout the agricultural depression of the 1920s and into the Great Depression of the 1930s, as rural historians such as Jellison have shown. If it did not result in much actual change in the ratio of domestic to field work for many farm women, its success in symbolic terms is indicated by the growing prominence of discussions in the farm press about the appropriate limits of women's work in the fields, as well as by the growing association of female agricultural labor with shame.[53] And the public image of the farm woman in both official and popular venues increasingly merged with that of the sub/urban woman, invariably pictured inside the house. While such imagistic standards say little about what real women on farms were doing and thinking, they reveal a great deal about the perceived need to situate farmers' wives within acknowledged parameters of modern womanhood, even if such an accommodation was artificial or forced.

Of course, it was not only the farm woman's relation to productive, income-generating ventures that was at stake. The tug-of-war over her body and image was conducted on even more inflammatory levels, notably those concerned with her reproductive capacities. Even within the universally acceptable boundaries of child rearing and domestic work, farm women were subject to a cultural appropriation that revealed their excessive signification as vehicles of both agrarian and extra-agrarian dictates. The extravagant sentimentalization of motherhood that was common in the period, for example, was also apparent in the farm press;[54] yet, in addition to sublimating the full range of the farm mother's labor, her idealization as mistress of a farm-home sanctuary obscured the importance of her reproduction to both agricultural and urban market economies, as well as to ideological conceptions of Americanness. Farm women *had* to reproduce not only to ensure the economic stability of the farm but also to provide the "best" kind of people to populate the cities and, ultimately, to sustain a pure American race: that the farm created its own labor pool via childbirthing was a long-standing given, but it was also assumed by many reformers that the country, with its robust birthrate, would provide the city with the workers necessary to fill urban-industrial needs and with citizens, and potential leaders, of superior character and ability.[55] These attitudes were expressed not only by public intellectuals but also through popular idioms. One poem by John Charles McNeill published in the *Progressive Farmer and Gazette* personified "The White South" as a (rural) mother who guards "her heritage" and "Heredity," and whose "seed" shall "endure" as a safeguard against "creation's prime disgrace, / A mongrel, prideless, hopeless race."[56] Hence American-bred, *country*-bred, individuals were to counter the threat posed by masses of incoming foreigners, who—as evidenced by one photomontage published by *Ladies' Home Journal*, widely read in rural areas—would surely include among them those who are "unfit—mentally, morally, and physically."[57]

From the earliest years of the century, Theodore Roosevelt's entreaty to avoid "race suicide" unequivocally linked rural mothers to the containment of such threats. Alarmed about the declining white birthrate, Roosevelt brought into common currency a term that had been coined by sociologist Edward A. Ross in 1901 and that described, as Ross saw it, the loss of racial virility that resulted from American men's competition with inferior immigrants. Like Ross, Roosevelt was obsessively concerned with both manliness and racial superiority; his glorification of frontiersmen and the conquering of the West equated nationalist power with hypermasculinity. Significantly, his exhortation to white women of good stock to reproduce for the sake of the nation was part of a broader eugenics movement that, for some, also involved curtailing the reproductive capacities of the "feebleminded," a category that included women of questionable morals. Hence as scholars such as Gail Bederman and Wendy Kline have demonstrated, the fear of race suicide indexed a strong connection between race and gender imperatives, between the perceived need for more manly men—and, not coincidentally, fewer overtly "modern" women—and the necessity of manipulating women's reproductive capacities in order to fulfill those imperatives.[58] Farm women's generativity offered a matchless opportunity to advance the race and gender characteristics deemed appropriate: solid, proprietary farm folks were understood to be both white and natively vigorous, and in the popular imagination they had inherited the traditional pioneer values that included temperance and independence. Moreover, farm women's "natural" womanliness was preconfirmed by their large families, just as farm men preserved the association of physical hardiness with authentic masculinity.

Roosevelt's own privileged background might suggest that he would favor the especial replenishment of blueblood stock, but his attitudes toward nativism were considerably more complex, and surprisingly less class-bound, than that. He believed that all "ordinary, everyday Americans," excluding only criminals or obvious degenerates, must rise to the challenge of sustaining the nation's population: for instance, he systematically denied any moral justification for members of the upper classes to limit family size, and, unlike some other observers, he seemed unconcerned that larger families typically came from the less well-to-do classes. He even fretted over the low birthrate of female factory workers, indicating the consistency of his clarion call to parenthood. What was also consistent, though, and of particular interest here, was Roosevelt's association of race suicide with what he saw as the decadence of urbanity, including the pursuit of leisure that the city, with its dance halls and other entertainments, fostered. In a letter to incoming president Howard Taft, he bemoaned the "various legacies of trouble" Taft would face, including the "decline of the birth rate," which Roosevelt ascribed to "the drift . . . away from the country to the cities." City life produced an overly indulgent populace, Roosevelt repeatedly warned, leading to a physically and psychically shriveled society unwilling or unable to produce the children the nation required.[59]

It seems perfectly apt, then, that Roosevelt opened his 1905 speech to the National Congress of Mothers, wherein he called upon American women to fulfill their proper procreative functions, by invoking the superiority of the country in a manner that evidenced his standing as a Country Life proponent:

> In our modern industrial civilization there are many and grave dangers to counterbalance the splendors and the triumphs. It is not a good thing to see cities grow at disproportionate speed relative to the country; for the small land owners, the men who own their little homes, and therefore to a very large extent the men who till farms, the men of the soil, have hitherto made the foundation of lasting national life in every State; and, if the foundation becomes either too weak or too narrow, the superstructure, no matter how attractive, is in imminent danger of falling.

Roosevelt was careful to declare, in the very next paragraph, that "the question of how [citizens'] family life is conducted" is ultimately more crucial than "whether the man's trade is plied in the country or in the city," yet his prejudice was obvious. The remainder of the speech contrasted the women "among whom Abraham Lincoln called the plain people," who lived lives of "quiet, self-sacrificing heroism," with those who seek "perpetual amusement and the avoidance of care," and who live in "some flat designed to furnish with the least possible expenditure of effort the maximum of comfort and of luxury, but in which there is literally no place for children." The wrong type of woman, Roosevelt averred, constitutes "one of the most unpleasant and unwholesome features of modern life." The historical gap between his examples notwithstanding, and despite his claims that both city and country are valid places to create "a real home," Roosevelt's underlying message that *rural* mothers have a particular mandate to breed and multiply was clear.[60]

It was so clear that it drew some pointed reactions from country women. The Country Contributor referred to her own two children as her "two little specimens of race suicide," sarcastically indicating both her failure to propagate as heartily as Roosevelt would have liked and her perception of his outcry as particularly addressed to rural mothers. Yet she also denied that childbirthing could or should serve nationalist interests. "I haven't much faith in a generation of children born from a sense of duty to the country," she wrote. "I fear they might be pale-faced, pious little souls lacking the virility of the pioneer child who insisted on coming though there were ''leven in the fambly.'" Hence she denied that the hardiness and autonomy associated with the settlers, and which she claimed as a rural legacy, could be channeled by way of public mandates for procreation, ironically subverting the very link Roosevelt was attempting to establish. Other women lamented bitterly that, as one summarized it for a farm periodical, "less thought and consideration was given to the preparation for and rearing of children—human souls destined for eternity—than was given to the rearing of the stock upon the farm destined for the butcher's block!" As this writer argued, those most in need of reproductive control—those with knowledge of "poverty," "privation," and "hard labor"—were additionally burdened by Roosevelt's call to procreative duty, which denied women "the courage to decide this solemn responsibility for [themselves]" and "the strength to abide by [their] decision."[61]

Despite efforts by Margaret Sanger and other birth control advocates, such a decision was widely available only to the middle and upper classes: it was bourgeois women who were more fully able to realize the ideal of careful family management, including control over family size, that was keyed to increased prosperity.[62] Yet this reality was obscured in various ways by the rhetoric surrounding the birthrate issue, which attempted to glorify large families, and which effectively reframed rural women's procreativity as anything but a sign of impoverishment. For instance, the widespread assumption that higher education for females impeded their fertility endowed farmers' wives with the dubious distinction of a natural proliferativeness not dulled by unnecessary privilege or overcivilization.[63] And then there were the "Fitter Families" contests, held at country fairs, which merged eugenics with public health imperatives so as to advance the proper cultivation of stalwart human stock. Prize-winning families exhibited both a "clean" genetic history and a robustness resulting from an environment proven, via interviews and scorecards, to be healthful and nurturing—which, not incidentally, was likely to implicate the role(s) of the mother somewhat more than the father. (Significantly, the American Eugenics Society, like Roosevelt, idealized the rural family.)[64] Of course, the implication that rural women should reproduce heartily appeared to exalt them, while nonetheless investing them with one of the indices of lower-class status. Indeed, only the notion that farm people occupied higher moral and spiritual ground could lend dignity to their large families and differentiate their promiscuous reproduction from that of the vilified urban poor.

Hence farm women were implicitly and confusingly positioned by conservative commentators as working-class breeders of white, middle-class mores. As we shall see further in the next chapter, one of the ways that such a stratagem was facilitated was through the rhetorical overlap between farm language and the language of human reproduction: as the good farmer sows and reaps, so the worthy farm wife tends to the familial, and national, "crop." Ironically, though, the very terms of modern agriculture suggested the inapplicability of the parallel. "Progressive" farming assumed a causal link between efficiency and the quality of the yield, based on increased understanding of and control over breeding techniques and crop strains—issues of biogenetics. Excessive and uninformed propagation of animals and foodstuffs would, many understood, flood the market and result in the farmer's demise.[65] Yet for farm women the same logic did not apply, given the importance of their fecundity to agrarianism, to labor more generally, and to the state. In their case, a "progressive" attitude was linked to hyperfertility, despite the higher standard of living for the farm family, and the better life for the mother, that could result from the farm woman's access to effective means of family planning. (The choice, as one outraged female commentator would have it, was between race suicide and mother suicide.)[66] Thus farm women's corporeal needs were subsumed within the dictates of the larger body politic.

Suggestions that the farm woman's body could or should serve as a manufacturer of bourgeois whiteness, in addition to its sheer value in building a hearty labor pool, thereby demonstrated its symbolic density as compared with that of women in other social categories, even as child rearing was, ironically, somewhat less central to the farm woman's labor overall. The importance of regulating rural female sexuality was further indicated through heightened awareness in the farm press of farm girls' susceptibility to the white slave traffickers alleged to be prowling American cities in the years around 1910. Sensationalist stories of capture stressed the country girl's especial naïveté and purity and fueled the outrage of moralists, suggesting that a misuse of rural femininity was particularly reprehensible.[67] This is not to deny the existence within some rural communities of radical positions in regard to a woman's sexual and reproductive rights, as recent work on sex radicals of the late nineteenth century has demonstrated.[68] Rather, the point here is that farm women's real and perceived differences from both urban working-class and bourgeois women opened up an interpretive space that enabled critics with varied social agendas, many of whom were external to farming, to engage in wide-ranging readings of their cultural roles. This was part of a larger, complex process wherein the urgent necessity of resuscitating farming's status was effected in part by constructing farm families as a special, hybrid social class.

This theoretical hybridity—one means of bridging the gaps between, for example, a mythical agrarian ideal and more constraining agricultural realities, or between farming as a way of life and farming as a business—also found expression in attitudes about consumer goods, which were capable of signifying both desirable bourgeois standing *and* the "unnatural" and therefore ethically drained realm of mass production. Here, too, farm women, in particular, were thickly enmeshed in the tensions surrounding farm families' supposed abilities, and desires, to conform to modern ideals—namely, to buy or not to buy. Once again, what we can learn from these discourses has less to do with actual farm women's buying habits than with the prevailing logic of consumerism, and the ways in which that logic reflected modern anxieties about the acquisition of goods and the female's role in that acquisition.

The relation between women and consumption had been famously theorized in Thorstein Veblen's *Theory of the Leisure Class* (1899); its adoption as a linchpin of commodity capitalism in the modern United States can be traced through the advertising of the period, much of which was pitched to women and all of which became more visible to farmers as the result of rural free delivery, established in 1896, and falling prices for newsprint. Increasingly sophisticated marketing, especially that which focused on domestic products, not only made buying seductive but implicitly defined the economic insularity of the farm, where goods were more often made than purchased, as deviant. At the same time, however, pro-agrarians were lauding farmers, and especially farm women, for what they imagined as a refusal to capitulate to commodity fetishism. Ralph Borsodi agreed that farm women deserved reasonable labor-saving machinery but nonetheless envisioned them as superior precisely because they *made* most of the necessary domestic goods, which bound them more closely to the rhythms of the natural world and prevented reliance on the factory. The Country Contributor evinced a similar attitude. "Next to the farmer . . . in actual value to the world," she proclaimed, "stands the woman who knows how, with her own hands, to feed and clothe her family."[69] The line drawn between what, if anything, farm women should buy and what they should make was a matter of perspective, and farm women were precariously positioned between traditional rural values, which discouraged consumption, and the new social, and even agrarian, models, which aligned progress with participation in the consumer marketplace.

In reality, consumption in rural areas was a site of contestation, as historians have shown.[70] Rural women both prided themselves on self-sufficiency *and* sought access to more goods and conveniences, especially those that would ease the acknowledged hardships of rural domesticity. The desire for telephones and radios, which would alleviate isolation, was paramount: farm women as late as the 1920s often expressed a preference for such communications technology over other purchasable goods. Yet the demand for indoor machinery, such as washers or cookstoves, was also strong. A ten-dollar prizewinning letter in the April 1910 issue of *Farm Journal* argued that the acquisition of running water should be considered "a necessity," more important for farm women than even "the right to vote." Rural wives writing to Secretary of Agriculture David Houston in 1915 asserted that, as one put it, "most of the women live the lives of slaves"; another remarked that "[farm life for women] may be summed up in two words—drudgery and economy. These seem to pursue her from the time she signs her name to the mortgage . . . until that other time when, weary and worn, she gives up the unequal struggle and is laid at rest." As they fed hired hands, tended gardens and poultry, made the family's clothing, and canned the year's food supply, often without electricity or indoor plumbing, many farm women were apparently caught in an endless round of backbreaking labor that seemed mostly invisible, given that the farm's success was measured in crops and animals. And the strain of economic necessity was compounded by the inability to conform to standards of respectability defined by dress codes. This same woman added, "I managed [to meet] the mortgage every year, but the strain was too great, and overwork ruined my health. Meantime I have had only one new hat in eight years and one secondhand dress, earned by lace work. We are of the better class and have to keep up appearances, but the struggle is heart-breaking and health-destroying."[71]

That farm women's bodies could signify labor and want on two levels—first through their "ruined health," and then through their failure to "keep up appearances"—points to the possible tensions between limited means and the approved social aspirations that defined farm families as a "better," more industrious, working class. As this writer suggests, the farm woman's own corporeal circumstances—the extent to which she worked in the fields, the number of babies she bore and with what physical consequences, even the question of whether she owned a decent dress in which to attend church—served as an especially potent reminder of the farm's condition. In short, the farm woman's corpus was itself a consumable object in the farm economy while also transacting and registering the family's social status—a symbolic condensation captured provocatively by an extension service contest photograph from 1927. The winners of this contest, rewarded for making the most attractive dresses at the least cost, are captured in their prizewinning creations, with the price of the dress goods pinned to their chests. While the image suggestively renders the female body as commodity, it also momentarily, and ambiguously, makes visible the invisibility of rural women's domestic labor (fig. 1.2).

Farm women certainly sought relief from both onerous work and the signs of economic privation through consumer goods, including machine-made clothing: as Susan Matt shows, through the teens and 1920s, those with means increasingly demanded the same range of affordable products that was available in towns and cities. The gradual evolution toward agribusiness as an ideal, with its emphasis on technology and efficiency, also contributed to consumerist tendencies.[72] Yet the shift to increased consumption was not without social consequences. Rural sociologists and other male agrarian commentators routinely blamed women's material desires for rural migration to cities; one suggested that the rural teacher, "[who] is usually a woman," imparts to rural children "a mind filled with urban interests and a craving born of urban purposes." Another argued even more pointedly that farm men evince "the traditional joy of open spaces and the freedom of spirit which goes with

Figure 1.2 Members of the Vermontville Home Bureau unit, 1927. (Item No. PR-PO-16, College of Human Ecology Historical Photographs, No. 23/2/749. Courtesy of the Division of Rare and Manuscript Collections, Cornell University Library.)

it" while farm women, in contrast, are driven by city-based longings "for domestic help, for pretty clothes, for schools, music, art, and the things tasted when the magazines came in."[73] A genuine farm sensibility and commodity envy, so the argument ran, were antithetical concepts, and in a sense this was true: "making do" was a cornerstone of the pioneer ethic that had been carried forth as a premier virtue on the American farm. As late as the 1930s, when the broader commodity culture had made definite inroads into rural life, self-sustenance could still be a matter of enormous pride for farm women, linking them to an illustrious past: as one woman put it, "I have made footstools of coffee cans, and book shelves from apple crates. I have smoothed and varnished floors, and refinished old walnut furniture that I bought for a song. I even learned to weave cane seats for stubby dining chairs that others have since admired. . . . We farmer folk who are standing by our land, are feeling a bit as the old-time pioneers must have felt."[74] In theory, then, for farm women the simple act of buying could be fraught with perturbation: while potentially elevating in its erasure of the obvious differences between them and their sub/urban bourgeois sisters, it also threatened to eliminate their uniqueness by tempering their performative connection to their intrepid and exceptional ancestors.

Changing attitudes within agrarian institutions toward rural women's consumerism only muddied the waters further. Matt traces a shift toward acceptance, and even encouragement, of consumerism following World War I, when "a moral vision of the marketplace, with its strong prohibitions against envy," was replaced by an endorsement of desire as a "legitimate instinct." The Rural Extension Service, for instance, was among those institutions in the 1920s that were newly acknowledging the need to bring the amenities of urban life to the country, in part to thwart rural exodus.[75] By that point, the official representation of the efficient, modern, *successful* farm wife—who carried out the same sequestered, mechanized model of housekeeping as her middle-class counterparts, serving her family through the judicious use of market goods and eschewing field work—was firmly established. But that imagistic model, as we have seen, was not accepted unequivocally by rural women, who often resisted the imposition of gender ideals imported from urban contexts. Ultimately, pressing farm women to conform to modern consumerist standards proved no less difficult than pressing them to maintain old-fashioned agrarian ones. The perceived need somehow to combine these imperatives, to admit the new consumerism while also validating rural thrift, was particularly evident in the popular culture media increasingly available to rural women. Magazines reaching a rural audience, for instance, as chapter 2 will discuss in more detail, tried to balance, among other things, conflicting ideals of farm womanhood and commodity culture. The same journals carrying regular fashion features with titles such as "What They Wear in New York City" also lamented the affectation associated with emulation of urban standards and ran pieces on stretching food resources, remaking clothing, and refinishing old furniture. And Edward Bok, longtime editor of the *Ladies' Home Journal*, virtually made a career out of preaching the value of a "simple life" that was somehow not incompatible with middle-class consumption.[76]

The reality, of course, was that most farm families were limited in their means and thus were unable to conform to market-driven precepts of technology, dress, or home decor, even if they so desired. (Wrote one farm wife defensively, "There are no farmers or wives but would enjoy modern homes if they could afford them.")[77] Whether they succumbed or not, however, the pressure for such conformity seemed directed at women, upon whom the material responsibility for maintaining the family's appearance, as well as meeting its more basic nutritional and educational needs, generally fell, and to whom advertising for many consumer goods was consciously pitched. Moreover, for those few farm families who did manage to achieve a more recognizably bourgeois standard of living in the 1920s and 1930s (primarily through surviving the consolidation processes of the New Agriculture, which resulted in many smaller farms being squeezed out), the social contours of farming were irrevocably altered. As William Conlogue observes, the modern farming model undermined traditional modes of thinking and living: "The new farmer disdain[ed] the conflation of management and labor in the figure of the farmer, the privileging of inherited farm practices, the recognition of immanent value in work and property as opposed to their exchange value, [and] the noncommercial networks of exchange within a community." And for female participants in the New Agriculture, advancement was equated with a newly privatized household, wherein, for instance, women were segregated from hired hands, and commercial goods tied them more to corporate enterprises than to their local farm communities. Hence the very isolation that some farm women had sought to alleviate in the earlier years of the century was in many ways compounded in the official version of the thriving modern agribusiness, which was larger, and thus farther from neighbors, than the old family farm had been.[78]

Such ironies only offer further evidence that broad cultural currents, rather than a measured evaluation of rural needs, shaped attitudes toward farming outside, and even inside, of rural communities: farm people were no more able than urban dwellers to resist fully the pervasive influences of corporatization, industrialism, and consumerism—the forces of modernity. Yet farm women, already characterized by an excess of productive and reproductive labor, and with less access to the scientific principles and technological advances that promised to redefine their husbands as mental more than physical workers, were insistently corporealized in a manner that suggests their especially acute figurative resonance vis-à-vis both the rural and the modern. Their very bodies—as ad hoc field laborers, as manufacturers of domestic products, as reproductive vehicles—reified and extended traditional American (farm) values. (As one pro-agrarian affirmed, "[The farm woman] bears our sturdiest children while she helps to feed us all.")[79] At the same time, though, the newer forces of modernity urged them to use those same bodies in different ways. The growth of commodity capitalism, together with the class consciousness that was nurtured by cultural constructions of farmers as a class set apart, magnified farm women's roles as signifiers, and moderators, of their families' diets, dress, and leisure time—the physical markers of class standing. The pressure to adopt more efficient modes of housekeeping and to re/locate women indoors also problematized farm women's physical routines and work spaces. And the birth control movement, although distanced from rural communities, nonetheless challenged traditional and contemporary male assumptions about (rural) women's procreativity, leading to growing agitation by farm wives for more reproductive control.[80]

The extent to which farm women were imaginatively positioned in reference to the specifically material concerns—the bodily markers—of rurality and modernity is suggested by a farm press poem published in 1921 by Lena Martin Smith. "I Like to Live on the Farm," it proclaims, "Where we may dare to eat real butter / And cream, fresh eggs and smoked ham, / Though we may not possess a single pair / Of cobweb silk hose!"[81] Such a vision, of course, dichotomizes rather too neatly the farm and the city, rurality and modernity, and denies the intermediary sociocultural sensibility that more astute commentators such as Mary Atkeson ascribed to the Progressive Era farm woman. Yet the very insistence on a country/city, rural/modern binary betrays both the interdependence of the concepts and the perceived necessity of maintaining their integrity in the face of possible contamination.

As we shall see in the following chapter, a more flexible articulation of these symbolic realms was accomplished in the women's agricultural press, where the figure of the Farm Woman gave way to the bodies of actual farm women, whose varied conditions undercut essentialisms. An investigation of this transformative process helps to elucidate, in Elizabeth Grosz's words, "the contributions of the body to the production of knowledge systems, regimes of representation, cultural production, and socioeconomic exchange."[82] Moreover, a close reading of farm women's debates about themselves within a medium that also relies on advertising images and sociopolitical sloganeering demonstrates the complex imbrication of ideal and "real" in the newly influential genre of the women's magazine—a genre that helped to position farm women as modern subjects.

Chapter 2

The Farmer's Wife and *The Farmer's Wife*

A Provocative Scene from Edith Summers Kelley's Kentucky farm novel, *Weeds* (1923), highlights a rather pathetic female character, Hattie Wolf, who subscribes to a cheap monthly publication called "The Farm Wife's Friend." For several pages and in scathing detail, Kelley describes Hattie's avaricious consumption of this journal, underscoring the obtuse and often surreal relations between actual rural life, especially in the poorer sectors, and the texts and advertisements aimed at women readers in the farming papers of the time. Among other things, Hattie's periodical covers such topics as "how to make the eyes sparkle . . . how to keep the hands dainty and delicate, how to live so that the world is sweeter and sunnier for your presence, how to make orange marmalade out of carrots and how to treat a cow with a caked udder." As Hattie, immersed in her "dirty, stinking" washtub, attempts to transcend her circumstances by concentrating stoically on a featured poem celebrating the joy of washing clothes (refrain: "And the Wind Is Right to Dry"), the narrator asks slyly, "Who can say that the mail order sheet does not bring joy and comfort into the rural home?" (131–32; see also 133–35).

Less extended, but equally suggestive, is a scene from Olive Tilford Dargan's novel *Call Home the Heart* (1932). Here Ishmalee, an impoverished farm daughter, encounters another monthly periodical, this time entitled *Woman at Home*; its obviously bourgeois perspective opens to her "a way of living so enticing in comfort, so engaging in form, so ravishing in color, that it seem[s] nothing short of celestial" (11).

Ishma is particularly entranced by the beautifully appointed tables regularly featured in the magazine's photographs and spends hours in the woods creating replicas of such tables with elaborately manipulated leaves and twigs—an ironic counterpoint to her meals at home, which must be eaten in relays so that the large family may take turns using the limited cups and spoons (10–12).

While these scenes are exaggerated in bringing together such magazines and the poorest of rural wives and daughters (who were less likely to be literate, or to have regular access to such publications), they nonetheless gesture toward the complicated relations between farm women and the journals that purported to represent, inspire, and inform them. Together they reflect the journalistic reality that both "farm papers" and general-circulation "glossies" influenced country readers: mass-market women's magazines such as *Woman's Home Companion* were popular with rural audiences, yet specifically agricultural periodicals also flourished between 1910 and World War II, as they had throughout the history of the republic.[1] Moreover, the emphasis in these scenes on the special relation between magazines and women anticipates recent studies by Jennifer Scanlon and Ellen Gruber Garvey, among others, stressing the role of periodical literature in shaping the image of the woman as housewife and, perhaps more important, as consumer.[2] Significantly, while Dargan's character apprehends the privileged realm depicted in her magazine only as a kind of unattainable fantasy, finding her satisfaction merely in gazing at the pictures and playing at table re-creations, Kelley's character harbors "deep-seated excitement" over her magazine and its advertisements, hoarding her pennies to purchase cheap gimcracks and useless pamphlets, and believing profoundly in her ability to improve her life through such acquisitions. In different ways, then, these scenes demonstrate the authority of magazines in prescribing an image of domesticity that was heavily inflected by class assumptions and that defined women by their purchasing power, including the power to buy the magazines themselves.

Notably, the characters in both of these scenes are also keenly interested in fiction, particularly romance. The inclusion of short stories in most women's magazines of the period, and in many farm journals, reinforces the reflexivity established when these novelistic characters respond to the periodical press. That is, both Kelley and Dargan assume and portray an interpenetration of discursive media, apparently aware that, for instance, books and magazines, fiction and advertising, may contribute equally toward shaping (farm) women's perceptions of themselves, reflecting and refining social values in complex and interrelated ways. Of course, we are intended to join with the authors in deriding certain types of discourse, including mawkishly sentimental stories and the gimmicky enticements of seedy advertisers, thereby throwing into relief the more serious-minded social purposes of Kelley's and Dargan's novels. On a deeper level, however, both of these writers, as we shall see in chapter 4, invite self-conscious interrogation of the various ways and means of representing farm women, of which the agricultural press offers a supreme example.

There are numerous reasons for examining the roles of magazines in the lives of farm women in the modernist period. In a most basic sense, such consideration can counteract the perceived dearth of information on rural women's lives. Perhaps more important for the purposes of this study, however, is that magazines, combining several different and often conflicting modes of discourse, potentially capture something less quantifiable than facts, namely, the attitudes and postures that index aspirations and emergent "needs" as well as realities. More specifically, magazines pitched to a rural audience in this period operate at the nexus of commercial mass culture and the more circumscribed arena of agrarian culture in both its corporate and private aspects; hence they help us to trace the strands of the complicated ideologies—of agrarianism, of domesticity, of nation—tendered to and absorbed by rural female readers. Like agrarian-inspired social fiction and photography, rural magazines register both aesthetic ("ideal") and documentary ("real") impulses, thereby offering a compelling context for considering the politics of representation as they applied to farm women. Indeed, since they reported on but also critiqued information offered by such federal- and state-sponsored organizations as the Rural Extension Service and the American Country Life Association, farm journals served as primary arbiters of attitudes about farm culture in the years between the world wars.

Historically, though, magazine scholarship dealing with this period has offered little in the way of enlightenment concerning farm women. Major studies of periodicals have focused primarily on mass-circulation publications, notably in an effort to explicate emerging discourses of mass culture and to posit magazines as essential vehicles for the transmission of shifting social values. Despite being read in rural areas, these mass-market journals had little to say directly to or about farm women; as Richard Ohmann points out, the apparent lack of a defined audience for such "general" magazines as *Ladies' Home Journal*, the *Atlantic*, and *Munsey's* masked their deliberate appeal to a white, middle-class, urban or suburban audience.[3] In contrast, specialized journals have received very little scholarly attention, and considerations of the farm press, in particular, have been almost entirely limited to the discipline of rural history.[4] Yet this proves to be a moot point, since specifically agrarian periodicals were almost exclusively for men, typically confining "women's" material to a single short section of recipes, inspirational poems, and tips for beautifying the farm home. Farm women, it seems, brandished neither the cultural influence nor the discretionary income necessary to sustain the variety of magazines aimed at sub/urban women and farm men.

There is one exception, however, and it is a significant one. *The Farmer's Wife*, a nationally distributed monthly published by the Webb Company of St. Paul,

Minnesota between 1906 and 1939, was the single magazine devoted exclusively to farm women in the early twentieth century. If its singularity alone does not make it worthy of study, its lively amalgamation of "ladies' magazine" elements and materials specifically related to farming bears scrutiny for what it reveals about the conflicting messages concerning domesticity and agrarianism with which its readers contended. Established as the sister magazine of *The Farmer*, a prominent men's agricultural journal, *The Farmer's Wife* (*TFW*) merged the business- and policy-related emphases of the masculinist farm press with the housewifely orientation of mainstream women's magazines, thereby tapping into an underrepresented audience with bourgeois aspirations and highly specialized labor concerns. Its folksy, colloquial tone bespoke the practical, no-nonsense attitude of farming culture, even as its features and advertisements assured readers that they, too, were worthy aspirants to middle-class respectability. While it clearly catered to a conservative white readership and thus might seem somewhat removed from the more progressive politics of, say, Dargan and Kelley, its content was considerably less orthodox than we might predict. More fundamentally, its impressive circulation statistics (1.25 million subscribers by 1930, with readership estimates reaching as high as five readers for every copy)[5] suggest that it wielded significant influence as it mediated between dominant perspectives on gender and labor and the realities of some women's lives on farms.

While it would be inappropriate to make sweeping generalizations about the typical American farm woman based on the contents of *TFW*, we can nonetheless investigate its concerns and attitudes as a means of exploring how a certain editorial conglomerate, heavily influenced by the Country Life Movement, filtered ideologies of womanhood, rurality, and modernity, and of how some women responded to those representations. Thus *TFW* allows us to perceive the contours of cultural debates that, while precisely situated, nonetheless had ramifications for groups and issues beyond the farm. Moreover, since the magazine unfolded and flourished with modernity itself, it also offers a glimpse, more generally, into how seismic social changes in the culture at large colored a populist publication catering to women.[6]

Agrarianism versus Domesticity

> I think The *Farmer's Wife* should please
> The ones its name implies;
> And if they like it, as it is,
> I think that they are wise.
> —Reader's contribution, Oct. 1909[7]

From the beginning, *The Farmer's Wife* was understood as filling a specialized niche in the marketplace. Edward Webb, who bought the magazine in 1905, hoped it would "improve the quality of life in the farm home" and "ease the loneliness that isolation brought to the farm wife."[8] Dan A. Wallace, its long-standing and most influential managing editor, believed strongly in raising the class consciousness of farm families and frequently used his columns to inform farm women about agricultural policy issues and to direct them to fight for their rights.[9] Advertising and feature articles conspired to suggest that the farmer's wife was a unique individual—one who shared the urban housewife's domestic-minded concerns, to be sure, but one who also embodied the nativist pride and dignity attributed to the farming enterprise, and who could influence her husband and children in ways advantageous to farming as a whole. Moreover, she was recognized as having distinct, valid views on both farm and domestic culture, views not always in line with dominant conceptions. In short, *TFW*'s pages seemed to suggest that the farm woman is deserving of attention in her own right. "This Is YOUR magazine," the editors declared in February 1915. "Is there any particular subject that you should like to have [us] discuss?" ("What Do You Think of 'The Farmer's Wife'?").

Readers apparently found this appeal to their special interests quite compelling, as indicated by their published letters. One of the distinguishing features of *TFW* is the substantial amount of space devoted to reader-response elements, including letters to the editor, write-in contests (with the best letters receiving a cash prize), and survey-based forums and feature articles. While such elements were part of many magazines of the period, *TFW*'s dedication to the inclusion of readers' perspectives eclipsed that of other periodicals and bore out Edward Webb's expectation that a magazine could indeed create a community of sorts for farm women.[10] Readers and editors frequently referred to the magazine's readership in communal terms ("[I] speak of it as 'our' magazine," wrote one contributor [May 1915]), and the constant appeal to the audience to help shape *TFW*'s perspective—"Tell us if we are right; correct us if we are wrong" (editor's column, Feb. 1924)—underscored the sense that readers and staff were engaged in the joint enterprise of representing the typical farm woman's interests. Unexamined assumptions about "typicality" notwithstanding (as I shall discuss further on), one powerful way that *TFW* responded to the farm woman's distinctive situation was by inviting her to be a participant in, rather than a mere reader of, the magazine's discourse, a strategy that reinforced readers' views of themselves as active rather than passive.[11]

Part of the magazine's implied mission, then, was to foster a sense of deliberate self-consciousness among its readers, a self-consciousness that was effectively manifested at the editorial level: witness, for instance, the playful 1907 covers showing a smiling woman reading *TFW* (fig. 2.1),[12] or the opportunities proffered to readers

THE
FARMER'S WIFE

VOL. XII. ST. PAUL, MINN., JUNE, 1907. NO. 2

June
1907

25 Cents
a Year

Figure 2.1 *The Farmer's Wife*, June 1907. The same cover image was used for the months of May, July, and August 1907. (Image courtesy of the Minnesota Historical Society.)

to express their feelings about the magazine itself (e.g., October 1909; May 1915; June 1924). Of course, such reflexive gestures helped to consolidate *TFW*'s specialized audience, and thus might be seen as effective marketing ploys; however, they also foregrounded the kind of attentiveness to her own circumstances that the ideal farmwoman-reader was presumed to evince. Advertisements exploited this implied self-awareness, or the desire for it, in the curiously soothing but also prescriptive manner typical of much advertising in this period. A Chevrolet ad declared, "[T]he country woman needs her own car," since the farmer can seldom relinquish his vehicle for wives and daughters who want to go "to town or to a meeting or church" (January 1923). Another announced that Jell-O "is now sold in every small town general store" so that the farmer's wife may "serve the same fine desserts that have become so popular with her city friends" (Jan. 1921, 294). Such carefully targeted promotions, clearly designed to sell goods, nonetheless reinforced *TFW*'s editorial efforts to encourage readers constantly to consider their *identities* as farm women—their needs, their desires, their labor roles, their similarities to and differences from their urban counterparts. Interactive uses of the magazine—such as scorecards through which women could "rate" the conveniences of their farm homes (April 1920), the healthfulness of their houses and barns (Sept. 1920), or the quality of their community schools (Jan. 1925)—furthered this goal, as did the articles published specifically as suggested topics of discussion for rural women's clubs, which became increasingly popular through the teens and twenties and which *TFW* supported as a means of counteracting rural isolation.[13] And, of course, women were invited to write in on a wide range of pertinent issues. One of the most touted reader contests in *TFW*'s history revolved around a question cleverly designed to urge readers to reflect on their simultaneous roles as mothers, wives, and farmers: "Do You Want Your Daughter to Marry a Farmer?" (1922). The 7,000 responses, summaries of which generated four separate feature articles, were also compiled into a booklet that was published and sold separately for ten cents. Advertising for this booklet proudly publicized the contest's relation to *TFW* and claimed that the responses constituted "the most amazing and truth-searching statement about farm life ever assembled" (July 1922, 49).[14]

In the context of the overwhelmingly masculinist agrarian discourses of the period, *TFW*'s nurturing of its readers' self-cognizance must be understood, at least in part, as an activist impulse. This is clear to see in its frequent airing of frustrations regarding the social status of farm families. Notably, readers were aware of themselves not only as members of a community cohering around *TFW* and as participants in the larger farming concern but also as objects of observation by a broader culture, a culture rife with stereotypes and essentialisms about farm women. Readers' letters were often a locus for objections both to negative and to overly idealized representations of country living generally and rural women in particular. "I am fed up with the trifling treatment farm women receive at the hands of journalists and other writers," wrote one contributor, who objected to a "coarsely illiterate" farm woman being quoted in the national press as representative of her type (Aug. 1938). An admiring letter claimed that *TFW* was a "heart-helping farm journal" precisely because it "does not give city drawn [and presumably simplistic] pictures of rural life" (June 1924, 4). Stories, feature articles, and editorial columns continually reflected and refracted this concern for the image of farming and farm women. An editorial titled "The Farm Woman as She Really Is," for instance, deplored the constant "misinterpretations" of rural life based on exaggerated fiction, occasional "paragraphs in the daily press," or visions of farms "from Pullman windows," all of which, according to the writer, tend to render the farm woman as a "drudge" (Feb. 1916, 252). Another editorial cited specifically the instance of a "showy metropolitan magazine" that based its sales pitch not on "a straightforward presentation of the special advantages of the metropolitan field which it serves, but [on] . . . a sneer for the rural field which it does not reach" (Sept. 1928). At the other end of the spectrum, those with unrealistic notions of the unrivaled joys of rural living were also brought to task—even if the idealized representations were generated by farm women themselves. In 1927, for example, a heated controversy erupted over what some readers perceived as an inappropriately sunny self-portrayal of one farm woman's daily workload as she cared for her husband and ten children.[15]

TFW's overt investment in issues of representation demonstrates its attempt to intervene in contemporary cultural conversations; it also betrays the tensions structuring farm women's roles, and their shifting perceptions of themselves, in the modernist era. As farmers and as women, *TFW*'s readers were implicated in two ideological image sets, those of agrarianism and domesticity, that were not always compatible and that were especially volatile in the years of *TFW*'s run, when appeals to the modern effectively redirected traditional paradigms. One useful way to understand the specialized positioning of *TFW* is through its accommodation, intersection, and reformation of these distinct realms, one premised largely on notions of labor and class and the other based primarily on gender. Even as these discourses jointly shaped the controlling perspective through which *TFW* idealized the rural woman as the guardian of conservative values of farm and home, their sometimes uneasy interaction also revealed gaps, slippages, and contradictions in that perspective. Not surprisingly, in these interstices lay a great deal of the magazine's interest.

But for now the point is that the farm woman's joint emplacement within these two cultural discourses made her, and the magazine that served her, exceptional, especially when we consider the less textured bourgeois sub/urban readership to which virtually all mass-market women's magazines in the period were pitched. Of course, in key ways *TFW* was similar to these journals. In particular, it shared the well-documented tendency of other mass-circulation periodicals to advance a consumerist model through which readers, and especially women, assumed middle-class respectability via the real or imagined acquisition of consumer goods. For instance, T. J. Jackson Lears has documented the means by which advertisements of the period asserted a domestic ideal with woman-as-housewife at its center, her worth measured by the cleanliness and efficiency of her home, the robustness of her family—so much so that an obsolete toilet seat, as one advertisement suggested, could signal her utter failure. And Scanlon and Garvey have argued that not just advertisements but all elements of the magazine (including fiction and editorial content) worked in tandem to reinforce not merely the selling of specific items but the selling of an ethos of consumerism to which women, in particular, were urged to subscribe.[16]

Yet the agrarian constituency of *TFW* resulted in a substantially different inflection of this domestic ideal. As we have seen, the farm woman was often aligned with production as much as consumption: she did not typically confine her energies to the home front, as her labor power was also needed in the fields or the barn. The ensuing tension between a prevailing domestic model whereby (house)wives were defined as passive and, increasingly, as consumers, and the predominance of farming culture, *working* culture, as an essential component of the farm wife's identity was embedded in the magazine's very title. Is the farmer's wife more of a farmer, or more of a wife? This tacit question remained at the heart of *TFW* and suggests the extent to which the magazine attempted to bridge the divide, conceptually at least, between assumptions about the "drudgery" of farm life—assumptions that were often contested by farm women themselves—and an elusive respectability delineated by leisure.

Complicating this dynamic, however, was the exceptional status of agrarianism itself in the national psyche. *TFW* took for granted that the same women who may, on one level, have longed for the trappings of urban housewifery—efficient cookstoves, indoor plumbing, store-bought clothes—were also heavily influenced by the national mythography upholding country living as intrinsically superior to urban alternatives. Of course, this idealization more often reflected sentimental American values rather than contemporary agricultural realities. As David Danbom has observed, "[T]here is reason to believe that the myth of the moral superiority of the American farmer . . . served to justify an existence that was difficult to justify rationally."[17] Yet that myth nevertheless imposed powerful psychic paradigms, even as American farming as traditionally practiced was clearly threatened by a range of social, technological, and economic forces. One result was that farm women could appear caught between, on one hand, the nostalgic invocation of a "natural" lifestyle that by definition seemed to eschew science and technology, and, on the other hand, a desire to conform to new standards of efficient, mechanized housewifery that threatened to compromise their uniqueness by aligning them more and more with city women.

Looked at from this perspective, the very concept of farm womanhood in the early twentieth century seemed fraught with instability—more generated, perhaps, than actual. Nonetheless, if the farm woman, even in theory, occupied a constantly shifting social terrain, the terms of which had to be continually re/negotiated but were never settled, then she managed to embody in part the disruptiveness of modernity itself. This may explain why so much ink was expended in considering her status. *TFW*, as a primary vehicle for this investigation, indirectly set the stage for a diverse range of inquiries into the larger social dilemmas of American modernity, including the place of agrarianism in a newly urbanized nation and the appropriate role of women in general. Its concentration on the farm woman as both *farmer* and *woman*, that is, enabled a highly situated response to widespread societal change.

Before considering how *TFW*'s dual focus on agrarianism and domesticity managed to call broader hegemonic ideals into question, however, it is necessary to consider first the ways that it conspicuously iterated those very ideals. To begin with, the magazine's title confirms the association of farm women with orthodox ideologies of gender organized around marriage. For most readers, the farmer's wife *was* the rural woman, and any liberal movements to which she belonged coexisted with her supreme assurance that being her husband's helpmate and the bearer of his children was her primary role. In the pages of *TFW* this role was constantly validated, as the magazine consistently advanced a highly nostalgic version of the farm family as the soul of a democratic and moral America. Headlines and essay titles throughout the teens and twenties state that "Rural Life Is Moving Forward" and extol "Master Farm Homemaking" as "A Great Job"; they admonish readers to "Hang Onto the Farm," proudly proclaim the "Ideals of Rural Society," and expound on "Why Rural Thought Rings True."[18] Literally dozens of pieces glorify country living, and a short list of titles will serve to index this preponderance of celebratory sentiment: "The Farm Woman and Her Advantages"; "Hail to Our Farm!"; "Westward Ho, Farmerettes!"; "Pride in Our Work"; "Superiority of Country Schools"; "An Appeal to Country Women to Share Joys of Rural Life"; "Daughter Chooses the Farm"; "Just a Glorious Farm Woman"; "The Faith That I Have [in Rural America]"; "I'm Glad I Married a Farmer"; "I Love the Farm" (poem); "Give Me a Rural Church"; "The Call of the Farm"; "Why I Love Farm Life."[19] This is to say nothing of the constant, indeed incessant, comparisons made between city and country life in letters, articles, and short fiction, virtually all of which reveal the "true" value of agrarian living.

According to the traditional agrarian ideology buttressing *TFW*, farm mothers had two primary responsibilities: to produce future farmers and, as a corollary, to nurture a love for rural life. The implication is that one sows what one reaps. *TFW* fostered a continuing conversation about how best to raise children not only so that they will remain healthy and happy but also so that they will perceive the superiority of country life and abjure the lure of the city. In addition, the beauty of the rural landscape is presumed to reflect and extend the wholesomeness of family relationships, including the marital relationship, as the following "creed" suggests:

> Yes, I am a farm woman.
>
> I live in the country and I love it.
>
> As a farm woman I can have more complete companionship and partnership with my husband, than I could anywhere else.
>
> In the country, my family can live in closer fellowship than is possible elsewhere.
>
> In the country each one of us is important to the community life instead of being lost in the crowd.
>
> On the farm our work, both inside and outside, is creative. And I, as farm woman, have a share in the great task of putting agriculture on a sounder basis and in making rural life all that we want it and expect it to be.
>
> Taking it all in all, I would rather live in the country and raise my family in the country than any place else.
>
> Yes, I am a farm woman. (Jan. 1930)[20]

The apparent singularity of purpose expressed in this creed was hardly exceptional and occasionally took on rather bizarre proportions: in 1928, the year that *TFW* inaugurated its "Master Farm Homemakers" recognition program (modeled on the "Master Farmer" contest run by *The Farmer*), the editors went so far as to publish a composite photograph of the Typical Farm Homemaker based on the facial characteristics of the winners (July, 9 [fig. 2.2]).

This composite image, with its implied connection to the eugenics movement, points to yet another ideal manifest in *TFW*'s pages: not surprisingly, the quintessential master farm homemaker is white. Moreover, with her spectacles, string of beads, and healthful complexion, she is undeniably middle-class. By appealing to a nativist, bourgeois population—or at least to a white population aspiring to middle-class status—*TFW* participated in the subtle racism and class bias of both mainstream women's magazines and agrarian reform literature in the Progressive Era. (For instance, *Ladies' Home Journal* engaged in a social construction of whiteness that precluded identification of minority females as proper women, and the Extension Service, among other agrarian policymaking groups, advocated conformity to a domestic ideal that was by definition white and middle-class.)[21] While *TFW*, especially in its early years, occasionally exhibited blatant cultural stereotyping, notably of African Americans, its racism and classism were premised largely on the absence of attention to less advantaged and/or nonwhite women. And, despite its celebration of working-class values, *TFW* assumed the position that rural people

Figure 2.2 Composite image of a Typical Farm Homemaker, compiled from contest winners' photographs. *The Farmer's Wife* July 1928: 9. (Image courtesy of the Minnesota Historical Society.)

were upwardly mobile, a stance that precluded, for instance, sustained consideration of farm women in tenancy. Particularly insistent was the association of farm women with an American tradition based on European antecedents and steeped in patrician ideals, as an admiring article titled "George Washington, Gentleman Farmer," indicates (Feb. 1924). Yet another piece featured photographs of four white, smartly dressed young people recently returned from agricultural college—"the type of young farmers," the caption tells us, "who are 'putting the culture into agriculture'" ("Mr. and Mrs. American Farmer," July 1916, 27). Often this nativist, middle-class emphasis manifested itself in the aggrandizement of the neo-pioneer woman or the female homesteader, whose acquisitiveness was perceived as appropriately located in the land and whose labor, not coincidentally, was undertaken in a setting relatively removed from the shifting sociopolitical contexts—of uncertain race relations, of economic instability, of waves of immigration—that defined modern experience and threatened white twentieth-century farm culture.

So, for instance, a lengthy autobiographical article by a woman living in a log cabin highlighted this quotation in a boxed-off section of the first page: "Why Katherine Douglas Homesteaded: 'I was city smothered, city starved, city weary! Every atom of me was crying out for—enough. I wanted enough room; enough time; enough air, light, sunshine. I was cramped in sense and spirit until my very intellect threatened to go to sleep like a cramped foot'" (April 1915, 312). The association of the city with both social disintegration and a physically enclosed lifestyle enabled a corresponding association of the open landscape with a (white) Protestant work ethic that signified an "American" ideal. We may not have fancy clothes or even telephones, the magazine implied, but in the country we are more genuine, more dignified, more complete. Living on the land, then, was represented as an authentic existence for "true" American women. As another article put it in introducing a featured farm heroine, "Here is a woman who, although city born and trained, just naturally gravitated to the soil. She works harder than ever before and gets more out of life" ("How Some Women Succeed," Aug. 1925, 326).

These not-so-subtly racialized ploys had complex underpinnings, since they also served to legitimize aspects of the farm woman's routine that might potentially compromise her maternal-domestic station. That is, her chores around the farm, and her life out of doors generally, could be idealized in their own right as part of a uniquely "American" lifestyle. Katherine Douglas's essay explains that her move from department store clerk to homesteader involved "cut[ting] [her]self off from friends, telephones, stores, churches, [and] amusements," but also lent her self-empowerment through her work on the land, making her "an American citizen—an entity." Similarly, in 1928 the magazine reported on a "distinguished businessman" who declared that hearing the experiences of exceptional farm women is akin to "reading an autobiography of Abraham Lincoln" (July 1928, 9). Eleanor Roosevelt, in an interview with *TFW*, confirmed that "[o]ut of the hardships of rural life have come many of our great men . . . [and] women, too. . . . There must be something in country living that gives fiber, backbone, ability to think and to act—something that makes for success in this country of ours" (July 1933, 5). Even rhetorically masculinist ideals could be appropriated in order to align rural women with American myths of the soil, thereby dignifying their experiences, as in a short story about the real-life Women's Land Army entitled "Peggy Phelps of Unit 12: A City-Girl Soldier with a Hoe for a Gun Went Out to Conquer the Land" (July 1919). If farm women could not match precisely the image of Mrs. Housewife put forth by the glossier magazines, then at least they could be identified with nativist grit.

This is not to say that the typical representation of the housewife dominating mainstream women's journals—namely, that of the woman of relative leisure, whose purchases allowed her to regulate and beautify her home and its occupants—was absent from *TFW*. On the contrary, despite the wide acknowledgment that farm families suffered a low standard of living relative to other groups in the United States, and despite individual farm women often resisting such representations, the notion of housewife-as-consumer was alive and well in *TFW*'s pages. In particular, Lears's articulation of a "dialectic" between "Americans' new emotional needs and advertisers' strategies"[22] is easy to perceive in this farm women's journal, especially insofar as the farm wife was exhorted to purchase goods that would simultaneously ensure the health of her family, perpetuate a pink-cheeked country ideal, and solidify her standing as a mother—all of which can be perceived in a long-running advertising campaign for Cream of Wheat (e.g., "Farm children have so much! Don't let them lose out on an easy care like this" [Oct. 1930]).[23] By the 1920s, farm women, like their city sisters, were routinely judged by advertisements for their un/willingness to purchase such goods as the Hygeia nursing bottle ("Is your baby safe while nursing?" [Aug. 1925]), Lux soap (How can you afford so many new stockings? . . . Lux keeps your rayon things like new longer" [Oct. 1929]), and Postum caffeine substitute ("Is she to be a failure as a mother? Don't let fatigue poisons ruin *your* nerves" [April 1932]).[24] Perhaps the single major difference between most ads in *TFW* and those in other women's magazines concerned their often explicit appeal to farming circumstances, as in a full-page General Electric ad asserting that the old-fashioned washtub, "the bane of the farm woman's life," can simply be "put away" on a properly "electrified farm," leaving "more time for everyone to enjoy the pleasanter things of life" (March 1927).

Certain promoters were successful in melding the farm wife's distinct roles, suggesting that both her farming duties and her domestic duties could be fulfilled by the same product. Such was a 1912 ad for the new Kodak camera:

> **Kodak on the farm**
>
> Pictures of stock that you have to sell, pictures showing the development of animals at a certain age, of crops at a certain stage of growth, of buildings, and of ditches and fences and roads—all these can be used to advantage in systematizing and making your farm profitable.
>
> Pictures of your family and friends, pictures of the places you visit and the things you and your family are interested in—these will add to the pleasure of home life for all the household.
>
> And *you* can make such pictures. (Feb. 1912, 281)

But some of these specialized appeals, in their eagerness to sell goods, came dangerously close to undermining farm life. It is in these ads that we can best see the competing claims of, on one hand, the period's agrarian ideology, which idealized hard work and plenty of it, and, on the other hand, a domestic ideology that was premised less on physical labor than on the housewife's mastery of an interior space. Indeed, advertising in *TFW* frequently hinged on downplaying oppositions that were accepted in the dominant culture—indoors versus outdoors, private versus public, leisure versus labor—but that were not operative for the farm wife, who moved fluidly between such poles. Copy that elevated one alternative at the implied expense of the other, then, could be risky indeed, although it could also embody an emotional appeal that successfully exploited the presumed apprehensions of its audience.

Especially unsettling from this perspective were those ads suggesting that the farm wife, through her purchases, was responsible not only for the pleasantness of her immediate domestic environs and the happiness of her family but also for the welfare of her farm as a whole, and perhaps even for the future of farming as an occupation. "It's up to you to make life on your farm worth living," stated one ad for Colt gas lighting. "Don't blame your children if they decide that life on the farm is not worth while" (April 1925). Advertisements for land in South Dakota and Montana asked, "Can You Hold Your Children on the Farm?" and suggested that wider spaces, newer horizons, would make for the prosperity that would allow the reader to "bind [her boy] to [her] forever" (March 1927). Underlying such appeals, of course, are two implied fears: first, that a farm woman's children will leave her, presumably because her lifestyle is unattractive or unfulfilling, and second, that she will fail to perpetuate the farming culture that is so obviously to be desired. In a related vein, a pitch for Kellogg's Corn Flakes intimated that the housewife's failure to serve tempting food could mean the farm's demise, as the quality of the "grub" could determine "how long [the hired hands] remain" (Oct. 1911). Such advertisements betray the uneasy relations between domestic ideals and agrarian ones, if only because the extent of the housewife's presumed responsibility, the need for her domestic influence, is directly proportional to the invisible forces that pull children and hired hands *away* from the farm.

Editorial content occasionally shared in this awkward dynamic. *TFW* readers were urged regularly to use their influence to keep their children from abandoning farm culture, as the following banners indicate: "Educate Them for the Farm" (Aug. 1907); "Keeping the Boys on the Farm" (Oct. 1907); "Shall [Daughter] Choose the City?" [No] (June 1917); "Daughter Chooses the Farm" (June 1917); "Mother Confesses: Before It Was Too Late She Discovered How to Tie Daughter to the Farm" (March 1919); "How Ya Gonna Keep 'Em?" (April 1921); "If Daughters Go to the City (And If Trouble Meets Them Because of Their Unawareness or Foolishness)"

(July 1922); "[Resolved:] To Tie Children to the Farm" (Jan. 1923). Such pieces do not exactly reconcile domestic imperatives and agrarian ones; rather, they connect them by placing the former in service of the latter. Farm life *is* an ideal life, the magazine observed again and again, and the farm woman's most important role *is* located in her maternal-domestic influence; if at times her domestic duties seem compromised by the pressing concerns of the field or barn, then that merely demonstrates her capaciousness, her resourcefulness, her overall superiority to the urban woman whose purview is more restricted. The country woman, insisted one editorial, is "stronger, simpler, truer than the city woman" (Feb. 1916, 252). Indeed, declared a contributor, the farm woman "has often felt somewhat sorry for the city woman," who seems "shut out" of her husband's activities, making her "little more than a beautiful luxury of no vital importance to the man or the home" ("My Ideas on 'The Tired Farm Woman'" [Jan. 1923]). After all, argued yet another, "a city woman is not part of the business as she is on the farm"; confined to her "dry, uninteresting" indoor existence, she must feel "as if [she] were merely part of the household equipment" ("Why I Wish I Was Back on the Farm," Sept. 1926).

Ironically, the elevation of the country housewife over the urban one (which, of course, was a reactionary response to the perceived attractions of the city as well as to its dangers)[25] also provided a roundabout means of bringing domestic and agrarian ideals more in line with each other, notably through the suggestion that the urban housewife's anxieties could be not merely diminished but eliminated in the atmosphere of the country. Lears assigns a "therapeutic ethos" to the period's advertising, which emphasized the desire to "experience 'real life' in all its forms," and which suggested the need for an antidote to the alienating effects of urban-industrial culture: "To affluent Americans reared with the agrarian bias of republican moralism, urban 'luxury' could be a symbol of 'overcivilization' as well as a sign of progress. Freed from the drudgery of farm life, they were also increasingly cut off from the hard, resistant reality of things. Indoor plumbing, central heating, and canned foods were pleasant amenities but made life seem curiously insubstantial. . . . [T]he most comfortable people were also the most anxious[.]"[26] It is easy to see how the dynamic Lears describes, which he traces in the advertising of popular mass-circulation periodicals, might work to the advantage of *TFW*'s specialized audience. If the modern housewife is defined by her anxious need to make her home setting healthy, attractive, and full of "natural" goodness in its foods and other commodities, then the farm woman clearly had an advantage, for even the poorest country family could boast of such benefits, and the farm wife did not have to exert herself to gain them. Virtually all aspects of TFW, including editorial content as well as advertising, played up this perspective. "The Farm Mother Feeds Her Family Right," declared an advertisement for Shredded Wheat; since she "work[s] in the open, and "live[s] close to Nature and to Nature's food," she "know[s] the health and nourishment of wheat" (June 1934, 13). Similarly, a feature article exploited the meaning of "kindergarten"—"Child Garden"—to argue that the farm offers a wholesome and educational site for preschoolers, "in Which the Tender Powers of Young Minds May Unfold" ("Where Little Children Grow," May 1917). Such attitudes had the important benefit of blurring the boundaries between indoor and outdoor environments, reframing domestic space in a way that accommodated the farm wife's daily rhythms.

This last example also points to the rich rhetorical overlap between domestic and agrarian ideologies, which, on the surface at least, enabled the superimposition of homemaking and farming roles. The stereotypical association of maternity with the fulsomeness of the landscape extended into a series of wordplays centered on notions of nurturing, fertilizing, and sowing/reaping, all of which allowed for doubled references to homemaking/child rearing imperatives and agrarian operations. Farm women were represented as the tillers of a familial soil, raising a crop of moral citizens who would, in turn, become farmers (and "fathers") themselves. Such puns reinforced the notion that domestic and agrarian ideologies served, or should serve, the same ends: in the words of a published poem admonishing farmers for their narrow preoccupations, "You talk of your breed of cattle / And plan for a higher strain / . . . But what are you doing, my brother, to better the breed of men?" ("Answer, You Breeders of Men!" [Sept. 1927]). Both this poem and the magazine more generally advanced the expectation that the farm woman, in particular, should lavish attention on the domestic "crop"; her position, then, was articulated through a rhetorical maneuver that obfuscated apparent contradictions between domestic and agrarian duties, intimating instead that they were one and the same.

Perhaps most important, however, is the manner in which both the primacy of the farm and the sanctity of the nuclear family touched, once more, on the mythology of Americanness, suggesting that domestic and agrarian imperatives may be connected in service of the larger body politic. "I believe deeply in agriculture and the rural home," wrote a *TFW* editor. "[O]ur national welfare rests largely upon them" (March 1927). This coalescence of domestic and agrarian appeals under the umbrella of nationalist duty is nowhere more evident than in *TFW*'s World War I era preoccupation with the farm woman's responsibility to feed the nation. Under such headlines as "The Patriotic Potato!"(May 1918) and "Food Will Win the War" (June 1918), farm women were urged to contribute as much as possible to the farm's production (in the fields) *and* to conservation (in the home) in order to provide sufficient food for the troops. While this campaign pointed to the ever-present tensions—between production and consumption, between the field and the kitchen—inherent in the modern construction of the farm wife's identity, it also demonstrated the overtly successful melding of domestic, agrarian, and nationalist dictates. More accurately, this wartime bid for patriotism effectively, if momentarily, flattened the more contested terrains of agrarian and domestic discourses, suggesting that, if necessary, a "higher," more urgent ideal could trump those threatened by shifting cultural values.

To a significant (and predictable) degree, then, mainstream precepts dominated *TFW*'s pages, and anything that threatened those precepts was frequently glossed over. But by no means was its conservative message seamless. Rather, as I have already suggested, *TFW* registered ideological rifts as well as coherences—and it is essential to note that these were not entirely relegated to subtextual spaces. Sometimes quite challenging ideas were openly presented alongside orthodox ones. This was largely made possible by the magazine's dedication to reader involvement, which resulted in the periodic expression of minority opinions, such as letters by women who hated farming or who objected to the drudgery of housework and the joyless tasks of routine child care. While such perspectives were never allowed to destabilize the overall outlook of the magazine, which validated the nuclear family, the gendered division of labor, and the inherent dignity of the farm home, their presence was nonetheless influential. Occasionally, for instance, the negative remarks of a contributor led to a full-blown forum on a particular issue, with representation that was remarkably balanced.[27] And while the inclusion of minority voices, and the subsequent recontainment of such voices within the dominant perspective, might be seen as an editorial effort merely to titillate with conflicts that were destined to be resolved, subversive ideas about farming, domesticity, and even "Americanness" lingered in the background of the magazine's rhetoric, their very presence contesting the superficially unified perspective of *TFW* as a whole.

What I am asserting here about *TFW* distinguishes it somewhat from Christopher Wilson's argument about other mass-circulation magazines of the period—that they advanced a "spurious" realism based on an illusion of "power and participation that masked delimited options and prefabricated responses."[28] To the (substantial) extent that *TFW* invited and then published marginal perspectives, its proffered reader participation was more genuine than illusory. More important, while it did, like the journals Wilson discusses, advance a dominant and even controlling editorial viewpoint, it differed from other magazines insofar as this vision was already compromised by larger cultural forces that necessarily shaped it as openly defensive. It appears that *TFW*'s constant reassertion of a conventional agrarian lifestyle as "the best and most normal way of life" (editorial, Oct. 1921) was directly proportional to the perceived seriousness of the agricultural crisis. Yet that crisis was not ignored; on the contrary, the problem of how to modernize agriculture so as to retain a vibrant American farm community was continually addressed from a variety of angles in virtually every issue. Hence *TFW*'s primary message—the soothing reassurance that farming, and farm housewifery, is indeed a useful and dignified profession—was always situated in response to an openly acknowledged realm of conflict, disillusionment, and uncertainty. More than other popular women's magazines, then, *TFW* probed the limits of its own representational authority, resulting in a modernist stance that embraced, rather than eschewed, truly divergent perspectives.

It is no coincidence that alternative, less optimistic views of farm culture most often found expression in readers' contributions. The continuous agitation in reader-response sections for such amenities as better roads, neighborhood clubs, rest rooms for rural women shopping in town, and even vacations for farm women demonstrated the perceived need for more social interaction among farm homemakers, as well as more leisure. This is not to say that letter writers or other contributors routinely rejected normative domestic-agrarian ideals, but merely to underscore the extent to which *TFW*'s forums nearly always included mixed, or even quite negative, views on the situation(s) of the farmer's wife.[29] Significantly, many such contributions focused on the debased material circumstances of farm women, including their onerous workloads, their primitive domestic equipment, their vulnerability to repeated childbirths, or their inability to clothe or educate their children appropriately. Thus the overdetermined and often sentimental versions of domestic agrarianism dominating agricultural reform discourses, and to which *TFW* frequently adhered, were also challenged within its pages by specific women advancing oppositional images and attitudes. Such elements constitute what Donna Haraway calls "epistemologies of location, positioning, and situating," as they pit "the view from a body, always a complex, contradictory, structuring and structured body" against "the view from above, from nowhere, from simplicity."[30]

Indeed, in *TFW*'s pages the actual physical circumstances of an individual woman sometimes eclipse for a moment the larger essentialisms dominating mainstream notions of the farm home. While many such contributions simply demonstrate the vast spectrum of economic and social differences among farm women (small families vs. large, profitable farms vs. subsistence arrangements, etc.), the most striking ones—perhaps because they so dramatically challenge prominent ideals—emphasize hardships, and even suggest that farm life is not to be desired. The banner over the letter of one contributor, for example, proclaims "I Need Human Contact" (Sept. 1926, 415), while another letter writer offered this advice: "If [your husband] slaps you, you slap him back. . . . Demand money and keep on asking until you get it. . . . Keep on being mean until he changes, it might take a year to break him" (April 1913). Among those women who responded to the 1922 contest by saying that they did *not* want their daughters to marry farmers—and it is worth noting that a full-length feature article was dedicated to the 6 percent who responded negatively—the following comments were published: "Farm life is a narrow and ugly life"; "Dull monotony of prolonged household drudgery becomes intolerable"; "Farm life is a life without recompense" (Oct. 1922).

Somewhat surprisingly, advertising and editorial content also contributed to this darker dimension of the magazine, notably by acknowledging farm women's material difficulties and advocating change. So, for instance, in the early years of *TFW* (especially 1906–1907), graphic marginal advertisements sponsored by various temperance organizations offered help for dealing with drunken husbands, and part of a 1920 editorial page was devoted to an approving description of an exhibit at the Montana State Fair featuring a miniature cemetery with tombstone epitaphs reading "Mother—walked to death in her kitchen"; "Jane—she scrubbed herself into eternity"; and "Susie—swept out of life with too heavy a broom" (Jan.). Not infrequently, women's labor contributions were championed and their physical needs were addressed under such banners as "Dignifying the Work of Farm Women" (on the economic valuation of domestic chores) or "Why Not the Cooperative Laundry?" A 1921 editorial reported on a farm wife who wore a pedometer and found she walked 12 miles a day doing domestic work (15–18 miles during holiday periods and at threshing time). She walked 400 miles in a month, proclaimed the editors, "and in five years—hold your breath!—circumscribed the globe, right in her own home! We move the installment of a lot of pedometers. Or, better yet, a general improvement of household equipment" (May). Of course, such pieces reflect the era's investment in improved efficiency and productivity, which was stressed in virtually all labor arenas, not merely in terms of farm work or modernized housekeeping. But in *TFW* this efficiency mantra dovetailed effectively with other, often more openly negative, representations of farm women's physical existences, contributing to a wide-ranging, and progressive, preoccupation with women's materiality.

As an example, agitation for a better standard of living through improvements in domestic equipment, an issue that, as we have seen, was recognized generally in women's agricultural circles, acquired especial prominence in *TFW* and illustrates the attention devoted to the farm woman's corporeality across the magazine's diverse discourses (e.g., advertising, editorial content, readers' contributions). The prevailing complaint was that farmers failed to consider their wives' work seriously, assuming that it was more important to improve the efficiency of field labor than of household labor. Women even pointed out that farmers' prosperity typically meant more work for their wives, who had to feed the newly hired hands who were the result of the farm's extra income and increased acreage. That the husband must be flattered, nagged, or tricked into sharing his wealth to provide such labor-saving amenities as indoor plumbing, cookstoves, or washing machines was often treated as a given. One short story published in July 1914, for example, relates the tale of a farm wife who sells her husband's hogs to procure health- and labor-saving screen doors for their home; when her spouse discovers her deception, and perceives the comfort to his family that the screens provide, he vows to reconsider the household's distribution of money ("Millie Waters's Declaration of Independence"). Staff writers and reader-contributors regularly pointed out the necessity for such equality, arguing, for instance, that "It is just as necessary that the food be prepared as that it be provided; that the house as well as the fields be kept in order" (Dec. 1907, 126). Another wrote, "Happy is the man who sees to it that an equal division of the spoils is made" (April 1908, 200). An essay title in April 1913 asked, "Are Farm Women Getting a Square Deal?" and the piece opened by comparing "the meager facilities for doing work easily and effectively in the average farm home with the magnificent equipment employed in doing the work on the farm" (352). As early as May 1908, *TFW* took this issue to its front cover with a whimsical but nonetheless earnest poem about the exertions of the old-fashioned washtub, accompanied by a distressing photograph showing a frazzled farm woman in her front yard laboring over her outmoded laundry equipment; the poem ends by "blessing" the farmer who considers his wife's labor needs as well as his own.

Thus even as the magazine reinforced abstract models of domestic-agrarian soundness and plenitude, it also routinely showcased farm women's concerns, which fractured iconographic images insofar as those concerns centered on bodily discomforts related to labor, health, childbirth, and child care. *TFW*'s organized write-in forums, for instance, revolved around such topics as domestic machinery ("Labor-Saving Devices" [Oct. 1911], "How Did You Get Yours?" [June 1928]); conditions of rural childbirth ("Motherhood in the Country" [April 1918]) and rural medical care ("The Rural Medical Situation" [May 1929]); the USDA's Rural Extension Program ("What We Ourselves Want: Ways in Which the Smith-Lever Funds Can Serve Our Homes" [Sept. 1914]); and relations between rural women and laws of, for example, inheritance ("The Farmer's Wife Speaks" [Jan. 1928], part of a yearlong series entitled "Do Your Laws Protect You?"). Even those forum topics that might be deemed aesthetic, rather than practical, in nature pointed to farm women's investment in material representations of their lifestyles ("Ideal Farm Home Contest" [Oct. 1926]) or their contributions to the nation ("The Quest for the Pioneer Woman" [Nov. 1927, March 1928], concerning the appropriate design for a statue commemorating women of the frontier). Such topics served literally to ground more abstract essentialisms in the realities of farm women's existences. In the process they also foregrounded the farm woman's special status by addressing, rather than glossing over, her combined agrarian and domestic forms of labor, challenging simplistic assertions about the roles and concerns of the modern woman.

Perhaps most compelling from the point of view of subscribers, however, is that *TFW*'s participatory format appeared obliquely to serve farm women's interests and material needs—especially the expressed need for companionship—as much as it discussed them. Ellen Gruber Garvey has researched the ways in which ad-dependent women's periodicals in the early twentieth century ran contests encouraging readers to play with the advertising copy, thereby training them as attentive consumers.[31] While the editors of *TFW* did not focus readers specifically on the magazine's advertising, their contests and write-in opportunities nonetheless functioned similarly, encouraging readers to re/invest their attention in women's domestic-agrarian issues, thereby solidifying the magazine's specialized readership and engendering a kind of discursive community among women whose life circumstances made them prone to isolation. Hundreds, sometimes thousands, of women responded to particular survey questions posed by the editorial staff, providing the raw data for major feature articles; moreover, unsolicited letters on a variety of domestic-agrarian subjects were given substantial monthly space (typically five or six pages in a thirty-page issue). That individual letter writers routinely responded to previous contributors demonstrates the extent to which *TFW* succeeded in nurturing a sense of intercourse and fellowship among its readers.

But perhaps the epitome of *TFW*'s dedication to establishing a virtual community for farmers' wives was signified by its 1926 sponsorship, together with the American Country Life Association, of what was claimed to be the first national conference for farm women. Naturally, its proceedings—which highlighted the responses of attendees to a variety of questions about farming and housewifery—were given significant space in the magazine's pages.[32] It seems that *TFW* did what it could, then, to put farm women in dialogue with its editorial staff and with each other, constantly striving to evoke a sense of actual, physical contact. As the editors declared, "You are our 'folks' . . . and we need—oh, so much!—to see you face to face, eye to eye; to 'visit' with you and talk over many things that are dear and vital both to you and to us" (May 1915).

This attention to the concerns of real-life women (whose opinions, significantly, were usually expressed in their own words), combined with emphases on their material circumstances, effectively counterbalanced *TFW*'s tendency to promote idealistic notions of farming and farmers' wives. The iconic figure of the Farm Woman, that is, was systematically challenged by the individual farm women who both read the magazine and largely constituted it through their letters and auto/biographical narratives. From this perspective, it seems especially significant that *TFW*'s feature stories and articles were generally written not by its managing editor (who was typically a man) but by its female field editors. The more prominent and long-serving ones, such as Ada Melville Shaw, Clara M. Sutter, and Bess Rowe, enjoyed loyal readerships and were themselves farm women of long standing. (Ada Shaw, for instance, had homesteaded in Montana, and Clara Sutter ran a poultry farm in northern Iowa.)[33]

These field editors regularly fanned out over the United States, gathering material for different departments (poultry, health, handicrafts, etc.) and meeting with rural women firsthand in order to plan and execute feature articles showcasing their problems, concerns, and achievements. Clearly this arrangement suggests that a premium was placed on "authenticity"—that is, on the representation of actual farm women by those who were presumed qualified to interpret their circumstances. Indeed, readers were assured that these field editors were "experts in their line" and were "actually doing the things you talk about. They are the sort of women you would delight to visit within your home" (March 1920).

Hence a dedication to realism was also a prominent aspect of *TFW*; just as it tapped into discourses of both agrarianism and domesticity, it also tempered its own romanticization of farm and home through a regular, sometimes defiant, consideration of physical actualities. Of course, the assumption of eventual triumph, both for individual farm families and for farming as a whole, was integral to the magazine's philosophical stance; yet success was often merely the anticipated ending of a struggle that, in and of itself, took center stage. One letter writer illustrates perfectly this dynamic. After describing the hardships preventing her family—including ten children—from moving beyond a rented farm, she nonetheless declared grittily, "Ours is not a Success Story . . . not yet" (Jan. 1927, 25).

Stories, Fictional and Not

TFW's substantial body of fiction serves as a particularly illustrative model of the magazine's careful efforts to balance both agrarian and domestic ideologies, and realistic and idealistic representational imperatives. Considerable space was devoted to this popular aspect of the journal: a typical issue in the 1920s and 1930s contained two or more short stories of several pages, at least one of which was a serial. Somewhat ironically, though, this fiction justifies separate discussion not because it limns a discrete discursive realm—as has sometimes been claimed about popular magazine fiction[34]—but because it constitutes such a coherent extension of the magazine's preoccupations. Much of what I have already demonstrated concerning *TFW*'s multilayered response to contemporary dialogues about agriculture and women resonates within the magazine's fiction as well; sometimes the selfsame topic was treated in fictional and "real" arenas within a single monthly issue.

Predictably, *TFW*'s stories echoed the dominant rhetorical structure of the magazine by adhering to an entirely conventional mode of linear narration, confirming the sense of forward momentum that was an essential component of *TFW*'s appeal and strategy, a precondition of its expressed faith in the secure future of farming.

While it certainly carried much normative, place-neutral women's magazine fiction, most interesting for our purposes are those stories with strongly articulated agrarian settings and themes, of which at least fifty were published in the magazine's thirty-year run.[35] *TFW*'s farm stories bring together virtually all the interests of the magazine as a whole, including, for instance, tensions surrounding the perceived opposition between country and city, and between farm men and women about the valuation of domestic labor versus field work. They also address popular women's topics—such as the revolt against an insensitive husband, or the generational dissension between mothers and daughters—within the particularities of agrarian circumstances, tailoring recognized social issues to fit farm circumstances. Often combining sentimental versions of domesticity with agricultural concerns and backdrops, these stories collectively constitute a mode of their own—what we might call romantic agrarian fiction. This is not to say, however, that they adhere strictly to conventional ideologies; on the contrary, some resist convention in interesting ways. In the aggregate, they present another discursive location within *TFW* in which romantic notions of farming and womanhood met with the real-life issues of rurality. If their romantic aspects often seem to triumph, these stories nonetheless test the boundaries of sentimental accounts of farm culture and introduce new possibilities for its social organization, especially where women are concerned. Reading them as a coherent body of work lends them legitimacy as cultural documents even as attention to their nuanced relation to other aspects of the magazine contributes to recent scholarship on the interactive nature of the popular periodical.[36] Moreover, it is especially useful to consider this particular fiction, and the values it imparts, as a context for reading more self-consciously progressive, and literary, agrarian novels by women.

Janice Radway, in her study of women's reading of pulp romances, has argued that a useful cultural analysis of such reading must take into account not merely how women understand individual texts but also "how they comprehend the very act of picking up a book in the first place."[37] Although it is impossible to reconstruct the reading experiences of *TFW* subscribers in the manner Radway does for her group of contemporary romance readers, much of what Radway has to say seems relevant here. Some of *TFW*'s letter writers suggested that fiction, more than other parts of the magazine, should function as a diversion. Yet, as with Radway's test group, their pleasure in reading fiction depended largely on its amalgam of escapism and realism. For example:

> [T]he stories [in *TFW*] help to make the magazine spicy and interesting and I'm sure that the average country woman stands very small chance of reading too much good light fiction. We all need it to a certain extent. It keeps us from

> thinking "shop" (our own, I mean) all the time; therefore, it helps to broaden the intellect.
>
> [My favorite story] was interesting because of the splendid lessons [it] brings out—lessons by which we all should profit. Their home was a model one filled with love and unselfishness toward one another. . . .
>
> Then [the heroine's] powerful insight into human nature shows what can be accomplished toward keeping the boys and girls on the farm and at the same time enjoy their lives there—a question that every farming community confronts. (May 1915, n.p.)

> The stories are clean and true to life lived on a higher plane than is usual nowadays. Your pages reach and help us plain people. (July 1924, 36)

These comments stress that *TFW*'s best fiction is stimulating and uplifting, diversionary but also relevant—comments also made by Radway's romance readers. And significantly, *TFW*'s farm fiction, in particular, shares three traits that Radway ascribes to the popular romance. First, as with pulp romances, *TFW*'s agrarian romances conflate a real (i.e., possible) realm with an imaginary (idealized) one, "signaling 'escape' while suggesting to the reader that the imaginary world is congruent with her own"; second, they require minimal interpretive skills, ensuring that the reading remains pleasurable rather than laborious, and reinforcing the reader's sense that the text's "meaning" is preestablished and static; and third, they reaffirm conventional values, even within the context of "new" characters or situations, by telling a tale whose outcome is "always already know[n]." Clearly these traits suggest a fundamentally conservative activity, even as Radway also admits the possibility that romance reading can be "incipiently oppositional," since it allows women "to refuse momentarily their self-abnegating social role"—an idea corroborated by TFW's readers.[38]

But *TFW*'s farm fictions, like other aspects of the magazine, occasionally trouble gender boundaries, betraying some uneasiness regarding customary roles for farm women; this suggests that they offer resistance on other planes, despite their overt advancement of traditional norms of agrarian womanhood. Moreover, *TFW*'s farm fictions are, in one essential particular, quite different from pulp romances, which Radway's test group identifies as "stories about a 'man and woman meeting, the obstacles to their love, and their final happy ending.'"[39] While many of *TFW*'s farm stories indeed involve courtship and marriage plots, what makes them specifically agrarian romances is that their paradigmatic love interest is not a man (or, in those few stories with male protagonists, a woman) but the country itself. This is easiest to see in the numerous stories positing the country as a "home" to which the protagonists re/turn after a period of separation and/or unrest. Significantly, the deferred gratification of re/union with the land is figured in metaphorically romantic terms, as a necessary fulfillment that is both physical and spiritual. A very early published story serves well as a template for this idea. In "June's Venture" (1907), a young girl is forced to flee her bourgeois life in the city and finds in the country not merely contentment and worthwhile labor but better health and even God. "The country's the place, isn't it?" she asks rhetorically, and we are told that her new environment seemed from the first "like home." While it is tempting to dismiss this text as too brief to be of real interest (it fills only three columns), it is nonetheless instructive as a distillation of fundamental plot elements that would be elaborated upon over the next three decades in virtually every farm story in *TFW*.

Indeed, even other types of narrative formulas could be redirected in service of this romance-with-the-country archetype. By the 1920s (when the typical *TFW* agrarian romance had become, incidentally, much longer than "June's Venture"), a customary lovers' plot was often grafted onto this essential affirmation of the country as consummation. In stories such as "Peggy Phelps of Unit Twelve" (1919), "Swapping Jobs" (1925), "Good Ground" (1929), and "Over Grandmother's Patchwork Quilt" (1930), sexual re/union is contingent upon, and continuous with, the protagonist's acceptance of rural life. Other stories, such as "The Thing She Could Not Do" (1911), "Nella Runs Away" (1916), and "The Desert Shall Blossom" (1928), emphasize this conjunction even more sharply through a heroine who has temporarily turned her back on the country and whose return is predicated on the dawning realization that a country man, and hence country life more generally, constitutes her ideal. "Kathleen of the 'Come Home'" (1912), in which a young Irish couple is caught on a quarantined ship off the U.S. coast, further enhances this basic pattern by adding nationalism to the mix. The husband's illness temporarily threatens the couple's dream of coming to America, "where's land to buy," but his recovery reaffirms marital bliss, agrarian industry, and national pride. Obviously, this equation of heterosexual harmony, and even America itself, with an equilibrium located in the rhythms of rural life allows for traditional notions of family, rurality, and even nation to function as mutually reinforcing categories. The country-as-lover motif is thus accommodated within a matrix of ideological relations that sustain it as "natural."

An important subset of this type of story carries oppositional undertones but ultimately validates the same set of significations. Many of *TFW*'s farm fictions focus on the perceived gap between the farm woman's labor and her husband's cognizance of that labor; the "correction" of the farmer's misperceptions restores marital harmony and, not coincidentally, makes the farm an even better place to live, materially as well as psychologically. The more benign versions, such as "A Matter of Dollars and Cents" (1916) or "Melissa Shortens the Trail" (1922), involve an unforeseen accident (in these cases, the wife's nervous breakdown and the illness of a child, respectively) that prompts the husband to see that first, he has been unduly harsh in his expectations of his wife, and second, he has compromised his family's health through a refusal to adopt such improvements as running water. (Naturally, the stories end with his promise to change.) One especially interesting variation on this plot is related by a hired hand who alone perceives the farm wife's purity and goodness; overhearing her being wooed by, but resisting, an old city lover, the unnamed narrator hopes that "the Boss," who has recently undergone life-threatening surgery, will finally learn to give his wife the "love and tenderness" she deserves ("A Close Squeak, by the Hired Man" [April 1924]). Since the Boss overworks his men and has generally attended little to his wife, this story locates both agrarian and heterosexual ideals in the rustic narrator, whose labor on the farm is genuinely physical, and who loves the farm wife fervently but from afar. While the farm wife in this story indeed has a difficult lot, we are nonetheless assured that a man—and one whom she never suspects—appreciates her value. Even here, then, in a story about an *unhappy* marriage, the theoretical parallelism between domestic and agrarian harmony is upheld.

More frequently, however, stories about farm men "coming around" depict a wife in open or subtle revolt against her husband, manipulating circumstances to enable his subsequent enlightenment. These stories approach a feminist arena in their advocacy of shared resources for women and men, and in their depiction of women as more clever and resourceful than their husbands suspect. For example, in "The Flight of a Wife" (1906), "The Price of Acres" (1911), "Millie Waters' Declaration of Independence" (1913), and "Mrs. Wilbur's New Fourth" (1914)—these last two published in subsequent July issues—a wife achieves momentary superiority over her husband when she maneuvers him into seeing her side. Not coincidentally, she also gains material advantages (better domestic machinery, occasional holidays from chores, etc.) that promise to make her life in the country fully rewarding. Often such stories are humorous, as suggested by one 1917 title (albeit of a story whose farm themes are less pronounced than most): "The Shoulders of Mrs. Atlas: Father, at Home for a Whole Day, Gains New Light on the Subject of Mother's Ease."[40] While comic perspectives may appear to undermine the seriousness of the true-to-life concerns played out in such tales, the comic also delineates a safe space for exploring subversive social alternatives, as scholars have established in a variety of contexts.[41] And the combination in these stories of fantasy and reality, of the *unlikely* but *possible*, frames domestic-agrarian problems within a theoretical ideal in a way that reflects *TFW*'s ambiguous efforts both to reflect readers' concerns and to shape their aspirations. To the degree that these stories link an enhanced quality of life to the necessary education of men, they fashion women as more progressive—even as they combine domestic relations with agrarian specificities so as to cast satisfactory country living and genuine marital happiness as coextensive.

However, it was not only males who came in for criticism. Some cautionary tales in *TFW* effectively strengthened domestic and agrarian values, and emphasized their complementarity, through relating their actual or imagined loss due to the mistakes of shortsighted women. "The Working of a Miracle" (1915) and "Mother Confesses" (1919) both tell of farm women who must unlearn their martyrish ways in order to regain their health and the esteem of other women—a sister and a daughter, respectively. To be a willing "drudge," these stories suggest, is to take the virtues of both country and family for granted while also jeopardizing one's own self-respect. And woe to the woman who stands between her daughter and a worthy farming mate. "Nancy's Experiment" (1920), "The Man My Daughter Chose" (1923), and "The Road Ahead" (1935) push the formulaic generation-gap narrative in unexpected directions by pitting a "modern," urban-biased parent against a daughter determined to adopt a traditional agrarian lifestyle, complete with a reputable but humble farmer-husband. If the daughter is prevented from following her heart, we are to assume, both her domestic fulfillment and the future of farming will be endangered. Yet the older generation's failure to recognize the supremacy of country living is less threatening than it first appears: the daughters eventually triumph, ensuring that their parents' errors will not prevail. As one girl's lover puts it after the crisis has passed, "It was the farm against the fates, Nancy—and the farm *had* to win" ("Nancy's Experiment").

All these stories, including those with progressive elements, substantiate the notion that the farm's magnetism is a natural and ineluctable force: it must, indeed, "win." But of course, positing the country as the signifying realization of erotic, familial, and vocational desires did not necessitate a female protagonist. "Peter the Great Goes Home" (1920), "How Ya Gonna Keep 'Em?" (1921), and "Swapping Jobs" (1925) are among those *TFW* farm stories that focalize the same values through a male character. Perhaps it is these stories, in which *men* find connubial and occupational satisfaction in the country, that call to mind most compellingly Annette Kolodny's observations about the American pastoral landscape as "the female principle of gratification itself." Yet the more numerous *TFW* stories in which women protagonists re/turn to the land effectively affirm the same mythos. Indeed, Kolodny's metaphor of "the-land-as-woman" asserts an "experiential reality" of the landscape that is "variously expressed" through images of "eroticism, penetration, raping, embrace, enclosure, and nurture, to cite only a few."[42] In TFW's farm fiction, the female protagonist's apparent choice to align herself with the land merely obscures the underlying theoretical principle that woman and the land are already one and the same. That is, since the female character's adoption of a rural lifestyle is virtually always aligned in these stories with conjugal or familial experience and even duty—in short, domestic imperatives are always intertwined with agrarian ones—then her acceptance of that lifestyle is also an acceptance of traditional women's roles (erotic, maternal, sympathetic). Put another way, immersion in rural experience both necessitates and enables her achievement of her womanly (domestic) potential. *TFW*'s agrarian romances, then, extend the long-established figuration of pastoral gratification as feminine—an ideological position reflected in the magazine's subtle suggestions that women are somehow even more at home in the country than men.[43] Of course, Radway has shown that women who read pulp romances are attracted by a female protagonist's apparent choice of a set of circumstances that nonetheless reinforce orthodox ideals of womanhood. That same dynamic would seem to be at play in *TFW*'s agrarian romances: believable, apparently individualized female characters dominate stories that exploit, in Radway's terms, the "ritualistic reaffirmation of a fixed myth."[44]

Yet if such story lines depend upon a metaphoric conception of the relation between women and the land, they could also pry open that relation in a manner calculated to highlight the subversive potential of farm women. For example, a conflation of pastoral fulfillment and women's domestic roles may also prompt a sustained focus on women's actual, working (i.e., "fulfilled") bodies—and, as we have seen in other parts of *TFW*, that focus can be directed *against* the grain of normative mythic structures. At the very least, the farm woman's identity, even in its most conservative formulations, isolates and underscores production and reproduction as potentially imbricated, challenging an ideology of separate spheres, not to mention Marxist theories of labor. In this vein, a large group of *TFW* stories disrupts standard dichotomies by depicting farm women, who work the land as well as the social landscape, as a literal force to be contended with. "Sylvia Comes Home" (1917), "Peggy Phelps of Unit Twelve" (1919), "The Resurrection of Lemuel" (1925), "Tied-Down" (1927), "Not for a Million Dollars" (1928), and "Ma Dunnaway Meddles" (1937) all feature farm women with the vision and strength of character to effect change in their communities, sometimes within domestic contexts, but just as often outside of them. Other stories attempt to dramatize more liberal notions of women's relations to the land, often through disallowing their protagonists the reproductive identities that make women into figurative extensions of nature rather than forces that might impact it. Stories such as "An Early Spring" (1923), for instance, directly connect women's self-actualization to their ability to work the land without help from men, indirectly earning male respect despite their distance from traditional roles. And both "The Fads of Philancy's Friends" (1906) and "A Country College" (1909) demand that women imagine for themselves experiences beyond, or completely outside of, the realm of expected wifedom and motherhood.[45]

Such stories are uneven in their efforts to challenge agrarian-inflected gender roles, yet they share an impulse to claim rural spaces as potential sites of alterity rather than conformism for women, an impulse that was also evidenced, as we shall see, in women's rural novels. Moreover, in their suggestion that social strictures limiting female development may be more easily overcome in the country, these stories share a position frequently expressed by *TFW*'s editors and contributors. In the words of one *TFW* letter writer, "[T]he bright [woman], who might be a nobody in a large city, can be a real power in a small farm community" (May 1922). Positing the countryside as the site of such freedoms was one means of claiming contemporary relevance for rural women, as well as literally relocating, *resetting*, modernity.

TFW's farm fiction is not simply reactionary, then, though it would be claiming too much to say that its reformist or feminist impulses outweigh, or even match in intensity, its fundamental validation of received attitudes toward domesticity and farm life—that is, its status as agrarian romance. And it seems that the perception of overall conservatism generated by the fiction gained much of its power from other discursive elements of the magazine. In addition to the pro-country ideology of its advertising and editorial matter, *TFW* was heavily invested in *stories* generally, whose promise of closure, together with the magazine's dedication to rural life, resulted in "happy" endings that could only be conceived, ipso facto, in terms of pastoral fulfillment. Hence the rhetorical force of *TFW*'s agrarian romances was substantially compounded by the numerous nonfiction narratives that traced similar arcs of conflict and resolution, as the following titles of nonfiction pieces suggest: "How I Helped Him on the Prairie" (1919); "We Three Women Kept the Farm" (1921); "How We Went Back to the Farm" (1927); "She Was Her Own Farm Relief" (1929). Indeed, looked at from a certain perspective, *TFW* is brimming with stories, real and fictional, that persistently narrativize farm women's experiences so as to reaffirm accepted domestic and agrarian endings. Among the most popular nonfiction manifestations of this story emphasis were the monthly "How Some Women Succeed" pieces, which related the real-life struggles of agrarian women and which were modeled on similar success narratives in the male agricultural press.[46]

But while this tendency toward narrativization is not unusual in mass-circulation magazines of the period and certainly has much to do with the class positioning of *TFW*'s readership, what seems especially interesting is the extent to which the magazine collapsed the boundaries between fiction and nonfiction narratives. To be sure, some of *TFW*'s fictional texts stood out as self-referentially literary, making use of, for instance, embedded narrators or protagonists who were aspiring writers.[47] Often, however, fiction and nonfiction narratives were so similar in theme and structure that the line between them was blurred, so much so that it is sometimes difficult to discern at first glance whether a particular story is presented as "true" or not. For instance, certain words are used in ways that appear deliberately to destabilize this dichotomy, as in the following titles of nonfiction narratives: "Trail's End: The Story of a Girl's Experiences in Her Log Cabin" (April 1915); "This Farm Woman Defeats Drudgery: Mrs. Henry M. Dunlap's Romantic Story of How Her Kitchen Became a Place of Joy" (April 1919); "Grandmother Goes Down the Mountain: This Story Is True, Word for Word . . ." (1920); "I Bring Back the Old Farm: A True Narrative of the Restoration of a Valued Homestead" (Sept. 1923). Other established signifiers, such as the publication of photographs to accompany "real" stories and drawings or etchings to accompany fictional ones, could also be unreliable.[48]

This confounding of the real and the fictional had two crucial effects. First, it suggested that farm women could be their own heroines, occupying the same sentimental, but also empowering, space usually reserved for fictional characters. Real stories about farm women, like the fictional ones, inevitably ended on a positive note, and the numerous similarities between these stories and those of imaginary farmers' wives served to heighten the drama and consequent romanticism of actual farm life, even as they also reinforced the "realness" of the fictions. Second, this blurring of the real and the fictional buttressed the notion that farming itself is *the* great story, the master narrative not only of *TFW* but also of American culture. This is clearly evidenced in a five-part nonfiction serial piece entitled "The Story of American Farming" (1929–1930), accompanied by a headline reading "How it began, how it grew, how its problems arose—all this is found in a tale that is as interesting and thrilling as romance." An editorial blurb on page one of the initial installment is worth quoting in its entirety:

> The story of farming has been told often, and in many ways. It has been the theme of the novelist. It has furnished inspiration to the poet. As a way of living it has been bitterly derided, and also praised beyond measure. The present and the future of farming have given grave concern to economists and statesmen. Politicians have ever found the ills of agriculture a bait with which to gather votes. The farm problem is the one subject on which everybody either has, or is supposed to have, worth-while opinions.
>
> In his "*Story of American Farming*" Mr. Hughes gives us a picture of farming as a great living group of industries, interwoven with all other industries. He portrays an entire world in the process of industrial revolution, with American farming in the forefront of change, and enables us to see why many of today's problems are pressing for solution, and that they are but natural phases of change and growth.
>
> The story opens long ago, with a swift-moving picture of another great civilization based on agriculture, the parent of our own civilization of to-day. And if it sometimes seems to wander far afield from the farm itself, it is only for the reason that farming, and the interests of every farm home, encircle the world, mingle with every other business, and touch and react to every other human interest. (Nov. 1929, 6)

Ironically, this self-conscious shaping of ostensibly objective history into romantic story manages to suggest not that farming is idealized but that farming is indeed ideal. And it is precisely the blend of realism and romanticism here—the acknowledgment of difficulties over which we have triumphed—that makes the story of farming a successful metonym for the story of America itself.

Of course, the force of narrative momentum notwithstanding, a close reading of *TFW* also suggests the difficulties inherent in attempting to contain an increasingly fractured set of attitudes about both farming and women within a focused, reassuringly upbeat rhetorical trajectory. Occasionally contributors objected to the "fairy tale" quality of certain stories that overstepped the mark.[49] And titles such as that of Mrs. Warren Taylor's autobiographical narrative—"I Am Dairying for Dollars: At the Same Time, I Keep Home and Family Interests Intact" (1919)—demonstrate the pressures on *TFW*, and on its readers, to reconcile, for example, women's modern roles as business partners in the threatened agrarian enterprise with nostalgic, domestic-oriented measures of female value, all within a "tale" of success. Naturally, such problems were not confined strictly to narrative structures (although we might argue that the quintessential farm success story formed the implied backdrop of virtually every text published in *TFW*). The rather sprawling title and subtitle of one news feature similarly suggests the variety of considerations that must be balanced in promoting a particular role for the farmer's wife: "Women Operate Farm Machinery: This Work Presents Several Attractive Features Besides Being a Partial Solution of the Farm-Labor Shortage" (1918). This article argues, among other things, that field work for women not only will sustain the nation's agricultural production but also will provide health benefits, open to women "a wide field of new and varied interest," give them better perspective on domestic work, and improve marital relations. Hence while pressing agricultural needs perhaps made it easier to accept progressive valuations of women's abilities and interests, new ideas about farm women's roles still had to be carefully situated within established social patterns and ideals—in this case, the assumed comradeship between husband and wife and the advantages of working in the open air—as well as within formulaic rhetorical structures. This constant calibration of agrarian and domestic injunctions, and of real-life problems and romanticized roles and images, simmered beneath the surface of *TFW*'s apparently smooth master rhetoric enshrining rural life as the only life for women.

Richard Ohmann has identified this dynamic—in which conflicting images and appeals are overridden by a "'mystifying unity' . . . that whispers reassurance"—as the defining element of the discourse of mass culture that magazines disseminated as early as the 1890s.[50] In this sense TFW was perhaps typical of other mass-circulation monthlies, assuaging the anxieties of a readership faced, in this case, with competing and contradictory ideas about both women's roles and rural life. Yet *TFW*'s specialized focus also made it an exceptional instance. For one thing, the "incoherences" that it bridged (to adapt Ohmann's terminology) were unusually charged, given the place that agrarianism held in the nation's collective unconscious. Moreover, in its singular status as a publication dedicated to agrarian *women*, it incorporated an added layer of complexity, since its readers identified themselves simultaneously as members of an entrenched farming culture *and* as part of a gender group whose roles were being reshaped in ways that extended beyond the particularities of the farm. The value of *TFW* is that it allows us to trace the interrelations of these shifting ideological formations—these "structures of feeling," to use Raymond Williams's phrase—over the course of some thirty years through a variety of discursive and imagistic means.

What *TFW* reveals is that rurality—despite, or perhaps because of, its fundamental conservatism—offered a rich site for considering the intersections of labor, gender, and American identity. Farm culture was anchored in fixed ideals and images yet forced to contend with the developing, and often confusing, discourses of feminism and agricultural reform that swirled around it, all at a time when conservative commentators were re/claiming farming in the interests of nationalism. Rife with contradictions and heavily invested in the question of its own representation, farm culture in the early twentieth century marked the intersection of a working-class institution in social and economic upheaval, a traditionally gendered division of labor threatened by feminist movements in the "outside" world, and an "American" ideal always and yet newly at stake. For women these tensions were particularly acute. To claim the identity of both *farmer* and *wife* was to embrace a problematic combination of productive and reproductive roles, all the more difficult in the context of status-conscious reformers who sought to distance the New Agriculture from popular notions of farmers as impoverished workers. As a site of contested labor *and* gender identities, then, caught between the nation's storied agrarian past and its new enchantment with technology, consumerism, and urbanity, farm culture was an arena of deep divisions and confusing crosscurrents, especially for women. Retrospectively, it is easy to see this moment in agricultural history as a blip on the radar screen, a temporary precariousness of positioning that never succeeded in completely upsetting the fundamental conservatism that remains a defining aspect of farm culture in the United States. At the time, however, the struggles over the future of farm life and, more specifically, the farm woman's role(s) must have seemed contentious indeed, a battle among various compelling forces that remained very much undecided. Reading *TFW* helps us to recapture the ambiguity of that moment and makes it easier to see why some progressive women in the modernist era may have been attracted to the farm as a site of interpretive, representational, and even radical possibility.

Chapter 3

Women, the Farm, and the Best-seller

IN 1900, L. FRANK BAUM enjoyed immediate success with a children's book about a Kansas farm girl whose fantastical adventures led her to a glittering and mysterious Emerald City—where she insisted, in the face of its splendors, that there's no place like home.[1] A recent exhibit on Baum and his legacy by the Library of Congress calls *The Wonderful Wizard of Oz* "the first totally American fantasy for children," combining charm and enchantment with such suggestive elements of the period's social and physical landscapes as a prairie cyclone, a con artist from Omaha, and a man made out of tin.[2] The innumerable stage and cinema productions, sequels and print artifacts, and other consumer objects based on the story throughout the early decades of the twentieth century made Oz a fetishized commodity indeed, furthered considerably, of course, by the 1939 Metro-Goldwyn-Mayer movie starring Judy Garland.[3] The nearly forty-year period from the novel's initial publication to Garland's Academy Award for her role as Dorothy corresponds, not coincidentally, with the temporal range of this study and serves to remind us of the marketability, as well as the oddly submerged prominence, of the back-to-the-farm theme in modern America.

That most of Baum's narrative takes place away from the farm is important, as it underscores the ways in which farm culture operated as an implied alternative to, and even an antidote for, a presumably decadent but nonetheless highly alluring urban space and consciousness. To be sure, Dorothy ultimately clicks her magic slippers and ritualistically asserts the superiority of her farm-home, but there is no mistaking the central position that Oz holds in the narrative's structure and, consequently, in our imaginative longings. Moreover, this marginal placement of rurality relative to the dazzling city of modernity persists. Our lingering tendency to associate the modern with urbanity ironically reenacts the teleology of the yellow brick road: in literary-historical terms, it leads us away from the country, obscuring the extent to which farm novels flourished in the period between 1900 and 1940. Yet, contrary to literary studies that have long suggested the primacy of the cityscape to modern(ist) experience and representation, abundant evidence demonstrates that modern readers were drawn in large numbers to novels set wholly or substantially in rural locales.[4] Booksellers' records suggest that rural works by such writers as Louis Bromfield (*Early Autumn* [1923]) and O. E. Rölvaag (*Giants in the Earth* [1927]) enjoyed sizable readerships; some, such as Edna Ferber's *So Big* (1924), were national best-sellers. These novels have not, on the whole, survived the sifting and sorting process that results in a recognizable modern American canon, yet that in itself is of interest, especially given that some of them garnered substantial critical attention in their own time. As a body, though, these works have tended to delineate a mainstream literary arena rather than a high cultural one, and the transformation of many of them into early movies perhaps reflected the sense that they were closer to mass entertainment than to serious aesthetic production. The single exception to this rule would seem to be the widely admired agricultural-pioneer novels of Willa Cather, which, as I suggested in the introduction, enjoyed some relation, if oblique, to the literary vanguard. Most farm novels, however, occupied cultural territory quite distinct, in style as well as substance, from that of the period's most critically celebrated works, many of which, like those of Theodore Dreiser, Sherwood Anderson, F. Scott Fitzgerald, and John Dos Passos, focused on city or small-town settings and sensibilities.

Indeed, farm novels were so squarely posited as *popular* that they were heavily embedded in the period's conflicts surrounding the perceived encroachment of a middlebrow culture—what critic Dwight Macdonald identified disdainfully in 1960 as "midcult." Various scholars, of course, have detailed the reactionary responses to lowbrow and middlebrow idioms that dictated the wholesale rejection of what the public likes, and especially what it reads, as aesthetically inferior.[5] One highbrow critic of the era, quoted in the *Atlantic Monthly,* declared, "I should consider myself disgraced if I had written a book which in these days had sold a hundred thousand copies."[6] Compilations of best-sellers, which had become a standard marketing tool of the bookselling industry in the early years of the twentieth century, routinely included titles of rural novels, thus reflecting and enabling the assumption that they were something other than genuine literature.[7] Moreover, on the rare occasions when they were mentioned at all in serious literary venues, popular rural novels were generally excoriated for their banality and sentimentality. The noted leftist critic Granville Hicks, for one, used the examples of ruralists Gladys Hasty Carroll and Phil Stong to argue that popular farm fiction is overly romanticized and thus irrelevant to a class-conscious American aesthetic, averring that "a clear and realistic novel about farm life would be cause for cheering." And reviewers championing popular farm novels sometimes did so precisely *because* of their comfortable predictability. A reviewer writing of Bess Streeter Aldrich's rural work *A Lantern in Her Hand* (1928), for example, found it "compounded to formula from beginning to end" but nonetheless recommended its "simple pathos." Similarly, Louis Kronenberger, reviewing Phil Stong's *State Fair* (1932), delighted in Stong's folksy rustic types: "It is pleasant and refreshing to read about them; and it is somehow proper for them to offset . . . the less fortunate farmers in Middle Western novels who are ruined by droughts or overproduction, whose wives go crazy from loneliness, whose sons are unwillingly chained to the soil and whose daughters get ignorantly into trouble."[8]

Kronenberger's comments, of course, betray the existence of farm novels that were less simplistically nostalgic than Stong's, and more closely tied to the realism and naturalism that were an integral part of American modernism (a topic to be discussed further in the next chapter). Such works, however, have been obscured by the tendency among the period's high cultural commentators to dismiss both regional literature and commercially successful literature, including rural fiction generally, as merely diversionary.[9] Despite the acknowledgment by some that the farm novel had become a fixture on the cultural scene ("The increase in novels dealing with farm life is a remarkable development," wrote Nelson Antrim Crawford in 1925), the genre's aesthetic legitimacy was often denied, partly through the preposterous claim that no *real* farm novels existed at all.[10]

For example, a 1929 editorial in the *Saturday Review of Literature* entitled "The Farm and the Novel" complained, "What our fiction has in the main portrayed is not life on the farm, but escape from the farm, or, when it is sentimentally inclined, return to the farm." And Allen W. Porterfield, in a lengthy piece in the *New York Times Book Review*, submitted and then methodically discredited the "seven" or so works that are "usually classed as 'farm novels.'" Hamlin Garland's *Main-Traveled Roads,* he griped, is not rightly a novel but a collection of stories, while Cather's *My Ántonia* "bears all the delimiting marks of regional literature" and, in any event, depicts not authentic Americans but rather Americans "in the making." The research for a genuine American farm novel would take too long, he averred, and, incidentally, it is doubtful whether a woman could "do justice" to the task of writing such a novel at all. No "adequately endowed novelist" had yet emerged, Porterfield insisted, who could write "the greatest story this country has to tell—that of the farm."[11]

Such commentary was not exceptional. Other rhetorical trends hint at the imposing presence of the farm fiction genre—the proverbial elephant in the room—while also registering its perceived inferiority. Somewhat more subtle, for instance, was the deployment of the farm, and by extension popular rural fiction, as a metaphoric means of denigrating prevailing tendencies in the world of mass-market books. In another prominent *New York Times* piece, Edward S. Van Zile excoriated the New Realism, which he associated with best-sellers, as a "barnyard school of fiction." These novels focus on the "fundamental weakness and depravity" of the "live stock," he asserted, featuring "barbaric dances, necking parties, hip-pocket lawlessness," and causing readers to "despair of the Republic." John Carter apparently relished Van Zile's metaphor, as he extended it in a response essay two weeks later. Carter likened a popular genre he disdained—the "collegiate autobiographical novel"—to "a sort of Two-Headed calf" and characterized its practitioners as puerile young men displaying "the querulous bitterness of a tricked rustic." Yet he also predicted that "the unsavory exploits of the barnyard," found not in the work of "mature realists" but within a certain popular brand of "oversexed realism," would "supply fertilizer" for more worthy literary efforts, resulting in "bumper crops of wholesome American fiction." "[T]he rush to the barnyard of which [Van Zile] complains," Carter argued, "is only a harbinger of a general return to the farm." Hence Carter sustained an abstract association of rurality with a healthy, legitimate national art, while simultaneously furthering Van Zile's alignment of popular novels, presumably including farm novels, with a "barnyard" aura that disqualified them from that same realm.[12]

Farm fiction was also implicated in the gendered discourses that used images of a corrupt femininity to indict popular tastes. A particularly virulent essay appearing in the *New Republic* called for "Birth Control in Fiction," arguing that American writers are "ruin[ed]" by a voracious but undiscriminating reading public that tempts them to produce large numbers of "potboilers" and "mediocrities" in pursuit of a best-seller. The language of the article, centered on metaphors of irresponsible reproduction, imagines popular novelists as excessively generative females in need of institutional control. Such writers must develop "a eugenic attitude toward their brain children," the author argues; at the very least, a period of one year between completion of a novel and its publication ought to be imposed, so that the novelist "might prune and train and polish his rebellious child." Not surprisingly, an immoderate birthing of insipid fiction is linked to women's magazines, notably the *Ladies' Home Journal,* yet the author also cites gleefully an example from popular farm fiction to clinch the point: "So long as these [popular] writers confine themselves to the evanescence of the magazine form, they are comparatively harmless. Their tendency today, however, is to perpetuate their species in volume. Witness Mr. Arthur Stringer, for instance, with his Prairie Wife, Prairie Mother, Prairie Child performances. It reminds one of the old nursery rhyme 'The farmer in the dell'. . . . What will be the next volume? Logically, The Prairie Grandmother!"

Unfortunately for Stringer, the titles of his books (*The Prairie Wife, a Novel* [1915], *The Prairie Mother* [1920], *The Prairie Child* [1922]) captured beautifully the unreflective, and feminized, procreativity here deemed at odds with the inspired genesis of the Great American Novel: they called to mind the vulgarity of breeding for profit while also hinting at the gushing, womanish sentimentality often perceived as typical in representations of agriculture. And this reviewer, through the "farmer and the dell" allusion, linked the notion of a monstrously reproductive (female) body to the farm itself.[13] Hence these remarks demonstrate, once again, how farming and the feminine could be suggestively aligned through concepts of *reproduction* and *control,* concepts that also proved powerful in attempts to rein in the transgressive excesses of a feminized popular culture.

But it is a consideration of the farm novel's status within the developing economy of literary awards in the 1920s and 1930s that best foregrounds its persistent standing as vernacular, rather than serious, literature. Literary prizes and honors were becoming more and more prevalent as a means of distinguishing among the sea of books newly available to eager consumers;[14] yet the inevitable relationship between such awards and an increase in sales—turning prizewinning books into best-sellers—raised the hackles of a literary establishment still desirous of articulating a realm for high art that would remain separate from commercial culture. As books increasingly became mass-marketed commodities rather than icons of an educated elite, the location of true aesthetic endeavor within a privileged cultural space became proportionally imperative. This reactionary dynamic prompted, among other responses, virulent opposition to the Book-of-the-Month Club, inaugurated in 1926 and accused of emasculating readers by replacing the ethic of autonomous, discriminating choice with mindless consumption.[15] In a related trend, literary awards were also disdained by many writers and intellectuals, who argued that such distinctions reinforced a pandering to popular taste that would result in inappropriately standardized creative work.[16] Farm novels, frequently the recipients of these laurels, were thus swept categorically into a discredited realm of compromised art.

Part of the problem was that many such prizes were established by publishing houses, obviously as promotion vehicles: Harper's, for instance, created the Harper Prize Novel Contest, which was first won, not coincidentally, by Margaret Wilson for her rural novel *The Able McLaughlins* (1924). The blatant commercialism of such contests prompted one editorialist to suggest that P. T. Barnum himself had missed "a great opportunity" in failing to invent the literary prize competition.[17] Yet the Pulitzer Prize, administered by the Columbia University School of Journalism and presumably beyond the reach of market forces, also came under fire. The Pulitzer Prize for the Novel (later changed to the Pulitzer Prize for Fiction), established in 1917, was awarded to a farm novel in ten of the fourteen years between 1923 and 1936.[18] In fact, farm novels enjoyed such dominance on the Pulitzer scene that John Chamberlain, in his "Books of the Times" column in the *New York Times,* surmised an "agrarian bias somewhere among the Pulitzer judges" and remarked that "sometime we should like to see a Pulitzer Prize go to an urban novel, say by Dos Passos or Dreiser, just to prove that the committee is not congenitally Jeffersonian in its tastes."[19]

The association of the Pulitzer, in particular, with an insistently feminized corruption of American literary standards was only reinforced by Sinclair Lewis's refusal of the prize in 1926 for his novel *Arrowsmith.* In a letter to the prize committee, Lewis wrote,

> All prizes, like all titles, are dangerous. The seekers for prizes tend to labor not for inherent excellences but for alien rewards; they tend to write this, or timorously to avoid writing that, in order to tickle the prejudices of a haphazard committee. . . .
>
> Between the Pulitzer Prizes, the American Academy of Arts and Letters and its training school the National Institute of Arts and Letters, and the inquisition of earnest literary ladies, every compulsion is put upon writers to become safe, polite, obedient and sterile. In protest . . . I must decline the Pulitzer Prize.[20]

To be sure, Lewis did not expressly condemn rural fiction, nor did he entirely adhere to his disavowal of literary prizes.[21] Yet it is worth noting that in the three years prior to Lewis's refusal, the Pulitzer Prize had gone to novels dealing with rurality, all of them written by women: Willa Cather received the award in 1923 for *One of Ours,* Wilson in 1924 for *The Able McLaughlins*, and Edna Ferber in 1925 for *So Big*. That popular rural fiction by women was implicated in Lewis's objections to the prize scene seems abundantly clear.

The press of the period shows how Lewis's refusal of the prize fueled the division between a high-minded critical culture and the average reader. A jeweler in Kansas City sent Lewis a hat, size 207, with an accompanying letter suggesting that Lewis might be in need of "an adequate roof" for the "enlarged quarters" from which his fictional creations emerged. And the *Philadelphia Record* offered the following commentary, which the *Literary Digest* proposed for a different kind of award—namely, for the funniest reaction to Lewis's haughtiness: "[C]ould there be a more exasperating affront to the Sinclair Lewises of to-day? One cannot but sympathize with his agonizing resentment. . . . Let those who will be corrupted by prizes which he conceives to be rewards for being 'safe, polite, obedient, and sterile'; but let no one presume to imply that [Lewis] is or ever will be anything but dangerous, impudent, rebellious and fecund in devices for shocking the Philistines. Woof! Woof! Isn't he the desperate fellow?"[22]

Others, of course, hastened to construct Lewis as a champion of art: H. L. Mencken, for instance, referred to Lewis's rejection of the prize as "a gallant and excellent gesture." An editorial in the *Nation* supporting Lewis stated that his reasons for declining "were as honest as they were interesting" and aligned literary prizes generally with a sheepish, unexacting clientele by pointing to the "rather pathetic faith of the public in the wisdom of judges"—stating, without apparent self-consciousness (given its own freehanded critical judgments), that "[n]obody knows what literary virtue is anyway."[23]

Lewis claimed to renounce the Pulitzer largely on the grounds of its wording: it professed to honor the American novel that "best present[s] the wholesome atmosphere of American life, and the highest standards of American manners and manhood." Such a moral yardstick clearly disqualified his own socially critical work, Lewis suggested, and promoted fiction that merely reproduced received ethical and societal visions. Significantly, the prize description was changed after World War II, but not before others had also noted its prescriptive effects. In particular, Caroline Sherman, assessing the development of the farm novel genre in 1938, was quite explicit in stating that the very terms of the Pulitzer Prize had "forced the committee to turn frequently to rural writers." She affirmed a strong relationship between farm novels and the literary prize scene overall, noting that rural books had also fared well with publishers' distinctions and the Prix Femina Americain. Yet Sherman, too, saw this "excess of prizes" as a corrosive influence, suggesting vaguely that it had undermined the "normal and stable development" of the farm novel genre, presenting the danger of "exploitat[ion] by superficial or unskilled writers who were attracted by its growing popularity." While she argued strenuously against the view of farm novels as simplistically romantic, pointing to several works that "tackl[e] hard country problems," she also found it necessary to celebrate American rural fiction for having "*survived* precocious prize-taking, popularity, and praise" (my emphasis).[24] Clearly, Sherman was responding defensively to the widespread notion that a certain type of success could prove damaging to books, effectively invalidating them as authentic literature. As she apparently understood, the field of cultural production, to use Bourdieu's term,[25] had somehow come to define rurality and popularity as mutually reinforcing categories, extrinsic to the aims and values of bona fide art.

Doubtless it did not help that a work such as *The Specialist* (1929), a humorous novelty book by Chic Sales on the niceties of building outhouses, eventually sold more than 1.5 million copies and "for years sat beside the cash register at every bookstore in America." Michael Korda ascribes its success not only to Sales's combination of scatological humor and homespun philosophy but also, more generally, to nostalgia for an unproblematic rural past.[26] This was the very sensibility assumed to drive sales of farm novels in the twenties and thirties, a great number of which, significantly, employed nineteenth-century settings associated with homesteading and agricultural pioneering. As Roy Meyer notes, rurality emerged as a prominent subject matter for American fiction at the historical moment when the United States became "a predominantly urban country."[27] Hence the relation between rural fiction and nostalgia was overdetermined, allowing for widespread assumptions that popular farm novels merely soothed readers through an evocation of simpler times.

And, of course, if farm-related books in general were cheapened by their association with a sentimental mass readership, then those written by women were only more so. It is no surprise that this popular literary genre harbored numerous female authors, which may have predisposed critics to devalue it. Certainly farm fiction was widely associated with bathos, perhaps because, like other forms of mainstream fiction, it was often serialized in popular magazines, considered a feminine medium.[28] Critiques of rural novels by women frequently focused on sentimental elements, whether positively or negatively:

> On Maristan Chapman's *Happy Mountain* (1928): "A dewy idyll of mountain life, fit to restore our faith in the classical canon of Romanticism, that to be rustic is to approach perfection."
>
> On Bess Streeter Aldrich's *Lantern in Her Hand* (1928): "[Mrs. Aldrich] does make bearing children, and loving them, and teaching them, and cheerfully giving up all the world that they might have it instead, seem worth doing. Novels will go on telling about these things forever, and people will read them, and laugh over them, and cry over them. And it will do people no harm."
>
> On Josephine Donovan's *Black Soil* (1930): "That it has slightly sentimentalized [some of its incidents] will scarcely disturb those whose memories are piqued by the simple details of a vanished past[.]"
>
> On Gladys Hasty Carroll's *As the Earth Turns* (1933): "Mrs. Carroll writes in a somewhat nostalgic vein, as if insufficiently aware of a changing world, but her novel is . . . somehow consoling."[29]

It would be impossible to tease out the precise relationships in each case among a text's female authorship, its commercial success, and its perceived nostalgia—that is, to determine exactly how those aspects were interrelated and how, collectively, they may have affected evaluation of the texts themselves. Unquestionably, rural novels by men, like those by women, were subject to the charge of sentimentality, although the extent to which such charges were cloaked in terms of effeminacy or emasculation suggests the corresponding degree to which rurality was linked to womanliness through the medium of a feminized popular culture.[30] It would seem, then, that women had a special, more layered, relation than men to the status and circulation of rural literature—as authors, as presumed readers, and, most important, as figurative exemplars of a debased mass appeal.

Ironically, though, best-selling farm novels by women, while thoroughly saturated in assumptions about sentimentality and an adulterated popular taste, could be surprisingly assertive in their social critiques. Wilson's *Able McLaughlins,* for example, despite its overly moral tone, explores the impact of domestic violence and rape within rural communities, while Lorna Doone Beers's *Prairie Fires* (1925) was widely praised for its depiction of the conditions faced by farmers attempting to organize in their own economic interest. Significantly, Beers's novel is also critical of romance and pulp literature generally, which it shows to have a deleterious effect in shaping the expectations of naive farm girls; this metafictional dimension suggests that Beers thought of her own work more as cultural intervention than as entertainment. On a more subtle level, Patricia Raub argues that best-selling rural novels by women collectively challenged the ethos of consumption that had come to dominate American culture, and that was especially associated with urban femininity. Such situated social criticisms connect these texts less to the country idylls of Phil Stong, Louis Bromfield, and other popular male writers, or to the naturalistic vein of rural realists such as Hamlin Garland, than to works by minority groups that couch progressive commentary in conventional, accessible novelistic structures.[31]

This is not to claim, of course, that all popular farm novels by women in the period are lost gems deserving rediscovery; on the contrary, many are undistinguished and are of interest only insofar as they illustrate trends, such as the public's appetite for stories of the agricultural frontier. Yet it seems productive to untangle the complicated web of images and discourses that automatically consigned them to a subliterary arena, if only to challenge the accepted scope of modernist literary production by considering the sheer commercial-cultural force of this literature, which was shaped by the quotidian, but also revealing, concerns of a middle-class readership. And there *are* best-selling rural novels by women that have been forgotten and are worth recovering. The representative works discussed in detail in the rest of this chapter are chosen for two reasons: first, because they are among the best of the neglected women's rural novels of the era, evincing highly marketable, but nonetheless provocative, combinations of romanticism and social commentary; and second, because they were deeply embedded in the newly consolidated middlebrow modes of literary promotion, dissemination, and evaluation. These texts richly reward reconsideration on the dual levels of their internal dynamics, which reveal complex attitudes toward modern life, and the external influences that shaped their standings and that illuminate the politics of literary modernism. The insights to be gained in foregrounding these works thus relate not merely to the genre of women's farm fiction itself, which has been overlooked as such, but also to the larger dynamics of the literary scene, to the ways that rurality figured in the issuance of a modern literary canon.

Rurality for the Middlebrow: Ferber, Ostenso, Roberts, Carroll

While the term "middlebrow" clearly conjures up a middle space, a terrain of mediation between conflicting poles, cultural commentators, as we have seen, routinely invalidated the middlebrow's claims to serious consideration and aligned it rather freely with a devalued arena of unreflective production and consumption. Yet recent scholarship on the middlebrow has unsettled rigid dichotomies between "high" and "low" culture, between elite and mass audiences, and between refined tastes and the crude dynamics of the marketplace, all of which helped to sustain the middlebrow's elision with inferior readers and writers. Scholars such as Joan Shelley Rubin and Janice Radway have sought to reassert the middle territory of the middlebrow, its genuine status as *in between.* Following scholars of nineteenth-century sentimental fiction, who have redirected discussion of that genre so as to highlight its frequently subversive dimensions, scholars of middlebrow novels have similarly sought to alter the terms of critical debate, framing middlebrow fiction as a legitimate attempt to balance seriousness and accessibility, and to embrace both the economy of critical valuation *and* the consumer marketplace. While the middlebrow's perceived status as the domain of women helped to fix its subordinate position historically, that also makes it of particular interest to feminist scholars today.[32]

Middlebrow novels are now taken resolutely on their own terms, and those by women have attracted much attention. In the introduction to their recent collection, *Middlebrow Moderns: Popular American Women Writers of the 1920s,* Lisa Botshon and Meredith Goldsmith challenge the middlebrow's association with conservatism and lack (of the "cachet and edginess of high culture" as well as the "authenticity of the low"), and stress instead its cultural power to "bridg[e] gaps" for audiences fragmented by varied class allegiances, racial and ethnic differences, and clashing regional loyalties. These novels, they argue, insert themselves forcefully and often daringly into contemporary social debates, even if, as Joan Rubin suggested in her classic study of middlebrow culture, they also trace the "reconstitut[ion]" of nineteenth-century genteel values.[33] The middlebrow is now recognized, then, as *productively* marked by conflictedness, tension, negotiation, balance, mediation—in short, by the occupation of an intermediary ground, the often untidy, imprecise, inconsistent ground of the average reader, who is capable of holding reactionary and progressive attitudes simultaneously.

Best-selling rural novels by women in the modernist period constituted a particularized version of middlebrow fiction. Trading heavily on the era's nostalgia for farm life, many of these texts use that nostalgia in the service of critiques of both the past and the present, especially where gender is concerned. Reinscribing the familiar while also engaging freely in social commentary, these works can be imaginative in their accommodation of modernity, mapping concerns about the threatening aspects of the contemporary social and technological landscapes onto the comforting terrain of rurality, thus tempering them for the ingestion of the mainstream reader. Their themes are often ambitious and cover a wide range, including, for example, the nation's absorption of immigrants into the social corpus and the dilemmas introduced by new attitudes about women's reproductivity, not to mention issues particular to the rural-urban binary, such as the increasing influence of consumerism and corporate culture in American life. Some of them even flirt with high modernist maneuvers and sensibilities. True to their status as middlebrow, of course, they eschew the more thoroughgoing radical gestures and attitudes evidenced in the left-leaning rural novels discussed in the next chapter. Yet that hardly invalidates their subtle and not-so-subtle social critiques, which were presumably all the more influential due to the wide audience they reached. As with all middlebrow texts, these works call for an interpretive framework that acknowledges the complexity of their ambitions as well as the richness of their critical and aesthetic textures.

Novels by Edna Ferber (*So Big* [1924]), Martha Ostenso (*Wild Geese* [1925]), Elizabeth Madox Roberts (*The Time of Man* [1926]), and Gladys Hasty Carroll (*As the Earth Turns* [1933]) provide an opportunity to explore the status of the middlebrow as a newly emerging cultural force in the 1920s and early 1930s while also tracing the prominence and provocativeness of women's rural fiction. These four novels achieved exceptional visibility: rated high on best-seller lists, made into movies and plays, lavished with critical accolades, and festooned with awards, they straddled the line between popular and serious art and helped to create a new definition of literary success. Indeed, their authors acquired a status as public celebrities that transcended the purely literary and that both reflected and enabled new interactions between the literary and other modes of mass entertainment and production. That these works are set in four distinctly different locales—south of Chicago, the Pacific Northwest, Kentucky, and Maine—also suggests that, to a national audience, rurality as a broad cultural concept was far more compelling than regionalist distinctions. While each approaches that concept from a slightly different angle, all use it as a means of thinking through the dilemmas of modern urban-industrial life, and even, in some cases, of modern aesthetics.

Edna Ferber's celebrated novel *So Big* was as big as its name suggests. Indeed, few works of the period more thoroughly demonstrate the publicity that could accrue to mass-market books and their authors, tapping into all the cultural outlets that both defined mass appeal and abetted it. Initially serialized in *Woman's Home Companion*, Ferber's book has been described as "the first really recognizable modern fiction best-seller, with a promotable author, a 'modern' story, and a big subject." Its title allowed for promotional puns that linked status anxiety to the novel's consumption ("How big are you? . . . Measure yourself against Edna Ferber's mighty novel"), while other advertisements exploited its trendiness ("Look over your neighbor's shoulder—he's probably reading it").[34] *So Big* was the number one best-seller of 1924, won the Pulitzer Prize for Fiction, was published widely in Europe, and was made into no fewer than three films (in 1925, 1932, and 1953). It also catapulted its author from the ranks of popular magazine writers to a highly lucrative fame based on a subsequent string of critical and commercial triumphs, including authorship of the novel *Showboat* (1926), which became a legendary Broadway production (1927), and the play *Dinner at Eight* (1932), written with George S. Kaufman and the basis for the 1933 film now considered a Hollywood classic.

Ferber became a conspicuous personality, mingling with such luminaries as Richard Rodgers and Katharine Hepburn, enduring press coverage of her nose job, and periodically complaining, despite her enormous financial success, that both her readers and her reviewers misunderstood the serious satiric nature of her work.[35] She was most often positioned as a commercial writer who managed to tickle the public's interest without offending its sensibilities. A notice of *So Big* in the *Dial* remarked on Ferber's own apparent "astonish[ment] at the phenomenal success of her book" (which Ferber had predicted to be a "Non-Seller") and asked, "Is the author unaware that a facile naturalism is greatly in vogue, that her pictures of Chicagoan society are equal to the best the Saturday Evening Post can provide, and that she puts no strain on either the emotional or the intellectual equipment of her very gentle readers?" Parodist John Riddell portrayed Ferber as a saucy steward of "billowing style," "swish[ing]" prose, and "flashing" adjectives, and his comments were accompanied by a suggestive caricature by Miguel Covarrubias (fig. 3.1). When Ferber died in 1968, a lengthy obituary in the *New York Times* appeared to confirm this dubious stature, calling her novels "minor classics" that are more "vivid" than "profound."[36]

In Ferber's heyday, though, during the 1920s and 1930s, occasional attempts had been made to characterize her works somewhat differently. Despite the claim by her friend and fellow rural novelist Louis Bromfield that Ferber was "an incorrigible romantic in the good nineteenth century sense," other well-known commentators tried to distance her from the sentimentality and bourgeois correctness commonly associated with mainstream books and readerships. Grant Overton argued that Ferber was a keen social critic who, in both *So Big* and *Showboat,* revealed "contempt for correctly patterned existences"; he averred that her "gusto" had helped her to transcend the realm of belles lettres, which he characterized as a sterile "disguise."

Figure 3.1 Caricature of Edna Ferber by Miguel Covarrubias, 1932. (Copyright Miguel Covarrubias Estate. Image courtesy of Harry Ransom Humanities Research Center, University of Texas at Austin.)

Similarly, William Allen White claimed that Ferber was a true "craftsm[a]n" and, significantly, a social historian who managed to chronicle and critique the emergence of her very audience, namely, the "new, raw, happy, moron middle class." These observations, however, were insufficient to dislodge Ferber from her acknowledged position as purveyor of, in Riddell's words, "[s]ugar-coated culture."[37] That her reputation as a writer remained firmly entrenched within "midcult" paradigms despite her criticism of bourgeois values may owe something to the fact that her very champions tended to be not artists or icons of the cultural elite but members of middlebrow institutions.[38]

Ferber's standing was determined ultimately by her accessibility, not merely in formalistic terms but also in thematic ones. Her fictional employment of panoramic American social landscapes, for example—the Mississippi riverboat culture in *Showboat,* or the Oklahoma land rush in *Cimarron*—called forth nostalgia and populist civic pride. The rurality of *So Big* functions similarly: despite its apparent regional specificity, the novel avails itself of the mythic qualities—health, autonomy, virtue—that the American rural signifies. Equally important was Ferber's knack for portrayals of women that pushed the envelope of conventional gender expectations while still validating the middle-class mores of her audience. Her first major success, a series of hit magazine stories about Emma McChesney, a divorced mother and traveling saleswoman, had "gratified the liberatory fantasies of even her most homebound readers."[39] If Emma represented a mixed bag of subversive and traditional female traits (her assertiveness and independence, for example, were softened by her domestic bent and her love for her child), then the female protagonist of *So Big* was a similarly palatable "New Woman." The confident and iconoclastic Selina Peake De Jong is made acceptable to her readers, if not to her less imaginative Dutch neighbors, through received agrarian symbols that mark her as fundamentally sound.

So Big had first appeared in serialized form as *Selina,* a title that acknowledged its protagonist's conceptual, if not always narrative, centrality. A bourgeois daughter of a professional gambler who is forced, at age nineteen, to make her own way as a rural schoolteacher in the Dutch-settled farmlands south of Chicago, Selina marries an illiterate Dutch farmer who leaves her a widow when their son, Dirk, is only nine years old. This turn of events allows for a formulaic trajectory in which Selina takes over their unproductive farm and turns it around single-handedly, much to the consternation of the local, tradition-bound Dutch farmers. She ages prematurely as a result of her labors but acquires in the process a personal dignity, as well as the prosperity that allows her to send Dirk to college. In the last third of the novel, however, Dirk is unable to follow her lead and squanders his ideological inheritance by becoming a financially successful but shallow bonds trader. Incapable of his mother's zest for life and impervious to her love of beauty, he ultimately realizes, but is incapable of overcoming, his deficiencies. The all-too-obvious moral is that it is the modest and indefatigable farm woman, rather than her polished, commanding son, who is "so big."

Selina's character, however, is less progressive than this synopsis might suggest; while charmingly memorable, she is neither innovative nor arresting. Her victory in making her farm pay—the result of gritty determination and business acumen—represents, by 1924, a rather trite rendition of the single-woman-makes-good stories so popular in women's magazines (and, with the agricultural inflection, in the farm press). Even the control that Selina manages to exert over her circumstances, and over some men, partakes of a certain brand of assertive "feminism" that had become commonplace in literature. A review in the *Times Literary Supplement* suggested as much, placing *So Big* with other "American novel[s] of the modern school" precisely because of its conception of "a world in which the strings are pulled by women."[40] Moreover, the novel's conflation, through Selina, of agricultural labor and an acute sensitivity to the aesthetic (she loves books, and mentors a local farm boy who becomes a famous sculptor) marks its heavy reliance on Jeffersonian myths of agrarianism, even if their location in a female character is untraditional. And while Selina's flourishing after the death of her husband clearly critiques the marital relation as limiting for women (she wonders if it all would have happened "had Pervus lived" [177]), her devotion to a son who seems undeserving affirms, rather than challenges, normative middle-class family relations.

But if *So Big* is of little interest in its depiction of a modern woman farmer, it is of great interest in its chronicling of the shifting relations between rurality and an urban-based modernity. While Selina's impoverished farm is the literal and psychic center of the narrative, the city of Chicago looms insistently on the periphery. It is not merely the place to which Selina and Dirk must travel to peddle their vegetables, and the site of Selina's assertion of her right thereby to earn a living for the two of them; it is also the location of long chapters in the novel in which, for instance, we follow Dirk through college and into his fatuous professional life. Through Dirk's trajectory (he moves toward a permanent urban existence, returning to the farm in adulthood only for brief visits) and through Selina's lifelong interactions with Julie Hempel, a wealthy girlhood chum, we are repeatedly eased from the farm setting to the city setting and back. Thus in the years between Selina's girlhood and her old age, we witness not merely the forceful transformation of her farm and the dissolution of her hopes for her son but also the growth of Chicago's industrialism. For some reviewers of the time, it was this angle of the novel that seemed especially compelling: "[Ferber] has portrayed aspects of Chicago more vividly and with greater distinction than any writer I know; she knows the history of the development of Chicago in the industrial age and she is able to convey in a few words the import of that development; she can describe flappers and debutantes, shop girls and stenographers, tell you how they dress, how they talk, what their working philosophy is, with illuminating flashes."[41] Perhaps predictably, this particular emphasis has consistently colored *So Big:* it seems significant, for example, that the most recent paperback edition, published by HarperCollins in 2000, pictures a cityscape on the front cover, and the descriptive blurb on the back makes no mention of rurality.

Yet the first half of the novel takes place almost entirely on the farmland outside the city; moreover, the division of narrative space between rural and urban settings in the later chapters undergirds the thematic emphasis on their growing interpenetration. In order to survive, Selina recognizes that she must make her farm goods attractive to city buyers; conversely, the phenomenal growth of the city itself means that, for those farmers astute enough to capitalize on it, a steady market is guaranteed. By the end of the novel, De Jong asparagus has become a featured offering on the menus of fine hotels, symbolizing the extent to which Selina's modern farm and the modern city rely on each other (217). But the blurring of the boundary between rural and urban realms operates at other levels of the narrative as well. While Ferber obviously validates Selina's chosen life on the farm and censures the empty urban society to which Dirk aspires, *So Big* avoids the simplistic back-to-nature ethos that would automatically render the farm a superior place. For one thing, Selina is drawn to the city's "foreign quarters" as well as to its architecture and shops: "[S]he liked the sights, the colour, the rush, the noise" (217–18). And Julie Hempel's father, August, the millionaire who becomes Selina's benefactor and friend, is associated with an earthiness that his city-based success cannot displace: a former butcher who has parlayed his knowledge of the stockyards into profitable holdings, he is still addressed by the local farmers and merchants as "Aug" (15) and is appalled by his son-in-law's refusal to leave his office ("His clothes they never stink of the pens like mine do" [147]). Selina and Aug, one living in the country and one in the city, are united in their shared sense of the dignity and value of manual labor, a realm from which their children, by virtue of the parents' success, are entirely removed. If anything, the novel indicts neither city nor country, but rather the privileged and unreflective sons and daughters of the newly prosperous: these two characters, each in a different way, offer a foil for Dirk's rather facile assumption of bourgeois respectability.

This respectability delineates not only a "clean" space apart from sweat and grime but also, analogously, a nativist space that appears removed from ethnic markings. Aug must refrain from sneering when he pronounces his grandson's name, Eugene, which he associates with a clean-cut, upper-crust, ethnically sanitized milieu (147). And the increasingly insular social circles that Dirk inhabits are criticized by Selina not because they are located in the city but because they are so uniformly generic, disallowing Dirk's association with the wide variety of vibrant types that Selina's father had told her could make one "rich" (7). That two of the most validated minor characters of the novel—Roelf Pool, the farm boy–turned–sculptor, and Dallas O'Mara, a painter—move fluidly across class and ethnic barriers, and are comfortable both in urban settings and at Selina's side on the farm, suggests, again, that both city and country may produce and support a vivid, substantial humanity. Indeed, the novel's very definition of success seems to hinge on the imaginative sympathy that dissolves borders, whether cultural or geographic—a trait that Selina possesses in abundance but that Dirk lacks.

Hence *So Big*, less a rural novel than a novel about the effects of modernity on rurality *and* urbanity, evades the simplistic nostalgia for the farm that some other works with substantial rural elements exploited. But Ferber's text is perhaps most compelling in its very recognition of the way that such a nostalgia or sentimentalism operates, namely, as a means of creating a liberatory space that relieves present pressures and glosses over the details of the literal or figurative past into which it enters—in this case, the hardships of rural life. In the very scene in which Paula Arnold, Aug's debutante granddaughter, refuses Dirk's love because of his class status, she ironically embraces the farm itself, which she clearly perceives as offering a momentary respite from her diet-conscious, fashion-conscious society existence: "I'll stay [to dinner]," said Paula, "thanks. If you'll have all kinds of vegetables, cooked and uncooked. The cooked ones smothered in cream and oozing butter. And let me go out into the fields and pick 'em myself like Maud Muller or Marie Antoinette or any of those make-believe rustic gals" (179). Paula's inability to locate the asparagus once she is out in the field ("You dig for it, idiot," says Dirk) and the ridiculous picture she makes as her luxurious shoes sink into the mud suggest her utter ignorance of the labor that has shaped Selina's life. For Paula, the farm represents not reality, an existence to which she might bind herself through marriage to Dirk, but rather a place of relaxation and "make-believe." Significantly, then, *So Big* also traces the progression from a time when the rural districts were beneath the notice of wealthy city dwellers (Selina is as good as dead to her city friends when she assumes a job as rural schoolteacher in the early years of the century) to a time when rurality could be envisioned, for those of a certain social standing, as a site of diversion. But this pleasurable "recovery" of a cultural landscape flattened of its difficulties is a luxury that can be afforded by very few.

And indeed, the novel suggests that class formation structures the expression of nostalgic sentiment, if not nostalgia itself. *So Big* posits nostalgia—as opposed merely to memory—as deliberate, sustained immersion in a constructed past that has lost its essential meaning. When Paula's society set, to which Dirk sometimes belongs, begins staging foxhunts in northern Chicago, Selina is suitably amused:

> "A fox hunt! What for?"
>
> "For! Why, what's any fox hunt for?"
>
> "I can't imagine. They used to be for the purpose of ridding a fox-infested country of a nuisance. Have the foxes been bothering 'em out in Lake Forest?"
>
> "Now Mother, don't be funny." He told her about the [English] breakfast [Paula had given].
>
> "Well, but it's so silly, Dirk. It's smart to copy from another country the things they do better than we do. England does gardens and wood-fires and dogs and tweeds and pipes and leisure better than we do. But those luke-warm steamy

breakfasts of theirs! It's because they haven't gas, most of them. No Kansas or Nebraska farmer's wife would stand for one of their kitchens—not for a minute. And the hired man would balk at such bacon." She giggled.

"Oh, well, if you're going to talk like that." (240)

That this particular use of the past (or of an alternative present) is available only to those with leisure and means is clear. In contrast, Selina's class status shapes her more straightforward relation to history, especially her own, as something to be neither regretted nor romanticized. For instance, despite Dirk's accusation that Selina's "useless" mementos of her past expose her empty "sentimental[ism]," they include, among letters and dried flowers, the "pair of men's old side-boots with mud caked on them" that she wore in the fields (149–50). If nostalgia requires overlooking painful aspects of the past and their relation to the present, suggests Selina, then neither she nor Dirk, as she occasionally reminds him, can spare the price.

This attitude would also appear to validate contemporary literature that eschews facile "reminiscences" of an undefiled agrarian America and instead chronicles agriculture's relation to a changed, and still changing, nation—the book that Ferber wrote. This hardly means that *So Big* avoids romanticism; on the contrary, the very sweep of its historical vision is romantic, as commentators mentioned. But it treats Selina's early years of toil on the farm with a distinct realism ("Here was all the drudgery of farm life with none of its bounteousness, fine sweep, or splendor" [91]), and it self-consciously notes its own refusal to capitulate entirely to fairy-tale paradigms even as, ultimately, it paints Selina as a larger-than-life figure:

> It would be gratifying to be able to record that in these eight or nine years Selina had been able to work wonders on the De Jong farm; that the house glittered, the crops thrived richly, the barn housed sleek cattle. But it could not be truthfully said. (102)

> It would be enchanting to be able to record that Selina, next day, had phenomenal success, disposing of her carefully bunched wares to great advantage. . . . The truth is that she had a day so devastating, so catastrophic, as would have discouraged most men and certainly any woman less desperate and determined. (128)

Even more important, perhaps, are the criticisms Ferber reserves for certain aspects of contemporary culture, which suggest the degree to which *So Big* is a novel of the present rather than a "lost" past. Those who oppose progressive farming methods, the narrative suggests, or who fail to see that their timeworn practices are counterproductive, will not survive. Early in the text, Selina's husband repeatedly refuses to entertain her ideas for improved drainage techniques, remarking with false thrift, "What was good enough for my father is good enough for me" (87)—an attitude that leads to his death of rheumatism because he will not spare the money for indoor lodgings during long, wet nights in the city's market district (107–10). But Ferber's scorn touches on country and city institutions equally. The modern university, a means and symbol of bourgeois advancement, is a target for satire, especially insofar as both the professoriat and the student culture glorify book learning and undervalue practical life experience (158–66). And Ferber is particularly trenchant, and funny, in her analysis of the standardization that has crept into virtually every avenue of modern life. The girls in Dirk's office, for instance, though they come from lower-class homes, affect the same look and mannerisms of Paula and her friends: "Their very clothes were faultless imitations. They even used the same perfume. [Dirk] wondered, idly, how they did it" (213–14). For their part, Paula and the "North Shore Girls" all look "amazingly alike" (210–11); men, too, exhibit a marked conformity to type ("Nine out of every ten of these men possessed millions. Whenever corned beef and cabbage appeared on the luncheon menu nine out of ten took it" [200]). This homogenized culture is on a par with the modernity signaled by the encroachment of the city, which, by the end of the novel, threatens to "clos[e] in" on Selina's "rich green acres" (217).

Of course, resistance to such leveling factors is what makes Selina's character superior to Dirk's: "[I'm] nothing but a rubber stamp," he acknowledges miserably in the end (251). But such resistance is also a mark of the novel itself, which, for all its stereotypes of characterization, nonetheless attempts to move beyond a merely nostalgic, and therefore empty, evocation of agrarian mystique. As the first identifiable best-seller of modern America, *So Big* suggests that mainstream audiences approved of a vision of rurality less trite than those that had been offered to date, and that took account of the volatile forces of urban industrialism.

Martha Ostenso's 1925 rural novel, *Wild Geese,* is less overtly interested in urban-industrial landscapes, but it was, like Ferber's text, deeply embedded in the modern culture industry. Ostenso, a twenty-four-year-old Norwegian American who had spent her teenage years in Canada, triumphed over 1,389 other competitors to win what was considered in 1923 to be quite a hefty literary purse: $13,500 awarded by the Dodd, Mead Company, *Pictorial Review,* and the Famous Players-Lasky Corporation to "the story best suited for publication as a magazine serial and as a book and for motion picture adaptation." Predictably, when *Wild Geese* was published in book form in 1925, the fantastic profile of the contest itself—not just the size of the cash award but also the multiple media in which the winning work was to be presented—preoccupied the critical establishment. "Any novel which will satisfy the requirements of a reputable publisher, a popular periodical, and a motion picture producer" is at least "an interesting phenomenon," declared the *Saturday Review of Literature;* others claimed, however, that *Wild Geese* "suffers from the stress of such varied exactions," or that it "bears within itself traces of its dual purpose: to be a novel and to be a film-piece; and . . . it is faulty in both."[42] Virtually no one was able to discuss the work without reference to the contest that spawned it, lending it a stigma of commercialism even as it was also praised in many quarters for its vivid realism. Today it is available only in a Canadian edition, a testament to both the ephemeral nature of popular literary success in the 1920s United States and the politics of place and nation that has informed the novel's subsequent reputation.

While Ostenso has been claimed as a Norwegian writer and, more prominently, a Canadian writer, both her ethnic placement and the fictional setting of *Wild Geese* are more fluid than fixed. The novel was written, during a period of six weeks, in Manitoba, where Ostenso had formerly attended university and taught school for a brief time; most of her life, however, both before and after *Wild Geese,* was spent in the United States. More to the point, the bleak prairie setting of the novel is unmarked in nationalist terms; no mention is made of Canada, although biographical information has suggested that Ostenso imagined the location of her story to be near Lake Winnipeg.[43] The Gare family, on whom this intense psychological farm drama is based, is also ethnically indefinite, especially in the context of the "Indians" and northern European immigrants who populate their small settlement. In short, there is nothing to intimate that the social or natural landscapes of *Wild Geese*, which differ little from those of Ostenso's later Minnesota-based novels, are more Canadian than American—a point that probably contributed, as Faye Hammill has recently argued, to Ostenso's liminal standing in the Canadian canon. Others have suggested that Ostenso purposely downplayed regional associations to appease the prize committee.[44]

Ironically, though, Ostenso's acceptance as an *American* author was immediate. Many reviewers seemed unaware of her complicated heritage and touted *Wild Geese* as part of a national literary tradition. Harry Hansen of the *Chicago News* commented on the novel's "living American theme," declaring it "the fulfillment of the rich, glorious promise of our native writing." Wrote Herschel Brickell in the *Literary Review,* "[Ostenso] is one more of the younger Americans worth keeping an eye upon." An article in the *Bookman* titled "Norse America in Fiction," while calling *Wild Geese* "a[n important] contribution to the immigrant belles lettres of America," also claimed it was part of "native American writing"; other reviewers stated without equivocation that *Wild Geese* relates "exotic types" to "the common life of the American farmer in the West," or that it offers "a new study of a type of American citizen." The assumption of the novel's nativism was furthered by those who located the story ambiguously in the "bleak north country" or "somewhere in the Northwest."[45] If *Wild Geese*'s perceived complicity with an American popular culture prevented its full acceptance by the Canadian literary academy,[46] its presumably Canadian setting was also sufficiently indistinct to allow for its alignment with American literary trends and preoccupations.

Discussions of the novel's position within an acknowledged body of rural literature also demonstrate, once again, the prominence of that body and its role in contextualizing best-selling books. Brickell praised *Wild Geese* as having "more plot than most recent farm-novels," and Ostenso was assumed to have "studied the early novels of Willa Cather" and "followed the successful lead of Edna Ferber in 'So Big.'" An article by Donald Douglas in the *Nation* compared *Wild Geese* to Walter Muilenburg's novel *Prairie* (1925) in order to argue that neither a romantic, "wild goose's-eye view" nor a realistic, "worm's-eye view" of farm life makes for fully satisfactory rural literature. Douglas's complaints about the novel notwithstanding, he assumed that *Wild Geese* is properly understood in light of a range of approaches to rurality undertaken by American novelists.[47]

Yet efforts to position Ostenso's novel within prevailing literary models seemed forced, largely because reviewers such as Douglas struggled to categorize it as either realistic or romantic; recent discussions have more usefully read *Wild Geese* in the context of American naturalism, which posits a tension between those apparent oppositions.[48] Certainly the novel combines a probing analysis of plausible psychological states—especially the restricted emotional and expressive range resulting from sustained abuse—with a sweepingly cosmic symbolism that relates the social world and the world of nature. The terms of that relation, however, tend to challenge, rather than sustain, sentimental archetypes.

The isolated prairie farm of Caleb Gare, a cruel and exacting tyrant who drives his family like beasts, is a harsh landscape on several levels. Here Caleb holds hostage his wife, Amelia, whose birthing of a son out of wedlock prior to their marriage is the source of Caleb's psychological mastery over her. Amelia, threatened with the possibility of exile from their moralistic community if her background is known, submits to Caleb's brutality and offers their children—Ellen, Martin, Judith, and Charlie—as a kind of sacrifice in exchange for Caleb's silence, which will also protect her illegitimate offspring, Mark Jordan, from the knowledge of his base beginnings. Both Amelia and the Gare children are like prisoners, worked to excess and housed and clothed in the most meager way possible so that Caleb may reinvest his profits in more acreage. The simmering resentment of the children, especially the teenage Judith, is brought to the fore by the arrival of a new schoolteacher, Lind Archer, who boards briefly in the Gare home and falls in love with Mark Jordan, who is temporarily caring for a neighboring farm. The presence of this cultured outsider is sufficiently disruptive to alter the entire current of feeling, and hence the balance of power, in the Gare household. In an emotional climax Judith impulsively hurls an ax at Caleb, and, although it misses the mark, Caleb's hold over the family becomes gradually more tenuous, until ultimately Judith escapes to the city as Caleb dies fighting an accidental wildfire that threatens his own lush fields of flax.

Especially significant is the sympathetic link established between Lind and Judith, and the subsequent series of oppositions highlighted by that link. Lind's intellectuality and sentimentality are met by Judith's raw sensuality, and Lind's affair with Mark Jordan, described in genteel terms (they talk about books [93], and she calls him "my dearest" [e.g., 158]),[49] could not be more different from the illicit, carnal encounters between Judith and her lover, Sven. (In a much-quoted scene, they meet in the woods and wrestle feverishly, "like two stark elements," after which Judith breathes, "Kiss me—now" [102–3].) The subversive forms of sexual expression that are foregrounded by Judith's character, including her attraction to Lind (e.g., 196), are entirely absent from or sublimated by Lind's character. Since Judith is the more compelling figure, and since her violence and transgressive sexuality are tacitly sanctioned by the narrative, it is her radical subjectivity, rather than Lind's conservative one, that comes to seem more authentic—all the more interesting since Judith despises the farm and sees the cultivation of crops as a "rude growth" apart from genuine beauty (235).

Hence both Judith and *Wild Geese* dismantle, rather than affirm, hackneyed tropes of agriculture and of nature generally. The more facile figurations of nature-as-symbol—the investment of the geese flying overhead with a mystic ritualism (e.g., 56, 301), or the thought that nature's perfection mirrors her love (217)—are assigned to Lind. In contrast, Judith's responses to nature are often more conflicted, and are far less conventional: "Then she threw herself upon the moss under the birches, grasping the slender trunks of the trees in her hands and straining her body against the earth. She had taken off the heavy overalls and the coolness of the ground crept into her loose clothing. . . . There was no movement, except the narrow trickle of the water from the spring. . . . Here was clearly undreamed of, such clarity as the soul should have, in desire and fulfillment. Judith held her breasts in ecstasy" (185; cf. 61). This autoeroticism, with its simultaneous suggestion of Judith's sexual union with nature itself, temporarily displaces even her attraction to Sven, whose interruption of the scene is experienced by Judith as a "disappointment." And the text codes Judith as the virtual embodiment of a nature that is not placidly generative but restless, unpredictable, untamed, at the height of sexual impetuosity: Lind notes her "beautiful, challenging body," like that of a "splendid she-animal, nearly grown" (196; cf. 160, 204). Her hypercorporeality and extraeroticism make Judith seem uncontainable, foreign to the submission symbolized by the forcible cultivation of the land. And indeed, "she recognized in herself an alien spirit, a violent being of dark impulses, in no way related to the life about her" (108). When she becomes pregnant with Sven's child, she sees herself as "belong[ing] to another clear, brave world of true instincts"; she is unlike her family members, who, "living only for the earth, and the product of the soil," are "meagre and warped" (283).

Judith, then, is the essential antagonist of her father, whom Lind characterizes as "nothing but a symbol of the land," to which most of the Gares have "a monstrously exaggerated conception of their duty" (92; cf. 35). Judith despises both Caleb and the labor he exacts, which are collapsed into the (farm)land itself as the reification of her father's actual and fancied power:

> Caleb walked in the approaching dusk like a thing that belonged infinitely to the earth. . . . Before him glimmered the silver grey sheet of the flax—rich, beautiful, strong. All unto itself, complete, demanding everything, and in turn yielding everything. . . . (156)

> [The hay] was product of *his* land, result of *his* industry. As undeniably his as his right hand, testifying to the outer world that Caleb Gare was a successful owner and user of the soil. (213)

In contrast, Judith—for whom loving the farm would imply complicity in her own oppression—prefers the landscape in its wild, unordered state and resents the further subjugation of the open prairie by what she imagines as "a male giant violating the earth" (138). She also knows that this is why Caleb entertains "a special hatred for her," because "she hated the things that were God to him—the crops, the raising of animals, the rough produce of the land" (216). That Judith remains unpunished for both the attempted murder of her father and her pregnancy, while Caleb, attempting to save his fields, sinks into the muskeg (a boggy area resistant to cultivation), sufficiently validates her perspective.

Certainly Caleb's character is unsubtle, as reviewers noted. Since he clearly differs from the kindlier surrounding farmers, of whom he takes free advantage, it is tempting to read him merely as an aberration, an example, perhaps, of the backwardness that rural isolation was thought occasionally to foster. But the emphasis of the narrative, especially in its gendered and generational aspects, suggests otherwise. Rather, *Wild Geese* points toward an alternative, and dark, vision of the long-presumed link between farming and social organization. The attitude of mastery that Caleb assumes over the land and over his family, as well as over local farmers who are less financially stable, is seamless, underscoring the logical, mutually sustaining relation between farming and patriarchy. If Jeffersonian ideals assume that the character traits required for sustenance farming—independence, autonomy, thrift—affect positively the organization of the family unit and, by extension, the civic body, then Caleb Gare demonstrates that those same traits may also produce quite different results. That is, *Wild Geese* exposes the fault lines in the Jeffersonian paradigm that Theodore Roosevelt had tried to resuscitate for a modern world. Specifically, it shows that the forcefulness and single-mindedness necessary to wrest a living from a harsh landscape may actually make men *un*fit for cooperative membership in families and larger communities.

Relations between farming and the family are constantly dwelled upon in *Wild Geese*. For example, Caleb despises those farmers whose imagined tenderness diminishes profits: noting that the hay remains uncut at Thorvald Thorvaldson's "ramshackle farm," he thinks sneeringly, "Perhaps one of [Thorvald's] daughters had a toothache and the hay had to wait" (179). He blackmails Fusi Aronson into selling him a desired tract of timber by playing on Fusi's affection for his less ethical brother (69, 82), suggesting again that a willingness to accommodate familial needs is a weakness in business. And Anton Klovacz, the consumptive whose fields are temporarily cared for by Mark Jordan, is also Caleb's victim, his genuine kindness, as much as his physical weakness, signaling that he is ill suited to oppose Caleb's ruthlessness. Anton's concern for his family's welfare stands in stark contrast to Caleb's selfishness, as Mark Jordan notes when, after Caleb has cheated Anton, he asks, "Is there anything in the world you care for as much as for yourself, I wonder, Caleb Gare?" (241).

Caleb's response—"Every man for himself, that's what I say" (242)—justifies his authoritarian hold on farm, family, and neighbors, which he clearly understands as interconnected insofar as they collectively increase his real and imagined worth. Yet it is the subordination of the Gare family, rather than the cultivation of the land itself or the imposition of Caleb's will on the broader community, on which the narrative expends the most energy. Lind observes "the unbelievable amount of work" that the Gare family performs, especially the women (262), all of which is uncompensated; indeed, these laborers frequently lack basic necessities, and the Gare children have been largely denied schooling. When the fieldwork increases, Caleb simply pushes his family harder, begrudging the wages for hired help. While Caleb's cruelty is exceptional, the arrangements on his homestead nonetheless reflect the economic logic that underwrites the typical family farm, just as his peremptory stance highlights its essentially undemocratic nature. (At one point Amelia accuses Caleb of preventing Judith from marrying for "the work [he] can get out of her" [121], and occasional glimpses of minor female characters, in particular, intimate that the essential inequities of the Gare farm, while extreme, are not fundamentally different from those on other farms [e.g., 128].) That Caleb's most serious antagonists are, ultimately, not other farmers but familial females—Amelia, who finally finds the courage to stand up to him, and, most important, Judith—points to the text's critique of patriarchal institutions that structure unequal relations of power between men and women. These include not only farming but also religion.[50] It is especially significant that Judith and her unborn baby escape with Sven, and that Amelia's illegitimate child is never exposed, while Caleb, the coercive, self-righteous male, dies.

Wild Geese seems naturalistic, then, as Rosalie Murphy Baum has argued, because it combines gritty realism and a sense of localized determinism with "an ideology of social reform" and "a strain of idealism."[51] The ending certainly intimates that Amelia and the Gare children will build better lives for themselves in the absence of Caleb. Yet the novel's alternative social vision seems to reside most fully in Mark and Lind, who assure themselves that they "don't belong" to this farming community, that its "sinister" aspect "doesn't touch [them]" (210). Their certainty suggests their perceived cultural distance from a brutalizing patriarchy, as well as their actual circumvention of the class formation that consigns the settlers to a life of hard agricultural labor. Mark and Lind, that is, come from a finer stock: they are professional people, brought to the settlement by circumstances that are not binding, and are therefore free to leave its cruel isolation and the resulting social and emotional disabilities behind them. Both Mark's status as an orphan (he has even cut ties with the priests who raised him, declining to become one of them) and Lind's level of education point to their fortunate evasion of traditional, oppressively gendered social models, implying a challenge to Fusi Aronson's "almost oracular" suggestion early in the novel that it is primarily the *landscape* that constricts the spirit (33). Though less vivid than the Gares, and despite their retrogressive gentility, Mark and Lind point toward progressive social arrangements that somehow bypass conventional structures. That they must return to the city to recapture those, and that Judith, too, feels that she must "find the sky and the wind in a more profuse place" (138), seems to indict the rigidified social matrix of the novel's farm community.

Soon after Ostenso won the prize for *Wild Geese* she was described as a "novelist who came out of nowhere overnight," the "Actual Heroine of a Present-Day Literary Fairy Story."[52] But while she maintains some visibility in Canada, she and her novel have been largely lost to American audiences, perhaps in part because her multiple nationalist affinities and her mix of genres call for complicated reading strategies. Like Ferber, however, Ostenso used rurality as a means of sounding out modernity's perils and possibilities, especially where women are concerned. Modern sexual and psychological crises, *Wild Geese* insists, are not engendered by the city alone.

Ironically, and perhaps inevitably, an early advertisement for Elizabeth Madox Roberts's *Time of Man* attempted to distance her work from the considerable commercial machinery that surrounded the texts of Ferber and Ostenso, among others, seeking to align it instead with a more genuine art: "No prize of thousands of dollars is affixed to this novel," the publisher claimed. "[N]o motion picture rights have been bought or ever will be. Instead, it comes to you as a masterpiece of contemporary American literature." *The Time of Man,* however, was also one of the first featured selections of the newly inaugurated Book-of-the-Month Club, which surely enhanced the novel's circulation and currency among readers. While the press copy touting the novel as a club selection contained endorsements by such literary elites as Sherwood Anderson ("I am humble before it") and Carl Van Doren ("A beautiful work of art"), it also listed prominently the members of the selecting committee, which included journalist William Allen White and the popular novelist Dorothy Canfield. This coupling of high-cult and midcult names testifies, of course, to the intersecting planes of literature-as-art and literature-as-industry, and to the efforts of the Book-of-the-Month Club to position itself as a guiding force for the reader struggling to navigate a hugely diversified literary field. But in retrospect it also seems to presage the precarious cultural positioning of *The Time of Man*—a novel uniformly praised, even within sophisticated literary circles, but also drenched in the folk idioms of a (southern) regionalism that still tended to denote a vernacular, rather than a cultured, art. To quote a recent revisionist historian, such parochially situated works were all too frequently thought to constitute a "minor literature associated with local places, 'little forms,' and women."[53]

Yet *The Time of Man,* a lyrical novel tracing the growth to consciousness of an impoverished female tenant farmer, conforms both to the aesthetic contours of high modernism and to its theme of tortured individuation. One early review of the novel suggested that its occasional stream-of-consciousness sections demonstrated that Roberts had "studied the approved literary gods of the day." Indeed, *The Time of Man* has been linked to the work of Woolf and Lawrence, and its protagonist, Ellen Chesser, has been read as exemplifying, for instance, a high modernist preoccupation with language and the im/possibilities of articulation.[54] The novel achieves a mythic sensibility in two ways: first, through the minute tracings of Ellen's awareness of herself as embedded within the natural world, even as she also perceives that world with a heightened sensitivity; and second, through the use of the truncated rhythms and archaic expressions of an indigenous rural culture that seems suspended in time. Given these traits, and the acknowledged force of the text's many finely wrought passages, we can only guess at why it has failed to gain more of a long-term following among purveyors of high modernism. By the late 1940s, Roberts's formerly best-selling novel was little read, and it seems significant that her reputation, despite periodic attempts at revival, today rests almost entirely on efforts by schools and humanities institutions in her native state of Kentucky. The few critical studies of her work have placed her firmly within the context of southern regionalism.[55] It would seem that somehow the localized elements of her fiction eclipsed in significance the so-called universalizing ones, a process that, as recent studies of regionalism reveal, was probably related to the gender of both the author and her central character.[56]

Then again, Ellen Chesser's psychology and narrative trajectory may have compromised her alignment with elite as well as popular modes. *The Time of Man* begins and ends with Ellen and her kin moving on to yet another location, another tenancy; yet despite their continuing poverty (a class-based stasis that forms a counterpoint to their constant physical movement), Ellen does not despair. Rather, to borrow a favorite word from the text, she endures, displaying a temper markedly different from, say, the exquisite disillusionment of Lost Generation protagonists. But if this attitude of steadfastness makes Ellen an Everywoman figure likely to attract a broad popular readership, her story still departs from the tropes of triumph typical of mainstream fiction, including rural fiction. With no access to the postures of conquest frequently attached to American farm narratives, Ellen prevails over virtually nothing, unless we consider that she manages to retain a strong sense of beauty and of self amid circumstances—tenancy, poverty, spousal infidelity—that consistently seem to render her life ugly and insignificant. Such a private victory, however, seems undramatic in the context of the period's more common tales of agriculturalists who dominate both the land and their social circumstances. This is perhaps why, of the four best-selling novels discussed in this chapter, *The Time of Man* is the only one that was never adapted for film.

And in fact, relatively little happens in the novel in the outward sense. Against a backdrop of ceaseless agricultural labor, Ellen grows up, marries, and has five children, one of whom dies; her husband strays but then returns to her; a minor narrative thread deals with his continued persecution for a barn burning that he did not commit. But such plot elements are peripheral, having meaning only insofar as they direct Ellen's thoughts, which are thickly varied and communicated through a fluid, poetic discourse. The contrast between her rich inner world and the outer one, characterized by narrowness of circumstance and expression, lends the text pathos but also a stirring beauty. At times this contrast is rendered through unconventional stylistic maneuvers, as when at dinnertime in the family's bare cabin a young Ellen relives her encounter earlier in the day with a well-dressed, superior college boy whom she admires:

> She thought of a room where there would be fair colors and she felt herself to be stepping down hard white stairs, walking on wide stairs, a low wind fluttering her sleeve. An angry burst of tone came from near the fireplace.
>
> "Your pappy ought to come on now and eat his victuals while they're hot."
>
> "He might be a friend I'd know all my enduren days. 'We'll take a walk,' he says. 'Any day you say.'" She saw little flecks of amber on brown threads of cloth, minutely seen.
>
> "Your pappy ought to come. What's he a-loiterin' for? In trouble I reckon . . . "
>
> "And so this is your axe[,]" [he had said]. The sinking fire made a pink glow on the cups, three cups standing together on the table. (71)[57]

That her rough material world impinges as little as it does on Ellen's inner life prompted some commentators to declare that any documentary aspects of the text are largely incidental, and that it "lives in the mind chiefly as a beautiful achievement in the art of the novel."[58]

Yet the agricultural context of *The Time of Man* was, in Roberts's view, essential. Privately she averred a distinction between a farm sensibility, which she imagined as "freer, lonelier, less acute perhaps, more dreaming and more wise," and a factory sensibility, which she saw as "prosperous, abundant, commercial, expedient." She also believed that "agricultural people are closer to their morality" and that this is connected to "their identity with the earth."[59] Hence Roberts perceived a link between ideality and the material bases of agrarian identity; through Ellen, we see how the agricultural woman, in particular, is bound up in rhythms of both earth and body that shape the nuances of thought and define a life.

The very keynote of *The Time of Man* is desire. Again and again Ellen *wants,* and this disposition unites the material world and the abstract realm of feeling and perception. Against the backdrop of the seasons, whereby relative plenty (summer) is followed by lack (winter), hunger is both physical and metaphysical. As a girl Ellen wants "a blue hat with a big white ostrich-plume" (54) and the answers to her questions (88); later, she wants "a house on a green hill" with "a bright new pump" (327) and to hold onto her husband (347). Even Ellen's amorphous longing for something beyond her powers of imagination is so pained, so abstruse, that it virtually becomes visceral: "Her own want was undefined, lying out among the dark trees and their dark images, and she reached for it with a great wish that shook her small body" (56). Especially important is her reflectiveness about the very nature of yearning, which frequently takes the form of a hardened image, as when "what she knew of the world and what she wanted of it sparkled and glittered and ran forward quickly as if it would always find something better" (382). Like the turning of the seasons, desire—"wanting things and then having things and then wanting" (97)—is, Ellen understands, a cycle that never ends.

The novel's earliest and most poignant symbol of this longing is Tessie, a gypsy woman whom Ellen's family had known on the roads but who is lost to Ellen when the Chessers quit their wandering and assume a tenancy. Ellen's childish yearning to see Tessie again is so strong that she risks a whipping by taking off in the night to try, unsuccessfully, to find her. For Ellen, Tessie's attractions are many: not only is she a warm, expressive presence in a culture that stints on open affection, but she is the repository of actual goods that Ellen envies, including, notably, books. Indeed, Tessie herself bespeaks desire, as the few books in her possession, and the church to which she once took Ellen for a brief, mysterious visit, point to her own awareness of something beyond the gritty life of the road. Though Ellen's parents are at pains to distance themselves from Tessie and her "parcel of road-trash" (28), Ellen never forgets her and still thinks of her, at the end of the novel, as part of the "something brightly shining" that "always went ahead" (382). Her desire to see Tessie again, to hear her stories and songs and touch her books, conflates materiality and ideality, calling forth the multiple dimensions of Ellen's longings.

Tessie is also bound up in the text's preoccupation with sexual desire, which, while predictably central to a coming-of-age narrative with high modernist leanings, acquires increased resonance because it figures as the life-defining paradigm for impoverished tenant girls such as Ellen. Questions linger in Ellen's mind about Tessie's relations with Jock, the man with whom she travels the roads; and Ellen associates Tessie with her own dimly recalled molestation by Screw, another gypsy (42), and with the first childbirth of which Ellen was old enough to be aware ("Eva Stikes a-screamin' and a-pullen on the bedpost" [44]). Tessie, then, serves as an initiation of sorts into the roles that will shape Ellen's life, and that mark *desire* as a disposition with negative physical effects sustained primarily by women. (It seems no accident that Ellen's sexual awakening occurs against the backdrop of a female neighbor's suicide following the exposure of her husband's adulterous affair.) Many passages emphasize multiple debilitating childbirths as an inescapable reality for the wives surrounding Ellen (e.g., 141, 156), and her own childbirth experiences are marked, notably, by a rhetorical starkness that contrasts with Ellen's own rich internal discourse: "One bright morning in early February Ellen fastened the small children into the kitchen, tying the latch with a string. Then she bore her [next] child alone, being finally delivered toward the noon of the day" (359). Ultimately she imagines herself not as fulfilling any of her own desires but as becoming a vessel for those of her children, her body signifying, and continually birthing, desire itself: "One day she saw the children . . . as men and women, as they would be, and more beside them, all standing about the cabin door until they darkened the path with their shadows, all asking beyond what she had to give, always demanding, always wanting more of her and more of them always wanting to be" (333). Thus sexual desire structures all other desires for destitute women like Ellen, since it structures the very relationship that consigns them to uncontrolled reproduction and, not coincidentally, continued poverty. This reality is depicted with especial poignancy in a scene in which the neighborhood women, reluctant to acknowledge publicly the patriarchal dominance and extreme want that shape their lives, invent face-saving stories exonerating their men and suggesting that their own needs are deliberately deferred: "'[My husband] gave me money to get a new winter cloak,' one said, 'but I said to put it in the bank. No need to waste, I say'" (333–34).

Such emphases demonstrate that this is no sentimental pastoral. Despite Roberts's assertion that *The Time of Man* "could never be an analysis of society or of a social stratum because it keeps starkly within one consciousness,"[60] Ellen's story suggests how unlikely it is that an indigent rurality could harbor many people with her keen impressionability. More common are those, like Ellen's parents, whose very personalities are flattened by constant deprivation and by the endless "stooping and dragging and hauling" (253) required simply to get by. And if the present is hardly ideal, the past, too, fails to take on arcadian overtones. In the single scene in which Ellen's father becomes voluble, his stories of his youth acquire gothic dimensions:

> "I recollect when I was a youngone," Henry resumed his memory. "We used to live in a house over against a knob and once the chimbley smoked all one winter so bad we looked black as buzzards. . . . That spring when Pap was plowen he turned up a skull bone. Sure thing, he did, a small-like skull as if it was a woman or a child. Out in the middle of a field. He brought it in the house but Mammy she wouldn't let it rest until she got it outen the house, but my brother Newt, he stood it agin the door to make a door prop. Then Pap threw it out to please Mammy and it laid out behind the henhouse all summer upside down, and once when it rained I see the chickens drink water out of it. . . .
>
> It was when I was sixteen that Tom Begley stabbed Shine Mather, stabbed him clean through the guts and laid him out as bloody as a hog. Then the mob came and hung Tom to a white oak down by the creek along past our house and me and Pappy and Joe Deats, we took Tom down and laid him out for the funeral. Quarrel over a shotgun, I recollect. . . .
>
> Next year or year after old Uncle Billy Rudd went insane." (178–80)

Henry's anecdotes momentarily defamiliarize both the landscape and the rural peasantry, challenging any implications of a surface idyll. And while, on one hand, the apparent timelessness of the novel's rural culture (only once is a telephone mentioned) allows for the mythic qualities that commentators noted and approved, on the other hand the effect of temporal suspension also reinforces the finality of class formation, the utter lack of appreciable progress that generations of tenant farmers have come to accept. When Ellen's son Dick, in the very last pages of the novel, expresses his desire for "books to know and read over and over," the "strangeness" of his longing "bewilder[s]" and "sadden[s]" Ellen; she is "startled," and his "want render[s] her speechless." As with Ellen's own childish longings, which remain "unappeased" (387), there seems little possibility that Dick's desires will be fulfilled. Endurance, it appears, is a far cry from hope.

Robert Penn Warren suggested that Elizabeth Madox Roberts's reputation was negatively affected by 1930s emphases on social realism, whereby the exploration of a single inner consciousness was perceived as the repudiation of constructive social critique. Because she dealt with the dispossessed without focusing on the economic and social sources of their dispossession, Warren suggested, Roberts's work came to seem out of touch with literary-political priorities. Roberts herself claimed that *The Time of Man* contains "no thesis . . . and no propaganda," yet its focus on an impoverished farm woman testified powerfully, as one reviewer put it, to "the existence of a static class in America."[61] That it was pushed eventually to the margins of both literary and popular favor perhaps suggests that neither elite nor mainstream readerships were poised to appreciate fully a combination of modernist aesthetics and an incisive exploration of lower-class realities.

In contrast, the more heartening sensibilities of Gladys Hasty Carroll's *As the Earth Turns* perhaps allowed for an all-too-uniform critical-cultural response. Appearing second on national best-seller lists for 1933 (trailing only Hervey Allen's historical blockbuster, *Anthony Adverse*), Carroll's novel could only be read as a work of traditional "Yankee Yeomanry" with characters whose "ruddy features" happily "emerge through the socialistic pallor of our times"—or so claimed Donald Davidson in the *Saturday Review of Literature.* Other reviewers touched similarly on the reassuring familiarity to be found in this "solid, unpretentious novel" of rural Maine; more than one suggested that city readers, bedeviled by modern, urban problems, would find respite in Carroll's nostalgic pastoralism.[62] Against the instabilities of the Depression, *As the Earth Turns* seemed to evoke something sure and substantial ("The *real* drama, the *real* romance, the success and failure of *real* people," proclaimed one advertisement), which proved both comforting and marketable. The *New York Times* crooned that Mrs. Carroll's "strength and ability" lay in her quiet manner of depicting seasonal and social change "without stress and without violence," suggesting her work's appeal for a mainstream audience in search of placid diversion.[63] Its nearly instantaneous success, facilitated by the Book-of-the-Month Club, which made it a featured selection for May 1933, prompted Warner Brothers to announce plans that summer for a film version, which debuted the following year and featured Jean Muir and Donald Woods.

But the particular cultural appeal of *As the Earth Turns* is perhaps best illuminated by the dramatic adaptation, created by Carroll herself, which was performed regularly as a summer attraction for ten years beginning in 1935 in the author's hometown of South Berwick, Maine. Performances took place outdoors, in the fields surrounding the Hasty family homestead, as period photographs show (fig. 3.2). All the parts were played by local residents—mainly farmers whose roots reached back several generations—and profits were deposited into a general fund for community improvement. Before World War II forced Carroll to halt production, her folk play received considerable notice in the local and mainstream media, and its audiences included celebrities such as Sinclair Lewis and the governors of both Maine and Vermont. In the summer of 1938, in the fourth year that the work was presented publicly, the *New York Times* reported that more than a thousand people had thus far attended, justifying a yearly increase in admission. Likened to Thornton Wilder's *Our Town,* and proclaimed

Figure 3.2 Open-air theater in South Berwick, Maine, site of summer performances of Carroll's *As the Earth Turns.* (Collections of Maine Historical Society, Image No. 1313.)

in Boston newspapers as "America's *Oberammergau,*" the production was hailed for its homely communitarian spirit and its moving rendition of tragedy and faith.[64]

But Carroll's folk play was also celebrated for apparently sealing the verisimilitude of her fiction: as one headline put it, it merely required "Native Ruralites [to] Just 'Act Natural.'" Since the very actors playing the parts were the local folks upon whom Carroll had drawn in writing her novel, the dramatic version of *As the Earth Turns* was at once doubly removed from, but also ironically closer to, the "reality" that had prompted Carroll's writing in the first place. Hence the play made visible the intricate relations between representation and the real while also validating the sense that the social setting Carroll evoked was, indeed, not created but actual. If the fictional world of the novel seemed frozen in time and space, Carroll's audience was nonetheless assured that it reflected to some extent a real-life milieu that could be recaptured in multiple ways.[65]

There is no question that *As the Earth Turns* indulges in certain idealized notions of rurality, especially in the model of farm womanhood represented by Jen Shaw, the novel's heroine. The eldest daughter of a father whose second marriage has left him with a sickly, querulous wife and an extended set of mouths to feed, Jen is the center of the Shaw household, having taken on, while still a teenager, the physical and psychic labor of ministering to the family. This includes Cora, her stepmother, and Mark Shaw, her silent but hardworking father; several siblings (George, Ed, Ralph, Lize, and Olly) in or approaching adulthood; Lois May and Bun, Cora's daughters; and six-year-old John, the only child of Mark and Cora's union. That Jen feeds, comforts, and cheers this varied group, while also doing virtually all the gardening, canning, laundry, and other housework, and never losing her patience or resenting her lot, places her firmly within a convention of idealized farm women who seem so superhuman as to strain credulity, as some reviewers observed. One aligned Jen with the sentimental tradition of Louisa May Alcott, noting that "[s]he is almost incredible, but not quite; for, even if there are no women like that, at least we like to think there may be."[66]

But if Jen pulls strongly on the reader's heartstrings, recalling images of a womanhood, and a rurality, that seem to belong to a less complicated age, it does not follow that *As the Earth Turns* wholly sidesteps engagement with modernity. Indeed, Jen herself is less one-dimensional than she appears, if only because she fails to carry forth the assumption that farm life is superior to other alternatives. Rather, she smooths the way for others less suited to rurality to remove themselves to the city, exhibiting a tolerance for difference that is less a stereotypical equanimity than a realistic approach to the varied personalities around her and to the imperatives of a changing world. Recognizing, for instance, that her brother Olly feels stifled on the farm, Jen helps to make law school a viable option for him and delights in his success, even as her father seems confused and somewhat disappointed by Olly's choice; she also supports her sisters, first Lize and then Lois May, in their decisions to seek office work and a more fast-paced social life in the city. That Jen herself pities Lize and Lois May, who seem wan and thin when they visit, is, from this perspective, irrelevant; it is not merely rurality itself, but Jen's *suitability* for rurality that the novel celebrates, just as it acknowledges freely that others may, and often do, find fulfillment elsewhere. This position is buttressed by the situation of Jen's oldest brother, George, whose assumption of his own farm results in misery for his wife and children, since he is a lazy, uninterested farmer who lacks the motivation to improve. Hence rurality is depicted as one option among many, and it is not for everyone, a sensibility that departs substantially from an unreflective endorsement of the country as an idyllic place to live and work.

Even more significant, however, is Jen's gradual courtship by Stan Janowski, to whom she is betrothed at the novel's end. When Stan and his Polish family arrive in the middle of winter to take over a neighboring farm, the small community is astonished—first, because the Janowskis are foreigners, and second, because they appear to know so little about their new enterprise that they arrive at a time of year when a suitable house cannot be built, forcing them to take up residence in a barn. Jen's kindness to Mrs. Janowski, Stan's mother, initiates a tentative friendship, and Stan eventually proves that he is as capable and dedicated a farmer as Mark Shaw, earning the respect of both Mark and Jen. Even Stan's strongly evidenced ethnicity—he plays "wild and foreign" music on his fiddle and seems effeminate compared with the local men (192; cf. 301)—is slowly accepted, paving the way for a deeper relationship between Stan and Jen. When Stan's parents, who are as ill suited to rural life as some of Jen's siblings, decide to return to the city, Stan remains, taking up permanently a rural lifestyle that he has come to love and winning Jen's heart in the process.

The decision that Jen and Stan will live with Mark Shaw, combining the Janowski and Shaw farms, is thus framed as a "natural" outcome, not only because it makes good business sense and solves the practical problem of Jen's indispensability to the Shaw household but also because it closes the novel through the conventional means of a marriage that will maintain the status quo. On the most obvious level, then, *As the Earth Turns* presents a prescriptive, sentimental plot that serves to reinforce the value of its heroine's chosen lifestyle. On a deeper level, though, the accommodation of a Polish farmer into this tight-knit Yankee community disrupts tradition. Early on Mark Shaw seems to know that, of his nine children and stepchildren, only Ed, Jen, and John are likely to make good farmers (12–13); this awareness that farming is no longer as self-perpetuating as it once was is further emphasized by the arrival of Stan, a "Polack," on the scene. Ironically, the novel's much-lauded "Yankee yeomanry" comes to depend for its continuation on an infusion of foreign energy and will. That most reviewers failed to note this twist points, perhaps, to Carroll's skill in couching trenchant observations about rural culture and the pressures of modernity within an invocation of tradition. It may also suggest, however, readers' willingness to overlook such sticking points in the urgency of their desire to relive a mythologized "American" rurality.

In other ways, too, *As the Earth Turns* betrays the incursion of contemporary actualities into the time-honored rural society of New England. Unlike Ferber's *So Big*, this novel never shows us a cityscape, but it manages to relay the imposition of modern, urban life just the same. While the cycle of the harvest year organizes the narrative structure (divided into sections named for the four seasons) and continues to order the outward life of those remaining on the Shaw homestead, this rhythm is increasingly difficult to hang onto in the face of an intruding outside world. The regularity of the Shaws' existence, presumably uninterrupted for generations, is now periodically unsettled by visiting urbanites, or letters from Olly that detail his exploits at the university. ("Letters made [Mark Shaw] apprehensive. . . . There had been no need of them [in years past], when trains were nothing in his life but a whistle in the distance. . . . It was a strange thing how so many of his children wanted to go off, as if farms were not good enough any more" [32].) Just as Lize tries to impress the still-homebound

Lois May with hints about her city beaux (Lois May was "only waiting, breathless, to begin the glamorous life [Lize] lived" [46]), Stan's little sisters, new to the community, dazzle their country schoolmates with descriptions of urban goods and steam heat that make country life seem insipid and antiquated in comparison. And when Ralph, a pilot, loses his life in a faraway plane crash, the disquieting realities of modernity take on a material presence in the form of his broken body, sent home for burial, lying in a coffin in the front parlor. Mark Shaw reflects grievously that he might have forced Ralph to remain on the farm but finds some comfort in knowing that he allowed his children to pursue their own paths (233; cf. 218–19). As Jen had put it on a happier occasion, Ralph could not have been held back: "'Give a boy like Ralph an airplane,' she said lightly, 'and he might be *anywhere.* All he needed was wings'" (52).

As the Earth Turns acknowledges, however, that farm women are granted less freedom and far less recognition than farm men, even as it also explores women's changing roles in a fuller manner than the stereotypes associated with Jen Shaw might indicate. Lize and Lois May both become urban office workers, and, despite their efforts to exalt their circumstances for those back home, the text makes it clear that they belong to the legion of poorly paid women who compete in the romantic marketplace to find a mate to relieve their financial hardships. Margaret, Ed's new wife, struggles with her desire to fulfill her teaching commitments in the country school in the face of Ed's insistence that, as a married woman, she should concentrate on their home ("She could do both and do them well, [she thought]" [122]). Even the placid Jen notes the inequity between men and women as she tends the unmarked grave of a farmer's wife who lost her husband and son to war: "To-morrow men would drive up and leave a basket of flowers and a flag for Joseph because he died in the Civil War, and for James because he died on his way home from it, but they would not have anything for Hannah because she had only identified her son James one hot summer day on the platform of North Derwich station, and raised all the food her husband ate for the twenty years he sat in a chair in her kitchen, and done washings for Mrs. Hale to buy monuments for them at the end" (148). When Mil, George's wife, tells Jen of her intention to leave George ("It's pretty hard to work myself to death and never get any credit, and be shut up in that kitchen washing and digging and have him come home at night and only find fault because there's no hot bread"), she merely makes more personal, then, the gender imbalances of which Jen is aware. That Jen does not try to dissuade Mil, recognizing that her own contentment with her farm woman's lot leaves her unqualified to pass judgment on Mil's desire for something more, legitimates Mil's perspective and underscores, once again, the novel's refusal to give rurality and its social structures a blanket endorsement (183–85).

In particular, the strong relations between farm culture and male dominance are everywhere apparent in *As the Earth Turns,* and the narrative's sympathy lies consistently with the women who must operate within the confines of disfranchisement. For Jen, this merely means carefully managing the men such that they come, without realizing it, to share her own way of thinking. But for those women who lack Jen's touch, or who are more deeply affected by injustice, gendered restrictions are less innocuous. The most interesting and extended episode addressing these dynamics concerns the family tension that breaks out when Ed Shaw refuses to contribute the final twenty-five dollars that Lois May needs to enroll in a business program in the city. Lize has agreed to house Lois May in her apartment, and Cora has spent months sewing a new wardrobe for Lois May, but the men, as an enraged Cora points out, are not so generous:

> Her face was crumpled with crying. . . .
>
> "You're awful good to [Lois May], Lize," she said choking. "You're just as good and sweet as you can be, and don't you think we'll forget it. All the women folks in the family has done a little something, and you've done the most; it's the men that can't see a foot ahead of them. It's the men that don't care what lives or dies as long as they're kept comfortable and get what they want. And they don't want anything for anybody but themselves." (60–61)

Ed, of course, claims that his hard-earned money is his own, and that Margaret, who will soon be his wife, is deserving of comforts; yet Margaret, when she hears of the trouble, is embarrassed, feeling that Lois May's education is much more important than furnishing her new house. In the end Ed comes around and provides the money, vindicating Jen's faith in his fundamental goodness, but not before twenty pages have been spent in detailing Lois May's and Cora's depression, Lize's fury, and Margaret's flustered discomfort in the face of Ed's initial decision, to which the women have no recourse. On the contrary, Ed's absolute authority is presented as a commonplace aspect of the farm:

> "Now that'll do," Ed said evenly. "I've heard all I'm going to. I've heard enough. It's all done."
>
> . . . Nobody spoke, not even Lize. Bun and John sat, frozen with awe, on the couch. It was the spell the man on the farm had the power of casting over his women when occasion demanded it. The rooster swelled up, stretched his neck, and crowed, when he had done it. The bull threw back his head and roared. Ed only buckled his boots and dipped water but it was with the same certain air of dominance. (61)

If Ed's ultimately sheepish acquiescence to the women's request in any way softens our vision of him, it cannot wholly gloss over this domineering attitude, which surfaces again in the early months of his marriage. Nor can it erase the image of a defeated Cora Shaw, "thin and small" and with eyes "streaming tears," bereft of the power to assist Lois May, her favorite child (67).

As the Earth Turns suggests that traditional American rurality is under siege from a range of sources, including not only those "outside" attractions of the modern world that lure away its children but also interior forces, such as an entrenched sexism, that are subject to intensified scrutiny in the context of the twentieth century's shifting social order. This latter is especially important, given the implication that the American farm was never purely bucolic to begin with. Carroll's happy ending, of course, which apparently reaffirms the value of country living, appears to smooth over such problems—but just beneath the text's surface lies a subtle exposure of the American rural myth. Indeed, in comments about her work Carroll distanced herself from an overly simplistic nostalgia, proclaiming a certain distaste for notions of, as she put it, "the old order of things." Rather, she asserted, we need "a new order of things built upon what was good in the old."[67]

Some reviewers argued that not much happens in *As the Earth Turns*—in the words of one, it is more a "family portrait" than a "narrative."[68] But it hardly seems surprising that women writing about farm culture might choose to focus on its "familio-centrism" (to use David Danbom's term) rather than on the tradition of the yeoman farmer's autonomy and its connection to his rights of citizenship. Insofar as historians understand the interdependence of the farm family as a more compelling actuality than the mythos of yeomanry,[69] the texts of Ferber, Ostenso, Roberts, and Carroll seem, despite their romantic elements, quite realistic. All four concern themselves largely with farming's impact on familial relations, especially on women; even those that highlight the tensions between rurality and a newly alluring urbanity (i.e., Ferber's and Carroll's) depict those tensions primarily in terms of the divisiveness that results within the rural family unit.

Of course, this focus on the family allowed these works to overlap a broader tradition of sentimental domestic fiction, much of it regional in scope, which almost certainly contributed to their popularity as much as it eroded their claims to serious critical consideration. Recent scholarship, however, argues for the political dimensions of sentimental literature and its means of consolidating notions of American identity, a focus that has important implications for the works addressed here, which challenge, rather than affirm, the long-standing nationalist mythos of agrarianism.[70] At the very least, these four texts contradict assertions that modern rural novels are concerned more with narrating humans' struggle against nature than with critiquing social relations.[71] As an alternative mode of American modernism, these middlebrow novels combine certain nineteenth-century values with twentieth-century explorations of societal problems, demonstrating that a critical edge did not necessarily undercut a text's popular appeal. To be sure, rurality sold—but it also allowed incisive commentators to make their points about the contemporary urban *and* rural worlds.

Chapter 4

Radical Ruralities

If We Were to plot fictional ruralities in the early twentieth century along a spectrum, with one end occupied by popular farm novels and their midcult ideologies, then the other end would be the site of an insistent radicalism. There, too, women were implicated in intriguing ways. Writers such as Edith Summers Kelley, Olive Tilford Dargan, and Josephine Johnson, whose acclaimed but largely forgotten rural novels are the subject of this chapter, appeared to resist not just some, but virtually all of the farm's traditional significations. While more mainstream female writers tapped into the comforting resonances of agrarianism and thereby softened their works' progressive tendencies, these women, all of whom had strong ties to the Left, seized on rurality as a social space that foregrounded gender and class inequities and therefore heightened the cultural tensions characterizing modernity. Moreover, unlike progressive male ruralists such as Paul Corey[1] or the better-known Steinbeck, they were less interested in narrowly agricultural reforms than in more broadly posited radicalisms that sought to reimagine social structures both inside and outside of agrarian contexts. While popular writers such as Edna Ferber and Gladys Hasty Carroll seem, despite their social critiques, largely to reinforce an agrarian ideal, Kelley, Dargan, and Johnson must be understood as consistently challenging it.

Of course, the poles represented by popular and radical rural novels in the early twentieth century derived much of their force and meaning from a culturally influential center that included critically acclaimed farm-oriented works by, among others,

Edith Wharton (*Ethan Frome* [1911]), Susan Glaspell (*Trifles* [1916], rewritten as *A Jury of Her Peers*), and Ellen Glasgow (*Barren Ground* [1925]), and was unquestionably dominated by Willa Cather. The consistency of Cather's literary investment in rural settings, and her works' resistance to the perceived extremes of formal experimentalism, sweeping sentimentalism, and overt social commentary (she reportedly deplored literature with a "social message"),[2] pushed her to the forefront of what can only be called a modern rural canon. While it is unnecessary to rehearse here the excellent and expansive scholarship on Cather, it must be acknowledged that her works constituted a literary force to be reckoned with. Indeed, they delineated a commercially solid, artistically legitimate ruralism that wielded considerable cultural weight, and that sustained the viability of rurality as a modern representational arena. To read the literary extremes of middlebrow and radical rural novels with the celebrated texts of a writer such as Cather at the presumed center is to read modern American literature and culture along a new and different axis, one that validates the representational choices of women in particular.

And those women had wide-ranging reasons for choosing rurality as a signifying setting—some easier to perceive than others. On the surface, for example, an exploitation of the farm's nostalgic overtones appears to make more sense for middlebrow novelists than for women writers on the Left, who would presumably avoid a backdrop with sentimental connotations. Yet it is important to recall that writers, reformers, and intellectuals, including rural sociologists, consistently validated the city and its thinkers as the locus of progressivism and reform: both modernism and modernity were widely imagined in urban terms. A turn to the country, then, especially as a platform for revisionist social criticism, might be considered a highly subversive move. More pertinently, the three self-consciously radical women novelists discussed here had personal experience with farms and their social and economic structures; their use of the farm as setting is thus in keeping with their lived sense both of societal constraints and of revolutionary potential. The point is not that these writers literally envisioned the country as the likely site for a reformed society, but rather that they perceived untapped possibilities for critical and aesthetic maneuvering both in the farm's "real" circumstances and in its accumulated symbolism.

To be specific, rurality as a setting invited rich commentary on nature versus nurture as it pertained to the roles of women. Significantly, all three of these novelists interest themselves in maternity as an overdetermined aspect of womanhood and explore the enhanced and often oppressive resonances between female reproductivity and agrarian ideology. They highlight, and even exaggerate, the farm female's laboring body in ways that stress the conflicts and continuities between production and reproduction. They also wrestle, though often indirectly, with the dominance of modern consumerism, which infiltrated even isolated and impoverished farm communities and was especially central to women's experiences. As we may recall, men routinely blamed women's alleged materialism for rural out-migration, and both Kelley and Dargan feature scenes in which very poor farm women are deeply moved by the commercial pitches of periodical literature; in a related vein, a minor female character in Johnson's text complains that her daughter-in-law is more interested in her new icebox than in honest work. Hence the blurring lines between traditional agrarian lifestyles and modern urban enticements underlay the explorations of class and gender formations that structure these novels.

But these texts do not merely critique existing orders. On the contrary, they offer alternatives to conventional ideas about gender, about economic and social parity, and even about the limits of artistic representation. Unlike the novels discussed in chapter 3, which, for example, advance gender "equality" by presenting exceptional heroines who appear somehow to transcend the boundaries of their socioeconomic worlds, these more subversive novels tend to renounce bourgeois fiction's cult of the individual and insist instead that the experiences of seemingly singular women matter largely because they illuminate the strictures of the social, political, and aesthetic codes by which women generally are constrained. Moreover, despite these texts' agricultural orientations, they reach beyond the particularities of the farm. Rurality becomes not merely a narrative setting but a signifying space that points in two directions at once: toward a heightened social orthodoxy that lays bare the injustices that a modern world must presumably rectify, and toward fresh theoretical frameworks capable of unsettling even some of the more progressive proponents of modern (urban) social movements.

That these texts failed to sustain the interest of readers much beyond their initial publication is due to a variety of factors. Kelley's, for instance, endured significant excisions by her publisher that resulted in a less boldly challenging book than she apparently intended, while Dargan's—the most overtly polemical—was consigned to the Marxist pigeonholes that mandated its eventual suppression with the rise of anticommunism. Johnson's farm novel, which received the Pulitzer Prize in 1934, was surely overshadowed by the gargantuan success of *The Grapes of Wrath*, published a few years later: as Michael Denning has argued, Steinbeck's narrative of Okie migration captured the national imagination in a way that more static-seeming narratives could not.[3] Perhaps most important, though, is that these three texts did not conform to dominant 1920s and early 1930s paradigms of radical or even liberal-reformist literature, accommodating, for instance, neither the New-Woman-Makes-Good model of bourgeois feminism nor the exploited-industrial-worker preoccupation of the literary Left, both of which were external to agrarian structures and interests. And of course, in an era when race texts were defined primarily as texts by and about African Americans, Dargan's and Johnson's speculative explorations of the privilege of whiteness did not seem especially compelling as race commentary. Notably, male intellectuals attempted to measure all three of these works via more standard (i.e., masculine) forms of protest fiction: Upton Sinclair tried rather desperately to drum up interest in his friend Edith Kelley's farm novel by suggesting its potential as a muckraking tract; the communist critic Granville Hicks reviewed Johnson's text according to the tenets of proletarian realism; and Dargan's work was of course treated as a work of Marxist propaganda.[4] But these novels' shared preoccupations with women, work, and representation, and especially with the layered cultural meanings of rurality, fell outside the bounds of recognized radical expression in their time.

This includes radical aesthetic expression. Kelley, Dargan, and Johnson were certainly aware of, but refused to comply with, an extreme experimental formalism that defined the ultra-avant-garde in literature; like other leftists, they were devoted not only to a collective social vision but also to more accessible, and hence politically viable, novelistic structures. Yet their use of rurality, firmly linked to a romantic American past and newly reinforced as such for modern readers, defied a different representational norm. Uninterested in invoking the rural merely as a reassuring cultural touchstone, they instead confronted head-on its contradictory dimensions. The tension between agrarian myths and the modern realities of agriculture (not to mention industry) is central to these texts, which present an unflinching representation of the underside of farm life and which are also heavily inflected by revolutionary attitudes about women's traditional roles. In short, these novels, which seem relatively conventional on the surface, foil readerly expectations: they align habitual signs and symbols with the unexpected—rurality with discontent rather than well-being, for example, or elemental, intuitive women with a rejection of maternity—and exploit fully the recombinational effects.

To be sure, Kelley, Dargan, and Johnson are not the only socially revisionist women writers to use and comment on rurality, especially in terms of its contrived opposition to urbanity; Nella Larsen, Zora Neale Hurston, and Tillie Olsen are also among those female modernists whose novels incorporate substantial rural elements. The three writers discussed here, however, are chosen for the thoroughgoing nature of their inquiries into rural life, in their personal activisms as much as in their fictions. Unlike the mostly male practitioners of a straightforward midwestern naturalism, for whom the farm serves as a backdrop for deterministic philosophical attitudes, these writers are interested in rurality as a cultural construct that galvanizes their class- and gender-oriented social analyses. For all three, the iconic American farm has become in the twentieth century not a dream realized but a promise broken, a dystopian locale made all the more disillusioning by the relentless rhetoric playing up its alleged superiority to corrupt urban cultures. For the sharecropper, white or black, and especially for the female, the farm is not the wholesome setting that more privileged proponents declared it to be. On the contrary, its pleasant surfaces hide a violent politics of exclusion. To cite Tillie Olsen's *Yonnondio*—which similarly, though more concisely, dismisses the farm tenancy system as just another sanctioned means of exploiting the needy—the sufficiency of food and sunshine, and even the glorious "drama of things growing," proves insufficient salve for the pain of social injustice.[5]

An Aesthetic of Unrestraint: Kelley, Dargan, Johnson

One of the distinguishing features shared by Kelley's, Dargan's, and Johnson's novels is their investment in hyperbole and excess, especially where the female body is concerned. All three texts lend their women characters a heightened corporeality that exceeds even the insistently physical dimensions of their everyday lives in barns, fields, and kitchens: Kelley's female protagonist, for instance, is allotted a lengthy and highly wrought lying-in episode; Dargan's is repeatedly described as nearly grotesque, larger and stronger than the local men; and some of Johnson's women endure horrible, extended deaths by fire and suicide. Since these scenes of exaggerated materiality serve uniformly to enhance a pessimistic outlook concerning the stifling circumstances of women on farms, the novels in which they appear might be understood as continuous with the naturalistic vein of rural fiction created largely by men—what one critic described in collective terms in 1932 as the "morbid, unpalatable novels of Middle Western farm life."[6] Surely Kelley, Dargan, and Johnson advance a negative portrait of farming that shares something with the work of Hamlin Garland, whose *Main Traveled Roads* (1891) was often cited as the progenitor of a "disillusioning" strain of harshly realistic modern farm narratives.[7]

Yet the magnified physical and emotional registers of these three texts, not to mention their highly dramatic events, align them suggestively with a very different genre, one that is still linked to realism but that bears special relation to women: namely, melodrama. Recent theorists have reconceptualized melodrama in newly capacious ways, seeing it less as a narrowly defined theatrical genre than as a broad mode of expression inhabiting fiction as well as film, and with special relevance to modernism; such attitudes open up the work of Kelley, Dargan, and Johnson to a host of fresh perspectives. Specifically, they offer a framework through which to articulate more precisely these texts' investment in both describing the quotidian and reaching for something above, beneath, or beyond it—an impulse that distinguishes them sharply from the naturalistic novels that take their cue from the arena of strictly observable phenomena.[8]

In his highly influential work entitled *The Melodramatic Imagination,* Peter Brooks asserts that the melodramatic impulse depends upon both "document" and "vision" and is "centrally concerned with the extrapolation from one to another." Indeed, argues Brooks, the melodramatic writer uses "the things and gestures of the real world, of social life, as kinds of metaphors that refer us to the realm of spiritual reality and latent moral meanings." Yet the representation of this social surface, serving as a springboard into an arena of psychic, and even cosmic, signification, is in itself writ large, extravagantly rendered, keyed to a higher pitch than its prosaic details might seem to suggest. The relation between melodrama and realism, then, is essential but "oblique," since melodrama "refuses to content itself with the repressions [and] the tonings down . . . of the real." Instead, it creates from "the banal stuff of reality" an "exciting, excessive, parabolic story"; thus melodrama "insists that the ordinary may be the place for the instauration of significance. It tells us that in the right mirror, with the right degree of convexity, our lives matter."[9]

Brooks's framework dovetails provocatively with Kelley's, Dargan's, and Johnson's apparent efforts to fuse the evidentiary and the visionary, and to wrest from the mundane an intensity that points toward a consideration of ontological dilemmas. While these authors clearly attempt to document through fiction what they understand as the harsh reality of women's lives on farms, they also seek to explore in deeper, more meaningful ways issues of social in/equity that extend beyond the particularities of rurality, and they do so largely through an aesthetic of exaggeration that signifies through superfluity and excess. But if these writers tap into a melodramatic sensibility, apparently believing that, as Brooks would have it, "[a] new world [and] . . . a new morality lay within the grasp of the revolutionary legislator and, particularly, in the power of [her] verbal representations," their texts decline to offer clean solutions to the social problems they present.[10] Thus they fuse realism and idealism in a way quite distinct from, say, the proletarian fiction of the 1930s, which offers a partisan (some would say facile) perspective on how to heal the diseased body politic. Instead, the novels of Kelley, Dargan, and Johnson are concerned less with answers than with questions, and with making ethical and spiritual dimensions insistently legible. Like other melodramatic texts, they respond to modernism's characteristic sense of loss, especially the loss of absolute moral authorities, by refusing to renounce altogether the promise of a potentially transcendent vision.[11]

That these three texts deal with domesticity and familial dynamics says something about their connections to melodrama itself as well as their particular reformist ambitions. Christine Gledhill, glossing Peter Brooks and various feminist theorists, traces the historical relations between melodrama and women, explaining melodrama's traditional categorization as a feminine genre—enabled by the association of women with extreme emotionalism—and highlighting family configurations as apt sites for its characteristically primal confrontations. In contrast to the "genuine" arena of masculine (i.e., restrained) realism, the melodramatic sensibility has been, of course, devalued.[12] Significantly, though, the very target of Kelley's, Dargan's, and Johnson's ideological interrogations is, at least in part, the domestic realm itself: their female protagonists engage in constant battle with gendered roles and expectations that are intensified by the traditional social practices of poor farming communities. Hence these fictions are not exactly in line with more typical domestic melodramas, which, in Gledhill's summation, exteriorize psychic states in a Freudian manner, making the family "a means, not an end."[13] To a great degree, domestic arrangements are more than a metaphoric vehicle in these texts: they are, in and of themselves, a subject of scrutiny. Perhaps more important, the narrative formulas that reflect and reinforce patriarchal culture are called into question; thus these novels utilize the highly charged discourse, symbolism, and circumstances of melodrama to challenge indirectly the stakes of representation itself.

Edith Summers Kelley's *Weeds* (1923), set in the impoverished Kentucky tobacco country, provides the most concentrated example of these dynamics, notably in the chapter entitled "Billy's Birth," which details the protagonist's first lying-in and which was excised from the originally published text. (*Weeds* was out of print entirely until 1972, and it was not until 1982 that the Feminist Press published an edition including this recovered section as an appendix.) Kelley's publishers in the early 1920s had apparently cut this scene on the grounds that it seemed "exaggerated," perhaps even "hysterical" (Kelley's words), and not sufficiently relevant to the story's Kentucky setting; they thereby evaded its potentially melodramatic effect and delineated the novel's chief audience as those seeking a realistic but nonetheless relatively tame regionalism.[14] Yet this rediscovered chapter, when considered in its intended position, uses a highly fraught scene to set in motion a stimulating and original resistance on several fronts. It defies virtually all received notions about maternity and domestic labor and confronts both previous literary constructions and "real-life" cultural perspectives, including those of Kelley's first husband, whose attitudes about women and childbearing lend a provocative biographical dimension to "Billy's Birth." It also destabilizes essentialist constructions of the natural world that have traditionally enabled symbolic alignments between women and nature.

Significantly, reviewers recognized in *Weeds*—even without access to the excised portions—a novel that pushed the envelope, especially as regards sexual matters; according to reviewer H. H. Boynton, this very quality constituted the text's modernness. He claimed that, despite its "dignity and force," Kelley's novel overemphasized "physical unseemliness and squalor"; others went so far as to call it "smut." To Stuart P. Sherman, writing in the *Literary Review*, *Weeds* was akin to Sinclair Lewis's narratives in the power of its social criticism: in addition to underscoring the need for cooperative farming organizations and education for country children in advanced agriculture, he proffered, Kelley's book raised the question of whether "scientific birth control or primitive methods of abortion furnish the better solution of the problem of a degenerating physical stock, due to excessive childbearing."[15] The text's emphasis on women's bodies was thus clearly acknowledged, though it was consistently channeled into more accepted avenues of debate (contraception, eugenics, sexual mores).

No one seemed fully to recognize the disruption in Kelley's novel of the hackneyed but still prescriptive link between agrarian paradigms and maternal-domestic ones; perhaps this is what the author referred to when she wrote her friend Upton Sinclair in 1924 that she was "afraid the propaganda in *Weeds* was not obvious enough" to result in recognition by progressive groups. She readily agreed with Sinclair, however, that her book constituted "radical literature," despite its only overtly leftist scene—involving cooperative action by local farmers against the "American Tobacco Company"—having been among those cut prior to publication.[16] Her other writings, many of which were never published, provide a useful context for considering the left-wing preoccupations of *Weeds,* notably in the areas of representational aesthetics, sexual and economic equality, and rurality. For example, in an essay entitled "Can an Artist Exist in America?" Kelley grieves over those old friends who have sold out artistically by writing financially rewarding but vacuous romances, and laments that American readers are uninterested in the poor as subjects for serious fiction. She also describes manuscripts of her own that failed to find a publisher, including a realistic sketch of slaughterhouse workers and two short stories of disillusioned people isolated and trapped on farms. And in "Helicon Hall: An Experiment in Living"—a reflection on the ill-fated commune founded by Upton Sinclair in 1906 (destroyed by fire in 1907), and where Kelley met and was briefly engaged to Sinclair Lewis—she celebrates not just the camaraderie among the Helicon inhabitants but also their socialist sensibilities; of particular interest are the arrangements whereby children were cared for in a separate space to free mothers for intellectual and artistic work.[17]

Perhaps most illuminating, however, is an autobiographical manuscript entitled "We Went Back to the Land," which details Kelley's life with her common-law husband, C. Fred Kelley, a sculptor who was unable to support his family through his art. Here Kelley relates their years of grinding poverty as tenants on a series of unsuccessful farms, beginning, significantly, with a tobacco farm in Kentucky and ending with a poultry farm in California. Kelley's letters to Upton Sinclair, who remained a lifelong correspondent, speak repeatedly of her inability to maintain a schedule of writing given the labor requirements of farming and household management, including the raising of three children. And in this unpublished essay, the tensions between artistic aspirations and economic privation, and between agrarian promise and the realities of agricultural life for poorer farmers, emerge again and again. These experiences, of course, resonate powerfully in *Weeds,* which was noted for its realism; but perhaps an even more significant link between the essay and Kelley's novel concerns the potential alterity of the farm as setting. Kelley makes it clear that she and Fred first embarked on agricultural ventures because they felt like "social misfits" in the city: their move to their first farm is associated strongly with their "burn[ing]" artistic ambitions, which they apparently assume will enjoy freer rein in the country. Thus the farm is posited less as a destination in itself than as a removal from the regiments and routines of commercial-industrial life, an attitude that suggests its capacity for Kelley as a symbolic locale of otherness.[18]

Though Judith Pippinger Blackford, Kelley's protagonist in *Weeds,* has never been more than a few miles from the farm on which she was raised, she similarly strains against conventions, and her rural circumstances become a site for alternative conceptions of the relations between both women and domesticity, and women and nature. "The sensitive plate" of Judith's "keen imagination," so seemingly misplaced among the "dull" minds that surround her (23, 13), might well describe that of her creator, who served as a model for some of the unconventional female characters of Sinclair Lewis.[19] Yet Kelley's Judith far exceeds the boundaries even of Lewis's transgressive female portraits. As a restless seeker who refuses to be satisfied with the familiar, and who defiantly and unrepentantly rejects both social and sexual mores for women, Judith is patently unorthodox—challenging, like Kelley herself, the connotations of the term "farmer's wife."[20]

Kelley's wide exposure to various radical-reformist tendencies naturally owes much to her early experiences with the residents of Helicon Hall, and it is especially important that she spent her early twenties as Upton Sinclair's secretary in the important period just after he published *The Jungle,* which had been widely admired for what was considered the first realistic presentation of a childbirth scene. But it appears that Kelley's radicalism was also shaped by conservative forces in her life. Germane to her depiction of maternity in *Weeds,* for instance, though not widely known, are the circumstances surrounding her own first childbirth in 1911, at which time she was married to Alan Updegraff, another member of the Helicon Hall circle and an aspiring poet. Updegraff's letters to Kelley during her lying-in display a self-absorption that suggests a fascinating biographical context for Kelley's representation of Judith's intense psychic solitude in "Billy's Birth." (Despite the physical presence of her husband, Jerry, Judith in her laboring is "quite cut off from all humankind" and is pointedly described as traveling through a "No Man's Desert of pain.")[21] While Kelley apparently wrote "Billy's Birth" in response to her sense that the literary world had not produced "adequate" depictions of childbirth, which, she argued, should logically come from female writers, and while this statement invites comparison of her childbirth scene with that of Upton Sinclair, it also implies that her own birthing experiences would have special relevance.[22]

Two of Updegraff's preoccupations, reflective of general cultural perspectives, become especially pertinent to the childbearing sequence in *Weeds.* First, Updegraff's letters to Kelley repeatedly invoke images of a mother besotted with love for her child. He imagines his wife "calling it 'baby'—how sickening!—and going into cute maternal raptures about its fingers and hair and disposition and toes and mouth, ad infin." Second, Updegraff argues that such intensity of maternal feeling is "natural" and expected, just as his own jealousy is also "instinctive" and therefore acceptable. The "nature" of femininity and masculinity cannot be reckoned with, Updegraff asserts, except through the "higher" act of "stand[ing] off and contemplating" such fundamental, and therefore inescapable, impulses.[23]

These ideas prove provocative in the context of Kelley's childbirth scene. Specifically, "Billy's Birth" is remarkable precisely for its insistence on the mother's birthing body as *un*natural, and for its refusal to consider maternity in any light other than that of *labor* in its strictest sense. An overlaying of metaphors suggests that Judith's harrowed body is brutally mechanistic on the one hand and subversively bestial on the other, leaving little room for conventional images of maternity as a triumph of both the mother's body and the body politic. In contrast to Updegraff, who stressed the special meaning of the terms "nature" and "labor" as they were normatively applied to women, Kelley seems bent in "Billy's Birth" on perverting these usages—or, more accurately, on affixing standard denotations of these words to the "special" contexts of women's lives. Thus birthing and raising babies becomes a *labor* no more promising, no more fulfilling, than the pointless round of planting and harvesting that circumscribes the poor farmer's existence. And the *nature* of women, specifically their assumed maternal nature, is no more fixed or predictable than the nature that repeatedly wreaks havoc with the crops.

Throughout *Weeds,* Kelley refuses to idealize not only the domestic existence of the rural wife and mother but also the life of the farmer, especially the tenant farmer. She exposes the Jeffersonian ideal for the elitist paradigm that it is, showing that the tenant farmer, lacking ownership of the soil he works, can afford neither contemplation nor experimentation; at one point Jerry Blackford bursts into sobs of frustration over his continued inability to provide for his family, despite his year-round, backbreaking regimen in the fields and barn (226–27). Moreover, while Judith's misery is closely connected to her imposed, and bitterly resented, domestic role, Kelley is at pains to suggest that the larger context of rural life sharpens and particularizes Judith's sense of oppression. Kelley repeatedly shows how Judith and her neighbor, Hattie, bridle under the weight of expectations related both to the patriarchal structure of the farm community and to the specific tasks relegated to farm women (e.g., 144–45). This includes not only the general alignment of outdoor work with men and indoor work with women but also more specific divisions of labor: at one point

Judith absolutely refuses her apportioned task of cleaning a tub of pig guts after the men have enjoyed the more satisfying job of butchering (236–37), and on other occasions she insists that she be allowed to enjoy the pleasures, such as riding into town for the horse sales, that are usually reserved for men (168). Kelley seems to be suggesting first, that agrarian women's containment within domestic spaces is especially acute, given that the rhythms of rural life are centered in the outdoors generally, and second, that the relative lack of evolution in farming methods over the generations (as opposed, say, to the huge changes in business and industry) has resulted in a correspondingly extreme rigidification of sociosexual roles in farm families.

In Judith, who is aligned from her earliest childhood with the open landscape—she is her father's best helpmate on the farm, "[in] harmony with natural things" (25)—Kelley creates a character who finds the domestic realm especially confining, as she "dislike[s] the insides of houses" and is always "glad to escape into the open where there [is] life, light, and motion" (116). But it is in relation to Judith's maternity that Kelley poses her most provocative challenge to women and agrarian ideals. Through Judith, Kelley not only refutes the widespread assumption that rural women were privileged, and deeply content, to mother the nation's future farmers; she also thwarts the trope of fecundity that conventionally aligns women with the land. "Billy's Birth" is the key to this dynamic.

The first paragraph of "Billy's Birth" is devoted to Judith's extreme distaste for her mother-in-law, "Aunt" Mary, who is likened to a "great cat that . . . purrs by the domestic hearth and nurses its kittens tenderly and considers that the world revolves around itself and its offspring, and spits and scratches at anyone who approaches the kittens." Judith cannot refrain from teasing this cat by periodically criticizing her husband, Jerry, in order to get a rise out of Aunt Mary—who has come, portentously enough, to assist with Judith's lying-in. Thus Aunt Mary represents nurturing as "natural" to female creatures, an end and an ideal; her smug certainty about the laboring process contrasts with Judith's fear, just as, immediately following the birth, her cooing over her new grandchild will act as a foil for Judith's disinterest. Early on, as the birthing progresses, Aunt Mary goes about briskly preparing for Judith's confinement and sagely advising her daughter-in-law not to "take on so" when the pains hit; above all, Aunt Mary's calm and meticulous performance of the household's daily chores while Judith suffers with her first contractions frames Judith's childbearing as just another routine domestic task.

Yet the protractedness of Judith's labor and the narrative space that Kelley devotes to it suggest that it is extreme work indeed, work that alienates Judith from her own body by, significantly, aligning it with notions of industrial mechanization. She is repeatedly likened to a machine operating against its own desires or needs: the birthing process turns her into a "steel and iron monster" that is "relentless and indomitable," and her contractions are like "the ever-recurring drive of some great piston" that grows "regular and incessant as clockwork." Jerry is frightened and awed by the exertions of his wife, and she appears to him to be "something superhuman, immense and overpowering," an instrument of "gigantic proportions." Her contractions turn her into an automaton with "no volition of her own," struggling "blindly . . . endlessly, endlessly, endlessly, without rest."

This metaphoric insistence on childbearing as work without agency is accompanied by an attention to the various connotations of *nature*, in terms both of sociobiological imperatives ("feminine nature") and of the natural world. Judith's confinement in "Billy's Birth" is doubly figurative, for the conjugal bedroom has become a scene of terror (the bed is described as a "grisly rack of torture") signifying the special constraints of female biology while also literally severing Judith from the natural world that has always provided her with respite: "These things [the dawn, the sounds of the animals waking, the freshness of the earth following the night's rain] in which Judith was wont to take delight were all as nothing to her now." Her distance both from the tranquil agrarian landscape as she has known it and from the sweet "feminine nature" that Jerry has come to expect is suggested by numerous references to her tortured, and distorted, brutishness. Jerry reflects that the guttural sounds she emits are not even those of an ordinary dog, but rather like the cries of "some wild, dog-like creature"; later he decides that a cow could not have endured her condition, and then is shocked by the implications of his comparison. Animals are no longer the friends and helpmates of Judith's youth on the farm but usurpers of her body, as she is likened to "a tigress newly caged," "an angry wolf," a beast with a "fierce snarl."

Ironically, when the doctor arrives, he announces that Judith's symptoms are "quite normal and *natural* so far" (my emphasis), and he exhorts Jerry to be patient, for "nature takes her own time." But Judith imagines that nature is not on her side at all, that in fact nature is her enemy: "Nature that from her childhood had led kindly and blandly through pleasant paths and had at last betrayed her, treacherously beguiling her into this desolate region, now sternly pointed her the one way out: the dread and cruel pass of Herculean struggle through tortures unspeakable." When the baby is finally born, this nest of metaphors relating re/production to a nature made abhorrently unfamiliar is intricately rendered: "It was over, and the doctor triumphantly held out nature's reward for all the anguish: a little, bloody, groping, monkey-like object, that moved its arms and legs with a spasmodic, frog-like motion and uttered a sound that was not a cry nor a groan nor a grunt nor anything of the human nor even animal world, but more like the harsh grating of metal upon metal." It is difficult to mistake here Kelley's emphasis on the *un*natural: on aberration, truncation, mechanization, aversion. Even Jerry has a "shiver of revulsion" upon seeing the newborn child. And while the penultimate page of the chapter seems momentarily to suggest that Judith succumbs to more typically maternal emotions (after a brief recovery period she is indeed "captivated" by the baby), Kelley ends the scene on a pessimistic note. Jabez, an unattached old man of the neighborhood with whom Judith shares a peculiar sympathy, pronounces the childbirth unfortunate, as it means that Judith will become "cluttered up" with "babies in the kitchen" when she should, in his view, be out "over the hills a-stalkin' turkeys . . . or else jes' a-runnin' wild with the res' of the wild things" where she belongs. "Ah well," he tells her, "it's nater [*sic*]. It's nater, that must have her fun with all of us, like a cat that likes to have a nice long play with every mouse she ketches."[24]

The metaphor of the cat, of course, recalls the chapter's opening references to the maternal instincts of the catlike Aunt Mary, but Jabez's comments here suggest a significant twist. Judith's forced containment within biologically and socially determined female roles is seen as concordant with a manipulating, inconstant nature that "plays" with humans in ways beyond their apprehensions, against their desires. (Perhaps not coincidentally, Jabez's comment echoes that of Alan Updegraff, who wrote to Kelley after their first child was born, "Natur [*sic*] has used the brat to change [you] into something I do not know.")[25] The excessiveness of Judith's maternal body, then, may be understood as an ironic extension of the harsh conditions—of heat, blight, flood, drought—affecting the land, showing that nature's caprice is manifest through superabundance as well as deficiency. Similarly, nature's restorative properties are also inconstant; Judith's "betrayal" by nature during her lying-in does not so much suggest that the natural world is entirely exclusive to women's lives and concerns as that nature's role as solace rather than avenger can be, at best, unpredictable.

Stacy Alaimo compellingly connects this thematic emphasis on the extremity of Judith's corporeality, and the involuntary work performed by her body, to the period's discourses about contraception (108–23). We might complicate that reading, however, by noting that the sheer space Kelley accords to Judith's labor process brackets the question of con(tra)ception for an extended fictional moment and instead underscores, as Jabez intimates, the connection between the female's loss of control over her laboring body and the vagaries of nature. Both nature and culture, it would seem, impose upon Judith's body[26]—yet ultimately Kelley works to dissociate a biological destiny over which Judith has little control from a social destiny that she can, indeed, challenge, evade, or perhaps even reject. Thus Alaimo's argument that the novel advocates "reproductive self-determination" may be complemented by an awareness of Judith's repudiation of social definitions of motherhood—a stance that may be, in the end, more deeply subversive.

Judith comes to perceive children as not only "a torture to bear" but also "a daily fret and anxiety after they were born"; hence when she temporarily becomes "mistress of her own body" by denying her husband sex, she also plans to free herself from a "degradation and suffering" that she associates with motherhood rather than mere childbirth (299–300). While she eventually succumbs to Jerry's sexual demands and even bears him another child, her disavowal of traditional ideals of mothering behavior, and of motherhood as her identity, is relatively consistent throughout the novel and is perhaps the more unsettling precisely because it is *not* typically marked by spectacularly dramatic scenes or by crystallized moments of self-consciousness. Even a cursory reading reveals Judith's ongoing indifference to, and occasional cruelty toward, her offspring, as there are virtually no extended moments of tenderness between mother and children. Rather, Judith "slaps [the children] savagely," perceiving them as "greedy vampires working on her incessantly, . . . never giving her a moment's peace, bent upon drinking her last drop of blood, tearing out her last shrieking nerve" (208). To Jerry's distress, she exhibits an unusual willingness from the very beginning to leave their first baby unsupervised (158), and on at least one occasion she completely abnegates her domestic responsibilities by walking away from house and children in the middle of the day (240). Moreover, her sense of her own "unnaturalness" is clearly connected not merely to her fear of pregnancy and childbirth but to her distaste for the nurturing role of mother: "[W]hen the child was born it was only the beginning. She loathed the thought of having to bring up another baby. The women who liked caring for babies could call her unnatural if they liked. She wanted to be unnatural. She was glad she was unnatural. Their nature was not her nature and she was glad of it" (240).

Kelley seems determined to show that Judith's tribulations as a mother are largely unmitigated by the emotional attachments that are presumed to transform motherhood and domestic work from an affliction to a delight: while Judith acknowledges that she loves her children, she also wonders, in a disquieting moment of comparison with her sister, why she cannot, like Lizzie May, "serve them wholeheartedly, devotedly, joyfully." Unable to be, like other women, "a willing victim" to the children's constant demands, she longs for "the nostalgia of the fields and roads"—but the very formulation of this desire as nostalgic reiterates the newly uneasy relation to the natural world that is the apparent result of Judith's maternity. Indeed, during the long winter months of "captivity" with her children, she "forg[ets] the old nostalgia, forg[ets] even to look out of the window" (217). She can no longer extract joy freely from the landscape but must make do with occasional moments when nature ceases to serve as a mockery of her state and momentarily recalls to her the promises of her youth.

"Billy's Birth" thus rearticulates Judith's relation to the natural world in terms that are closely bound up in her maternity. On the most obvious level, childbirthing initiates Judith fully into the domestic roles that sever her, experientially and symbolically, from the rhythms of the land that form the core of country life. If we understand her sensitivity to the natural world as genuine, a redeeming factor in a personality that her peers find otherwise suspect (e.g., 289–90), then the spatial and imaginative constraints imposed on her by domesticity are severe indeed. On a deeper level, however, Judith learns through the birthing process that nature is unreliable, inconstant, powerful in its beauty but also terrible in its vengeance. Whatever solace it offered before she became a mother is made doubtful in those hours of unwilling labor, when an alternative and deeply threatening landscape—a "No Man's Desert," a "sinister canyon"—unfolds before her, and when the (natural) product of her body "seems to the inexperienced eye a deformed abortion." Judith's connection to nature, therefore, becomes deeply ironic: through her maternity she is literally removed from the natural world, only to be reconnected symbolically in a startlingly subversive way. Just as nature itself cannot be reduced or contained, Judith cannot conform to social expectations—specifically, she cannot or will not take on the "natural" role of the nurturing mother.

The centrality of "Billy's Birth" to the novel's original design—intended as the twelfth of twenty-six chapters, it would have occurred, pagewise, almost precisely at the novel's center—substantially revises our understanding of Kelley's major themes in *Weeds,* which emerges as more daring, and more complex in its treatment of Judith's relation to the natural world, than previously thought. A few observations will suffice to suggest how its restoration colors subsequent events in the novel. For one thing, Judith's affair with a traveling minister several years later acquires new dimensions of meaning in light of "Billy's Birth." Their trysts, which take place in an open meadow, at first seem to release Judith from domestic pressures and promise a return to innocence, signified not only by her sexual license but also by her reclamation of the landscape. (She and Jerry had engaged in sexual intercourse out of doors prior to their marriage.) Alaimo asserts that Judith's sexual pleasure at this point in the narrative seems displaced onto a natural world that "penetrate[s] Judith's being" and "sway[s] her like [a] master passion."[27] Yet it seems significant that Judith herself understands this heightened erotic state as a "dream" of which "the waking hour was at hand" (276). Somewhat surprisingly, Judith's more genuine synchronicity with nature comes at the moment when she breaks off the affair, having chastised the minister for the abrupt affectation of conventional attitudes that has led him to call her a "scarlet woman":

> Now that she knew herself broad awake, she felt of a sudden glad, bold, and strong. A sense of freedom, of relief from some clinging burden that had grown clogged and foul, passed through her like a strong wind that scatters cobwebs and made her breath [*sic*] deep and lift her head high in the sunlight. Swinging the empty bucket with happy abandon, as a child its dinner pail, she strode with long, free steps across the pasture and along the ridge road, delighting in the sun and the sweet air, feeling clean, sound, and whole, her mind untroubled by regrets, unsullied by the slightest tinge of self-abasement.
>
> ... [She] went on toward home walking like some primal savage woman. (279)

The more significant displacement here, I would argue, is premised on Kelley's revision of facile tropes of fecundity: the simplistic alignment of Judith's sexual pleasure with a fulsome natural world is made transient, unreal, and is displaced by a more complex vision in which Judith's sympathy with nature both enables and reflects her momentary act of self-determination. But the text's refusal to allow Judith to sustain this feeling of accord with the landscape points to Kelley's thoroughgoing critique of essentialist versions of both maternity and nature. When Judith becomes pregnant with what can only be the minister's child, her failed attempt to induce a miscarriage through wild horseback riding reinforces her oblique relation to a natural world that clearly undermines, as much as it supports, her desires and needs. This extended and dramatic scene, in which Judith's galloping temporarily makes her "a girl again . . . happy and careless," nonetheless contributes powerfully to the sense that her existence in nature signifies nothing certain, nothing stable (282–85).

Similarly, when Judith finds herself unexpectedly pregnant by Jerry with yet another child, she retreats to the countryside, which she greets "as an old lover who has not lost his power to charm." But the diction here, too, suggests that this power is ephemeral, or limited in its healing capacities—for instance, she only "*half* forg[ets] the things that she had fled from" and feels "*almost* happy" (my emphasis). Indeed, at the height of Judith's pleasure in the landscape she "cringes" at the thought of the baby within her, and "For a long time she sat looking out over the winter landscape and seeing nothing" (240). Thus the connection between Judith's maternity (her conventional sexual "nature") and her thwarted relation to the natural world is played upon again and again, disallowing the potential role of communal earth mother that Judith's closeness to the land might encourage in a more culturally orthodox text. Moreover, the explosion of such stereotypes seems integral to Kelley's plan, for at one point the narrator slyly comments, "There is an idea existing in many minds that country folk are mostly simple, natural, and spontaneous. . . . There is no more misleading fallacy" (152).

A restoration of "Billy's Birth," then, both alters the overall sensibility of Kelley's novel—calling to mind melodrama's near hysteria as it "act[s] out the recognition of the repressed, often with and on the body"[28]—and makes more coherent its author's social commentary. Among other things, "Billy's Birth" suggests that the culturally defined role of "mother" is but another term for relentless and unfairly gendered labor, a sentiment borne out by Kelley's private descriptions of her own domestic difficulties and consistent with her earliest philosophical leanings as they were manifested in the socialist community of Helicon Hall. At the same time, this chapter redirects the focus of *Weeds*, underscoring its radical revision of masculine conventions of the agrarian tradition. Kelley allows a female character who is closely in tune with nature but uninterested in maternity and domesticity to play out the frustrations of that perceived illogic, exposing literary and cultural assumptions about the links between "women's nature" and the natural world as psychosocial constructions that nevertheless impose powerful experiential boundaries. Although Judith remains trapped within her circumstances (at the novel's end her future appears to her as a "sad, dead level of unrelieved monotony"), Kelley ushers her readers, at least, onto a new and challenging plane of awareness: in its most provocative moments, *Weeds* makes legible the gendered and gendering strictures of both the "real" world and some of its normative representational tropes.

Olive Tilford Dargan's *Call Home the Heart* (1932, published under the pseudonym Fielding Burke) raises different, if related, questions while similarly exhibiting a melodramatic disposition. One of six novels written about the 1929 Communist-organized strike of cotton mill workers in Gastonia, North Carolina, it is generally considered the best, despite uneven initial reviews that focused on a perceived conflict between the text's "artistry" and its propagandistic tendencies. No doubt such readings are invited by the novel's bifurcated structure, specifically its movement from Ishma Waycaster's childhood and young womanhood in the mountains, to her extended involvement in a textile strike in the town of Winbury, and back again to the perceived social safety of the mountains. The resulting sense of dual worlds, of competing social arrangements and ethical principles, allows the novel to enact through its very structure the dramatic choice between polarized alternatives that is a characteristic element of melodrama—even if, as we shall see, Dargan never passes judgment on which world is preferable.[29]

Critics, however, did. Contemporaneous reviewers of *Call Home the Heart* typically disparaged those portions of the text in which Ishma acquires a class consciousness and battles her own prejudices against an industrial backdrop, preferring instead those sections that detail the harsh yet comparatively romantic rural environment from which Ishma emerges and to which she eventually returns. Jonathan Daniels, writing in the *Saturday Review of Literature,* suggested that Dargan "flies unsatisfied from [her] own propaganda just as does [her] heroine," making the novel's ending a kind of retreat "from forthright indignation into the truer perspective of the artist." Another reviewer argued similarly that the novel's geographic and tonal shift from relatively idyllic rural-mountain life to gritty milltown scenes and back again felt "as if the second act of 'Tristan' ha[d] been embellished with a long interpolation by a Salvation Army band," after which the author, thankfully, "permit[ted] herself a relapse into art." Even Robert Cantwell, who, like most, felt that the book had genuine merit, found the "familiar" material of what he called the "down yonder" sections of the novel, in which Dargan captured "the poetic quality of native speech," superior to those parts set in the urban strike context.[30] For such critics, Ishma's ultimate return to her native home marked a victory that had less to do with a repudiation of Marxism than with a celebration of the conventions of local-color fiction.

In contrast, later critics have valorized the milltown portions of Ishma's story, which, despite their tendentiousness, can seem more dynamic and freshly original than the rural-mountain sections praised by earlier reviewers. Indeed, today's readers are likely to see Ishma's reversion to her "golden primitive" (her term for Britt, her mountain husband, and the lifestyle he represents) as a sentimental and unsatisfying resolution to a narrative that, in its urban-Marxist sections, raises forthright and progressive questions about class, gender, and race. As Sylvia Jenkins Cook has stated the problem, Ishma's final abandonment of the frontline power struggles in Winbury and her return to the less volatile social dynamics of the mountains seem like a "tragic falling-off in the heroine from strength to primitive weakness."[31] It is especially problematic, as Stacy Alaimo has argued, that Ishma's flight from Winbury is predicated upon a race encounter in which Ishma is revolted by the "engulfing maternal body" of a black woman.[32] Ishma's return to the mountains may thus be interpreted as her failure to sustain engagement with the most threatening aspects of industrial society, including the prospect of racial unity, casting the rural landscape as a site not merely of familiarity and romanticism but of reactionary sentiment.

While the dualisms invoked by all these critics remain useful, their views rest on assumptions that Dargan somehow lacked awareness of her novel's presumed disjunctures. The picture changes, however, when one considers that she may have deliberately invoked the conceptual binaries of rurality-stability-tradition and urbanity-revolution-modernity. Admittedly, such a reading downplays the text's overt politicism in favor of a broader interpretation that takes fuller account of Dargan's gender commentary and representational aesthetic. But this move seems justified by the lengthiness and complexity of the text itself, at least half of which takes place in the rural mountain setting away from the arena of Marxism and the strike. Indeed, the narrative space accorded early in the novel to Ishma's attempts to reconcile the constrictedness of mountain women's lives with the expansiveness that the landscape and certain rural social customs seem to signify suggests that Dargan was, like Kelley, conscious of both the literal and the figurative implications of rurality. As reviewer Daniels conceded, "No mere Communist would have given more than half of [her] book to building the rural life of the North Carolina mountains and in particular the woman's life of farm and house labor which has driven the stream of laborers into the mills."[33]

To be sure, Dargan was "no mere Communist": though she allowed her mountain cabin to be used as a meeting place for the local Communist Party, she never became an official member. And we know that her radical sensibilities were quite broad, despite the relative dearth of information about her life. A married woman who appears to have lived for long periods apart from her husband, she was a friend of such revolutionary female thinkers as Rose Pastor Stokes and Alice Stone Blackwell; she regularly took indigent women into her home and made plans to endow a shelter for them; and she interested herself in the social status and writings of African Americans, enjoying a forty-year correspondence with the African American critic William Stanley Braithwaite. She was also, importantly, dedicated to the preservation of rural-mountain culture (she published *Highland Annals*, a collection of tales, in 1925), and for years she worked a North Carolina farm largely alone, on which she also supported nine tenants.[34] Hence Dargan was linked to a variety of social and political movements, and rurality was at the center of her adult experiences. This raises the question of whether the Marxist doctrine advanced in certain episodes of *Call Home the Heart* has received attention disproportionate to its intended significance in a book that also, perhaps more fundamentally, explores the penetration of the new industrial society by rural people, especially women.

Like Kelley, Dargan at one point speculated that her novel's "subversive[ness]," which she located in the character of Ishma, might be overlooked or misconstrued.[35] The many shifts of place and space in the novel, which must be negotiated by Ishma and which connote different ideological perspectives, make of her mind a discerning instrument through which social options are considered, absorbed, rejected, revised. She is unconventional in many ways, by the standards of both mountain and town society, and her restlessness in both contexts indexes, as we shall see, her inability to be contained by orthodox codes and systems. That in the end she attempts to combine her old way of life and her new ideals—by suggesting to Britt that they create a haven on their mountain farm for impoverished town children—suggests that the novel may be less about choice than about synthesis. Perhaps more accurately, it implies that the interrogation and attempted destabilization of presumed dichotomies constitutes a substantial part of the text's cultural work.

In certain ways, of course, *Call Home the Heart* indeed renders mountain and town life as oppositional. As Dargan's immediate critics noted, the vibrancy of the mountain folk culture is established early on, such that the lives of the townspeople, though equally destitute in literal terms, seem especially thin in comparison. The rural-mountain sections of the novel include long interpolations of tales and songs (often sung by Britt, an accomplished musician), as well as descriptions of various types of ritualized performance—as when two old women, trying to garner attention, engage in a colorful "duel of ailments" (28), or when members of the Waycaster family, confronted by unexpected visitors, invoke the formulaic modes of mountain hospitality: "Jim was calling to Bainie, 'Crowd the pans in that oven! Any o' that ham left?' There had been no ham in the house for months, but Bainie knew her part. 'Not a sliver left,' she called back. 'Fat-back'll have to do ye, an' I'll make the coffee strong enough to stand up'" (133).[36] Both the performative storytelling traditions of the mountain people and their customary conversational manner, steeped in vivid metaphors and quaint turns of phrase, call attention to their idiom as heavily embellished, as fertile and organic as nature itself. Even old Granny Starkweather's tendency to bend the very Bible to her purposes ("Mark that [passage] fer skippin', darter," she would say to Ishma, or "I don't have to believe that, thank God!" [65–6]) is idealized as the mark of a creative, nonconforming mind. This pronounced emphasis on the mountain world's rhetorical expansiveness, even as its sociosexual rigidity and the primitiveness of its daily life are also emphasized, seems designed to throw into relief the mechanized lifelessness of the industrial arena.

Ishma's dissatisfaction with that urban arena of "shut windows and strangulation" (232) and her eventual return to the mountains near the end of the novel might indeed appear to mark, as certain critics raved, a victory for "art." The urban environment exposes Ishma to an entirely new, unimagined, and sometimes frightening social order, and while she becomes educated there in the ways of family planning and socialism and thus greatly expands her intellectual horizons, she nonetheless longs for the spiritual solace that the mountains provided, and the wealth of traditions and predictable social patterns that structured her earliest years. Yet to understand Ishma's rural and urban experiences as entirely or even largely dichotomous is to gloss over Dargan's emphasis on their underlying similarities. Moreover, to suggest that Ishma's flight home defines ultimately either her character or the novel's stance is to overstate the finality of a conclusion that seems anxious and irresolute: as the narrator reminds us in the novel's final line, "A cup, though full, is not the sea." In the end, Ishma hardly seems wholly content with her beloved Britt, "across [whose] voice ran another voice whose words were a path of flame"—the voice of Derry Unthank, her friend and intellectual mentor in the town below. "Why couldn't love be enough?" she asks herself wearily, even in the very moment of giving herself fully once more to Britt (428–32). To read back from this conflicted ending is to explore Dargan's refusal to compromise Ishma's complexity, premised on and reflective of the tensions in the changing world around her.

Ishma's native rural environment is, despite its ostensibly age-old culture, full of such tensions, many brought on by the forces of modernity, which disrupt the complacency of previous generations and create desires and aspirations that are difficult to satisfy in the mountains. While men such as Steve, Ishma's brother, are lured away by the promise of better jobs, Dargan focuses especially on the restlessness of Ishma and women like her, who buck against overwork, wretched poverty, and repeated childbearing—and who appear to Ishma's mother to be "quare" in their collective and perverse refusal to accept their lot (116–17). Ishma in particular is aware of mail-order catalogues and magazines, and in later years she explains to Derry Unthank that one of the reasons she left her husband and beloved mountains was that she "ach[ed]" for material comforts (295). Though she loves Britt, who shares her dedication to the farm, she resents giving birth to his son in the cramped family cabin, without privacy; when the ordeal is over, she fiercely, if futilely, insists that there will be no more children. At a particularly low point, when she is again pregnant and sick with disgust for her coarse lot, Ishma recalls with deep longing a certain "little room with a sunny window and blue curtains looped back" that belonged to Nanny Barton, a young woman who "'broke away' and went to college and studied law"; that Nanny never married, refusing the repeated proposals of one of the mountain bachelors, is an integral part of Ishma's recollection (142). The association of escape with material prosperity and freedom from domestic duty persists for Ishma, who eventually turns her back on the only world she knows and descends to the town with Rad Bailey, a former beau whom she thinks of as "a friendly force who would help her turn the lock and let her pass out" (155).

But if Ishma's daring departure seems to presage personal liberation, she soon discovers that life in Winbury is no less fraught with conflict, uncertainty, and constriction than life in the mountains. Significantly, Ishma is confronted not only by disturbing realities in the labor structure of the mills—"What a strange system, she thought, where to do your best meant hurting your neighbors" (272)—but also by the curiously subversive domestic situation into which she has entered with Rad, and through which Dargan masterfully extends her commentary on the constraints of gender. Ishma's pregnancy by Britt, of which Rad is aware, necessitates that they pose, despite their chaste relations, as man and wife, a situation that unexpectedly underscores the typical marriage arrangement and its performative spaces. Ironically, it is only in the privacy of their milltown home that their true relations can be acknowledged and, oddly enough, Ishma is free *not* to be Rad's partner; here, too, Rad's financial shrewdness allows for luxuries, such as running water, that release Ishma from many of her previous domestic chores. And yet their home becomes an exaggerated kind of domestic prison, wherein Ishma is continually punished by the specter of Britt and the presence of Rad, whose genuine affection for Ishma binds her through a sense of obligation. (When he suggests that she name her baby girl after his mother, she does.) The freedom she sought in coming to the city with Rad, then, turns into a heightened confinement in which the spaces and symbols of gender relations from which she fled in the mountains—house, bed, motherhood—take on a charged intensity.

In numerous other ways as well, the imagined distinctions between rural life and urban life, especially for women, are eroded. The first chapter devoted to Ishma's four years in Winbury provides an extended glimpse into the lives of neighboring women recently descended from the mountains in search of a better life; yet their suffering seems to have increased, if only because millwork destroys their health in ways that field labor did not. When Ishma gives birth prematurely to her baby and must find occupation for herself that still allows her to care for little Vennie, she becomes a nurse and helper to all the crippled and sick women in Spindle Hill, the impoverished neighborhood given over to the lowest millworkers. Ishma's patients are desperately in need: Grandma Huffmore is slowly starving herself so that her children may eat; Annie Weaver has a broken ankle, and her husband cannot leave his own work to help her; Mame Wallace, the mother of small children, is dying of pellagra. Especially pointed is the chapter's commentary on the dangers of overfrequent childbearing: Derry Unthank, a physician, labors to persuade married men to abstain from sexual relations so that their wives have some hope of regaining their health (178–207).

While some of these women profess to be delighted by the long-awaited pleasures of urbanity, their access to modern material comforts remains severely limited due to their economic hardships. As exploited millworkers, they are especially vulnerable to the cycles of purchasing and increased debt into which they are lured by the promises of the installment plan. Ishma's former mountain friend, Cindy Wiggins, cannot leave her dangerous millwork, she says, because she is "payin' on a sewin'-machine, a 'frigerator, an' a bedroom set" (213). And the city environment aggravates the desire to consume without increasing the resources by which consumption is made possible. Just as when Ishma in earlier years gazed at a mail-order dress that she could not purchase because her few dollars were needed to feed the family and prop up the farm, so these indigent town women are destined never to own the tempting array of wares that the city makes available to those with assured means. Nor, protestations to the contrary, do they cease to miss some of the simpler, freely accessible satisfactions of the mountains, notably the cold water, which makes the town's tepid taps seem insipid (191, 214). Unmet needs and desires, though hardly absent from the mountains, are, Ishma discovers, the very framework of urban existence.

But Dargan, like Edith Summers Kelley, disallows a facile association of the "natural" mountain life with something better or purer. Just before Ishma leaves the mountains, we are told, nature has ceased to sustain her; indeed, it has finally made her "lonely, hungry, impatient" (149). And a key town scene reiterates the sense that nature's restorative value is limited and is more readily available to the wealthy, and to men. Ishma hears of a free public park located on the outside of the city and, desperate for rest and replenishment, walks for miles with her sickly baby on her hip to find it. She indeed discovers a gorgeous park, with fountains and lush greenery, but it is privately owned and she is denied admittance; the free park, two miles farther on, proves to be muddy and desolate. While this episode reshapes nature as a commodity reserved for the privileged, it seems also to critique modern industrial society as the malignant vehicle of that reshaping (since nature is more widely accessible in nonindustrial contexts). On a deeper level, however, the scene challenges the symbolic associations that particularly link nature to women.

As Ishma sits under a scrubby tree, she laments not only her surroundings—the dirty, dreary little piece of land that fails fully to rejuvenate her spirit—but also the presence of her daughter, Vennie, whose fragility has bound Ishma especially tightly to her role as mother. Ishma wonders, "Was her horizon always to be Vennie's horizon?" and grieves for the "bright dream" that she had walked toward with Rad, a dream that was crushed by "the little house [of Rad's] and Vennie" (231). The constraints of Ishma's domestic roles within walls seem ironically to reverberate here in this open, natural landscape similarly void of promise, suggesting that there is no *place* for Ishma, no possibility of another vantage point. Significantly, she recalls a moment from her youth when she was thwarted in her efforts to widen her scope:

> She thought of a time when, as a girl of ten years, she had gone for a long climb up a mountain trying to reach a grey spur from which she knew she could see the far world. . . . Near her goal, she found herself between a cliff and a jutting boulder. . . . [S]he turned and opened her eyes. There in front of her, growing out of the cliff, was a stunted loblolly . . . [and she] couldn't see over it. . . . She could do nothing but look into the branches of that poor little pine that hid far valleys, the sunlit peaks, the long, dreamy ridges, and the pale path of rivers. Later she scrambled down to a lower ledge and her eyes found what they had sought, but ecstasy could not be re-born. (231)

The scene takes on histrionic proportions when, at the very moment that Ishma is lost in these reveries, Vennie wanders too close to the road and is killed by a passing car. Thus Ishma's effort to regain strength and perspective through immersion in nature proves futile on two counts: first, because her memories remind her that nature's succor is inconstant, and second, because her longings are conflated with what others will see as maternal negligence (e.g., 234). While Vennie's death functions, as some have asserted, as an overly dramatic deus ex machina that releases Ishma from domestic duties and allows her to enter more fully into a public role, it also suggests that maternal responsibility compromises, rather than extends, women's lives in nature and that maternity is incompatible with meaningful political work.

But Ishma is not entirely successful in the political arena, either, which only points to Dargan's refusal to countenance easy solutions—or to oversimplify the problems and promises of either urbanity-revolution-modernity *or* rurality-stability-tradition. Just as Ishma's mountain neighbors laughed at her efforts to practice progressive agriculture, many millworkers resist her attempts to organize them in their own economic interest. As class theory, Dargan suggests, Marxism is unsatisfactory in addressing the social complications posed by the ingrained gender patterns and race prejudices that plague both rural and urban societies. Significantly, Ishma herself embodies this ideological insufficiency. The pivotal and hyperhysterical moment when she recoils from the embrace of Gaffie Wells, a "very black" woman whose husband Ishma has saved from a lynching, undercuts her ostensible progressivism and is premised, as Alaimo asserts, on her problematic projection of maternity and excessive corporeality onto the site of blackness.[37] Yet it is essential that Ishma is deeply distressed by her own prejudice and even by her resulting flight from Winbury, which magnifies her uncertainties rather than resolving them. "What understanding could she have of humanity," she wonders on the novel's last page, "who had none of herself?"

Ishma's character, then, is surprisingly irreducible, as resistant to easy categorization as the supposedly dichotomous worlds she inhabits by turns. The extent of Dargan's challenge to facile symbolisms and simplistic binaries is evidenced, indeed, by Ishma's evasion of stereotypes, especially physical ones: her abundant strength and size, for instance, to which the narrative repeatedly bears witness, seem unwomanly, yet she remains attractive to men. In other ways, too, she challenges both conservative and liberal paradigms: a gifted nurturer of the sick, she nonetheless despises her own maternity, and as a champion of social justice, she surprisingly fails—refuses, even—to conquer her racist impulses. ("Ishma struggled with her prejudice," the narrator tells us, "but was too honest to deny it" [354].) Admired by country people and town people, by the impoverished and the genteel, by women and men, Ishma is fully at home with none of these groups. Her very complexity renders her unsuitable either as the personification of homely rural values or as the model urban social reformer.

Ishma's extravagant boundlessness, her inability to be contained within expected norms (Derry teases that she cannot fit all of herself into the cramped local houses, inevitably leaving out "a mountain or two, some miles of deepwood, and at least one waterfall" [232]), is also suggested by a long chapter in which, after she has left the mountains, Britt pummels the local preacher who has "churched" (i.e., excommunicated) her. The community's ballad maker, eager to commemorate the legendary encounter, realizes that "[a] ballit wouldn't do at all if it didn't end with a lady" (177)—yet Ishma's unconventional abandonment of Britt and their son makes it difficult to close the proposed song on an appropriately sentimental note. In the end, the singer solves the problem by concluding with a verse in which an imagined Ishma grieves over the husband she has left behind (177). The challenge Ishma represents here, however, is also the larger challenge taken up by Dargan, namely, the frustration of literary, as well as social, conventions. That the novel seeks to probe the boundaries of authenticity and representation is further underscored by Britt's encounter with the commercial music industry, in which he objects to being made a "freak o' the wilderness" yet is also led to believe that his music is marketable because he is a genuine mountaineer. "Since the war," Britt is told, "nobody ha[s] any patience with art all polished off. It was genius in the rough that got 'em to the box-office" (403).

"Art all polished off" is not at all what Dargan produced in *Call Home the Heart,* which disturbs contemporary readers with its race scenes, and which subtly subverts all sorts of conventional patterns, especially of gender: for instance, Rad turns out to be far more interested in bourgeois goods, and less capable of intellectual advancement, than Ishma, and Ishma's abandonment of Britt, whom she loves deeply, revises in provocative ways, as we have seen, the standard narrative of the jilted lover. One of the text's most disquieting but also penetrating moments involves Ishma's acknowledgment that to leave Rad, who had "heaped obligations upon her," would be "intolerably dishonest," though leaving Britt had been necessary and just (238). Such inversions of expectation reflect and extend the implications of the ideologically loaded settings of rurality and urbanity, which come to seem similarly unstable insofar as they are thought to signify entirely distinct social and symbolic realms. It hardly seems coincidental that Derry Unthank, the Communist doctor who ministers to the poor of Winbury, is also a farmer.

Ultimately, of course, in interrogating not only the poles of country and city but also woman and man, tradition and progress, Dargan pierces the very heart of melodrama, which relies for its significations on absolute binaries (e.g., virtue and vice, light and darkness). Yet she also utilizes the heightened affect of a melodramatic sensibility to enhance provocatively the contours of her protagonist's life predicaments. Hence she manages to explore the limits of her own ways and means. If *Call Home the Heart* appears occasionally to compromise a surface-level realism through unlikely scenarios or overly wrought characterizations, then the advantages gained more than compensate, for these elements point us toward re/considerations not only of an overdetermined rurality and urbanity but also of the prescriptive implications of representation itself.

Of course, we have already seen that there is more than one way to exploit melodrama's extremes. And at first glance, Josephine Johnson's tragic farm novel of the Depression, *Now in November* (1934), seems far less invested in a heightened emotionalism than either Kelley's or Dargan's texts. Yet its superficial equanimity belies its psychological intensity. A compact, lyrical work about the Haldemarne family's ill-fated efforts to fight the drought in Missouri, it faded from view relatively quickly, perhaps because it is focalized through the singular impressions of a female adolescent. One reviewer complained that its "quiet, modulated feminine voice" is too composed, too tranquil in the face of external disaster[38]—and, indeed, Johnson's heroine, even when faced by calamitous events, including gruesome and untimely deaths and a fire that all but destroys the family farm, seems to lack the anger and bitterness that well up in Kelley's Judith or Dargan's Ishma. But Marget, who is the middle Haldemarne daughter and the novel's narrator, strikingly exemplifies the melodramatic impulse to "force meaning and identity from the inadequacies of language."[39] She also advances powerful formulations of Depression-era rurality and its social and emotional underpinnings, which explode hackneyed figurations of womanhood and manhood within farm culture. The delicacy of much of Johnson's prose notwithstanding, Marget offers a robust challenge to the usual relations among women, land cultivation, and generativity.

To be sure, while critics universally admired the novel's "subtly cadenced" poeticism and its masterful depiction of "delicate and devious human emotions," many also found it forceful, if not always politically suggestive.[40] *Now in November* was immediately read against the canon of modern rural novels by women and was compared favorably to the work of Cather and to Wharton's *Ethan Frome;* Edith H. Walton, writing in the *New York Times*, called it "a farm novel of more than ordinary power and truth" that made the rural works of Phil Stong and Gladys Hasty Carroll seem "a little facile."[41] But critical emphasis on the novel's lyricism, which probably furthered its chances in the Pulitzer field, also helped to cast it, politically speaking, as somewhat slight—a characterization that unsettled Johnson's commitment to activism and that may have influenced her later literary production. (She next tried her hand at a proletarian novel that failed; later in her career she turned to nonfiction books and essays that anticipated the concerns of ecofeminism.)

Like Kelley and Dargan, Johnson was a woman of wide social sympathies—a champion of economic justice for the poor, full equality for African Americans, and, in later years, environmental awareness. Her thirty-year marriage to Grant Cannon, longtime editor of *Farm Quarterly* and author of *Great Men of Modern Agriculture*, helped to sustain Johnson's lifelong dedication to a human existence in nature that would be socially and economically equitable without exhausting natural resources. Long before she met Cannon, however, she was steeped in rural culture and, more specifically, in the rural reform issues of the 1930s. While not from an impoverished farming family herself (one journalist of the time described her parents' 110-acre farm as more of a "country estate"), Johnson understood the social paradigms of farming and consistently interested herself in the plight of poorer farmers, including those of color. She supported the Southern Tenant Farmers' Union, agitated for aid to migrant workers, came out publicly against the Agricultural Adjustment Act, and was involved in local efforts to teach children about the value of cooperative stores.[42] All this suggests that the farm setting of *Now in November* is not merely a timely backdrop for, as some have characterized it, a coming-of-age story that echoes European models.[43] Rather, the Haldemarnes' status as farmers is intrinsic to an understanding of their psyches: *Now in November* reveals Johnson's acute sensitivity to specifically American agricultural contexts, particularly to the ways that the presumed templates for girls' lives are rewritten in terms of Depression-era losses of both the farm as sanctuary and the marriage relation as a means of security.

Of course, this is not to deny the novel's poetic beauty or its investment in style as a means of carrying ideological weight. Nature's circularity is linked both to Marget's reflective personality and to her circuitous mode of expression: unlike her younger sister Merle, who "kept walking foot after foot down a straight path to some clear place," Marget's mind is forever "running a nest of rabbit-paths that twisted and turned and doubled on themselves" (13).[44] Her lyrical contemplativeness is posited as a reflection of nature's organicism, and the narrative as a whole, which ends by circling back to its opening line ("Now in November I can see our years as a whole"), imitates the natural cycles that it also relates—even as Marget stresses that nature exists apart from the human experience, relentlessly carrying on, "enlarg[ing] without mutation" (69).

This antiteleological structure coupled with Marget's fervent relation to the land has invited somewhat dated observations about "feminine" narrative strategies and the intersections of women and nature. But the text's formal qualities have other effects as well, effects that magnify the novel's setting. Specifically, its windingly meditative narrative style results in an apparent suspension of temporality that effectively foregrounds the spatial dimension. (One reviewer called the text "timeless," while a more recent commentator has described it as a series of "fragmented memories" variously fitted to form "pieces of a puzzle.")[45] Hence the Haldemarnes' home is underscored as not only a precisely demarcated geographic place but also an acutely experienced cultural domain. Since the Haldemarne daughters rarely leave their farm, and then only for brief but essential visits to neighboring farms, they know its spaces intimately (as evidenced by the precision of Marget's descriptions) and experience its mores as absolute and all-encompassing. Labor is incessant, Father's dictates are not to be questioned, and the lack of physical and mental diversion lends to isolated moments a visceral materiality, making "words and days and things . . . lie in the mind like stone" (9).

Moreover, this farm culture is the more desperately intense as it tries to maintain itself in the face of disquieting and ineluctable change. Mr. Haldemarne, clinging to the belief that a "misty gulf" separates men and women and that his daughters belong inside the house with their mother, stubbornly refuses to let Kerrin, his oldest daughter, take on farm chores typically assigned to men (63, 15)—this despite his urgent need for help on the land, which is revealed as less of a pastoral refuge than a repository of fear and grief. In the early pages of the novel Mrs. Haldemarne finds out that the old family farm to which they have retreated, which "at least, she had thought, was unencumbered, and sanctuary though everything else was gone" (5), is mortgaged, initiating a repeated emphasis on the lack of security offered by farming, despite the assumption by others that "farmers have got stuff to eat anyway" (204; cf. 75). Marget is painfully aware of the family's economic tenuousness, and of the myriad ways in which the land might be lost: "a drouth or a too-wet year or even a year over-good when everyone else had too much to sell" (68). After visiting the decaying farm of the neighboring Rathmans, who had seemed relatively impervious to market fluctuations affecting other farmers but who have now come upon bad fortune, Marget wonders whether "there was peace or safety anywhere on the earth" (172). And her father cries out in exasperation after his corn has brought a particularly low price, "God! don't they *want* a man to farm?" (224).

The pressures on farm families to sustain themselves despite massive social and economic shifts thus create a psychological climate that amplifies keenly the significance of every natural event, every seasonal variation, every family tension. Like Kelley, Johnson stresses the inappropriateness of the Jeffersonian ideal to American farming realities in this period: as Dorothee Kocks points out, Johnson shows that the farm cannot be a democracy in miniature, for it no longer guarantees the economic security on which solid citizenship depends, and its primary social unit, the family, is inherently undemocratic.[46] But Johnson also links the Haldemarne farm suggestively to its precise historical moment by allowing its economy of emotions—Marget's primary arena of observation and interest—to reflect the newly thwarted economic relations characterizing the "outside" world of Depression-era America. As a story of familial affection stinted or entirely withheld, of romantic love unrequited, of desire unsatisfied and effort unrewarded, *Now in November* mimics on an emotional plane the deflated currency, the stalled circulation of goods, the charged concepts of lien and mortgage and debt that also drive materially the lives of the Haldemarnes and others like them. The drama of a family's life thus becomes an imaginative, though oblique, means of representing not just the Depression's repercussions but the Depression itself.

In other ways, too, the novel engages surely but subtly with its times. Johnson's treatment of race issues, for example, is important though relatively understated: overt racism is kept in the narrative background, while Johnson foregrounds its effects and Marget's resulting understanding of the privilege that whiteness affords. The security enjoyed by the Haldemarnes, despite their overwhelming debt and increasing desperation, is brought home to Marget when she asks Ramsey, a neighboring black sharecropper with a wife and nine emaciated children, to lend them his mules for a day: "I told them that I'd come for help and they looked surprised, and all of a sudden it occurred to me that we seemed to them as the Rathmans did to us. Safe. Comfortable" (122). Later, when Ramsey seeks a loan to pay his rent but none of his white friends has the power to assist him, the Haldemarne women grieve over his hardship, and to their fear for themselves is added "the shame of being unable to help" (159). Indeed, Ramsey's role in the novel has less to do with black-white tensions than with highlighting whites' feelings of inadequacy in the face of an overwhelmingly racialized social hierarchy that they do not support but cannot effectively break. Thus the question of whether or not to help Ramsey meet his debts to a greedy white landowner becomes a question of how best to resist a racist, exploitative system without further hurting the individuals who are its victims: paying off the landlord would be like "propping an old wormed shed with good new poles, but better at least than having the roof crash down on Ramsey's head. You couldn't stand by and do nothing just because you thought it was wrong for a man to be trapped that way" (100). By throwing light less on black victimhood than on poor whites' sympathetic attempts to comprehend, and even alleviate, the realities of racism, as well as on their dawning awareness regarding racial privilege, Johnson locates her race commentary, unconventionally, in whiteness.

She also links racism implicitly to a systemic network of mystifying injustices and even absurdities. When Grant, the hired man, tries to convince Mr. Haldemarne to join other farmers in withholding their milk to protest the poor prices and possibly force them upward, Haldemarne demands, "What'll I do with a hundred gallons? . . . Can we eat milk? Read milk? Wear milk?" (129). Rumors circulate about old men watering their dried-up gardens with the milk that they cannot sell at a fair price (148), and Marget tries unsuccessfully to pierce the surface of these perplexities: "There must be some reason, I thought, why we should go on year after year, with this lump of debt, scrailing earth down to stone, giving so much and with no return"; but "the meaning . . . stayed hidden" (127–28). Thus Johnson depicts the Depression-era family farm as threatened on all sides by insidious social and economic forces that are simply beyond the conceptual grasp of the participant-observer.

Perhaps the most significant source of instability, however, is the disruption of orthodox gender roles that stems as much from women's changing aspirations in a modern world as from the agricultural conditions that require rethinking the gendered division of labor. Kerrin's desire to help in the fields and her fury and frustration when her father repeatedly refuses to let her participate in men's work contribute to her psychological breakdown. (She "felt things pounding in her, impotent and suppressed. . . . 'He thinks I can't do anything!' she'd shout at Mother" [15].) And the introduction of a potential love interest into this family of three sisters, which could become trite and formulaic, instead underscores the painful dismantling of gendered structures and expectations. Grant Koven's hire is necessitated by Mr. Haldemarne's loss of his usual man, who has joined the roadwork crew in search of more money; but in the excitement over Grant's arrival Johnson also makes visible the lack of approved social options that the recent exodus of eligible men presents for the Haldemarne daughters. Kerrin and Marget, somewhat predictably, fall in love with Grant almost immediately, but Grant prefers Merle, who will not have him; this concentration of misplaced feeling simultaneously reifies a general sense of Depression-induced disintegration and amplifies the novel's metaphoric commentary on how the normative gender roles of farm culture are newly thwarted.

The novel's men, for instance, are clearly severed imagistically, as well as materially, from the expectations that the culture engenders. Mr. Haldemarne is in a superficial sense the classic independent tiller of the soil, tenaciously working the fields to support his brood and "lov[ing] the land in a proud, owned way,—only because it was his, and for what it would mean to [his family]" (35). Yet he finds neither success nor even contentment in dominating the landscape and his household: he is bitter about his losses, joyless in his farming, and frustrated by his lack of control over Kerrin, whose flaunting of all of the conventions of womanhood he finds deeply offensive. Perhaps most important is Marget's perception that her father, in sharp contrast to the romantic image of the American farmer, is profoundly insecure, forever striving "to keep things from making him seem ridiculous, and fearful of anything that might tip over his dignity, poor-balanced and easily overthrown" (91). Grant, who is kinder and more temperate than Mr. Haldemarne, is nonetheless equally incapable of traditional forms of ascendancy in this agrarian culture, as his thwarted courtship of Merle mirrors his ineffectuality in organizing the local farmers. And Ramsey, when he can no longer maintain his tenancy, cuts through accumulated layers of symbol and myth by pointing out the emasculating reality that farming is no longer a way of life but a coldly economic enterprise: "'We ain't a farm if we can't pay up'" (156–57).

The women, too, fail to conform to type; it is especially significant that they are unable collectively to fulfill the "farmer's wife" paradigm. The kindly but ineffective Mrs. Haldemarne, for whom marriage is "a religion and long giving" (63), and whose subordinate position in the family is challenged by Kerrin and, less openly, by Marget (e.g., 15–16), dies horribly through a fire that also destroys the land, suggesting that both the independent farm and its social matrices are in danger of annihilation. None of the girls marries—not even Merle, the most domestic-minded, who rejects Grant for reasons unknown. Kerrin becomes more and more unbalanced as the novel progresses, increasingly aggressive in her pursuit of Grant; ultimately, by committing suicide, she forces the novel's sublimated emotional violence into the open. But it is Marget, whose narration focalizes the story and whose love for Grant is therefore most apparent to us, who is pivotal to the novel's revisioning of women's relations to marriage, procreation, and—by symbolic extension—the land. For Marget inadvertently undermines her own expressed desire for a typical courtship plot with herself as heroine, telling us, for instance, that there were many times when "the woods seemed all answer and healing and more than enough to live for" (68). In the end it is the land that sustains her, the land that gives her "courage somehow to face the mornings" (231), the land that is more fulfilling, and more enduring, than any lover.

But Marget's love affair with the land subverts the conventional agrarian romance by severing the typical tie between agrarian and sexual-domestic fulfillment. Indeed, her touching and lyrical narrative is a different kind of originative gesture, one that counterbalances, and even emerges from, presumably lost opportunities for re/production. While Marget's affinity for the farm's rhythms and her cyclical mode of recollection might appear stereotypically "feminine," Johnson destabilizes such trite associations by estranging her narrator from likely avenues of heterosexual love and its presumed maternity. Despite her tenderness, her keen sensitivity, and her potential for cultivation and creativity, Marget cannot be the sensual earth mother, the figure upon whom the farm's images of production and reproduction happily converge. Such a position depends, traditionally, on a corporeal act—not the act of mind and spirit that is signaled so forcefully by Marget's narration.

From the first page, it is clear that Marget is aware of how "shape and meaning" emerge through "looking down on things past"—that is, she perceives that her narrative creates as much as it relates (3). Early on she tells us, "Things were strange and unrelated and made no pattern that a person could trace easily" (4), and later still, certain questions are better left unanswered, for they "made the pattern of things more distorted than before" (62). The implied antidote to this confusion, of course, is the story itself, and the heightened performativity of Marget's storytelling signals an inventive agency that compensates for more constraining social and material realities. It is especially significant that her narrative, built upon an accretion of singular, fragmented moments, is entirely premised upon loss—of her mother, of the presumed security of the farm, and, most especially, of Grant. Hence this narrative, this creation, depends upon her *dis*engagement from traditional agrarian and domestic roles and ideals.

Ultimately she locates intimacy, fulfillment, and the potential for rebirth in the land itself: "Love and the old faith are gone. Faith gone with Mother. Grant gone. But there is the need and the desire left, and out of these hills they may come again" (231). It would be a mistake, however, to read Marget as merely romanticizing the landscape, or as displacing conventional female roles onto an essentialized, eroticized natural world. On the contrary, Marget's refusal to sentimentalize nature is a distinguishing aspect of both her personality and her narration, and forces us to understand these comments as an effort to find solace in a landscape that is nonetheless—like Judith Pippinger's—unpredictable in its healing properties. Indeed, Marget's vision of nature is even harsher than Judith's, for she sees it as not merely threatening in its capriciousness but thoroughly indifferent to human desire and endeavor: she asserts that nature is "both treacherous and kind," always "inconstant . . . go[ing] its own way as though we were never born" (8–9). The natural world cannot function as a projection of the human condition, or serve to justify social constructs, for, despite its ability to provide occasional comfort, it is ultimately unsympathetic, relentless, offering peace only in "sparse moments of surrender, and beauty in all its twisted forms, not pure, unadulterated, but mixed always with sour potato-peelings or an August sun" (226). Nor can Marget function, in the figurative (and feminine) sense, as a continuation of the world of nature, first because she is not a maternal figure and second because she is too much the observer: her immersion in nature, marked by her descriptive detail and her wonderfully fresh natural metaphors ("We were the green peas, hard and swollen" [59]), is nonetheless empirically based. For Marget, nature is an entirely separate realm, to be admired and even feared but never controlled; if she shares anything with the natural world, it is this detachment—the distance that enables her narration.

Significantly, Marget discerns, and even stresses, the distinctions between material realities and immaterial expectations, figurations, essentialisms. Despite her beautifully realistic descriptions, she seems modernist in her intuitive awareness of the gap between the physical and the metaphysical, observing, for instance, that words are inadequate and "pale" (35; cf. 145). And while she aches for Grant, it is the straightforward Merle whom she admires—Merle, who is secure enough to pass up Grant, who "did not fight half-heartedly with faceless shadows, masked forms she was afraid to name, but knew things for what they were and twisted them apart" (71). Marget's story both explores and performs a "twisting apart" of the romantic and the realistic, the mythic and the material, and she clearly finds the latter less constraining than the former: "It's a lie that the body is a prison! It's the mind, I tell you!—always the cold, strong mind that's jailer."

Thus while *Now in November* testifies to material miseries fostered by the Depression, it suggests that social and psychological constructs are ultimately more destructive. Specifically, Marget resents the social mores that prevent her from telling Grant that she is in love with him, prevent her from "do[ing] what Kerrin had done . . . touch[ing] [Grant] and get[ting] what sour comfort there'd be in this" (206). Kerrin, the sister who challenged most openly the dictates of her family, had made her feelings for Grant perfectly clear, and Marget recognizes a certain bravery in Kerrin's apparent recklessness: "Poor crazy Kerrin! All that she did I wanted at times to do, but had more sense or less courage—I do not know which it was" (169). But instead of touching Grant—and going mad with thwarted desire, like Kerrin—Marget is compelled to narrate. That compulsion, the desire to "pressure" the surface of things, "to make reality yield the terms of the drama of [a] moral occult," marks both her melodramatic sensibility and her refutation of the approved roles for females in her culture.[47] It also allows her to approach the landscape on her own terms, as neither its possessor nor its victim.

The preoccupations of these novels overlap with, but also extend, a range of contemporaneous radicalisms. As feminist texts, they are interested in the female body and its charged connotations, exploring the resulting dilemmas for women through a heightening of the harrowing experience of maternity (Kelley), a masculinization of the female body that unfits it for the cultural work of femininity (Dargan), and a sequestering of the feminine creative spirit from the biological aspects of womanhood (Johnson); moreover, their unanimous rejection of motherhood as a means of identification or fulfillment for women challenges even liberal feminisms. As class texts, they demand attention to the poor, and to the ways in which material deprivation ironically manages to intensify and disrupt gendered social constructs; they also link poverty decisively to women's uncontrolled reproductivity. As race texts, Dargan's and Johnson's works probe the construction of whiteness, representing, on one hand, a white woman bound by a race prejudice that she fully recognizes as constraining her ability to help revolutionize society (Dargan) and, on the other hand, a white neighborhood relatively free from such bigotry but nonetheless unable to pierce the racialized system that insulates whites from abuses endured by blacks (Johnson). The numerous touchpoints among these preoccupations foreground in these works the intertwined imperatives of gender, class, and race inequity that cannot be ignored by a modern, progressive nation, except at its peril. Kelley and Dargan would surely have agreed with Johnson when she declared, a few years after *Now in November* was published, that "America's own problems are as vast as her distances, but considerably more intricate. . . . And the tragedy, the true indictment of America, lies not so much in the darkness of this long list of wrongs, as in the complete nearness and possibility of their solution. . . . [They must be solved] in the name of peace and justice."[48]

My larger point, however, is that Kelley, Dargan, and Johnson were also of their time in their use of rurality as a cultural shorthand that allowed them to manipulate for critical purposes the psychological and emotional expectations of their readers. Rather than abjuring what might be deemed a nostalgic and therefore insipid literary-cultural space, they leaned into the comforting psychic resonances of farm culture—not to sanction but to explode them. In the process, they confronted both conservative and radical formulations of agrarianism, exposing the farm as neither a Jeffersonian haven of independent yeomanry nor a Marxist realm of triumphant use-value, both of which flatten or overlook the swelling social tensions and increasingly intricate economic relationships that dominate modern life, including farm life. Indeed, these writers seem to suggest that abiding semantic codes and recondite theorizations cannot serve or represent a complex modern reality.

Johnson's narrator intimates that there is danger involved in making the farmer's world into an abstraction:

> I could imagine a kind of awful fascination in the very continuousness of this drouth, a wry perfection in its slow murder of all things. We might have marveled and exclaimed and said there was never anything like it, never anything worse, and shaken our heads, recalling all other years in comparison with a kind of gloomy joy. But this was only for those to whom it was like a play, something to be forgotten as soon as it was over. For us there was no final and blessed curtain—unless it was death. This was too real. (113)

Even as these comments implicate novelists in the representational distortions that they critique, they seem also to champion the notion of an accurate social history. In the end, Kelley, Dargan, and Johnson wrote adamantly realistic texts, though they reached beyond a mere record of the quotidian to probe its effects on spirit and psyche, especially where women are concerned: perhaps ironically, the melodramatic aspects of their narratives only serve to enhance the sense that real lives and genuine experiences are at the heart of their social commentaries. Combining documentary and aesthetic impulses, then, their texts exert revisionary force on the symbolic imaginary of rurality. As a result, they validate, and potentially even alter, the experiences of actual women living rural lives.

Chapter 5

Rural Camera Work
Women and/in Photography

PHOTOGRAPHY EMERGED AS a popular medium at the same moment that agriculture was being newly scrutinized, standardized, and "reformed"; it is hardly surprising, then, that photographic depictions of rural life became a means of both registering and shaping rural "reality." As we have seen, publications by such agencies as the U.S. Department of Agriculture gradually attempted to re/direct women's roles through prescriptive images, many of them photographic; agricultural periodicals used photography in similarly authoritative ways, often as testament to the joys, and miseries, of rural life. It was not unusual, for instance, to see contrasting images of farm homes—some neglected, others neat and trim—published side by side in farm journals in efforts to spur women to achieve and maintain minimum levels of respectability.[1] In short, photography lent visibility to an impoverished rural culture even as it also furthered the dissemination of positive ideals of country living.

Also noteworthy in this era, however, was the new expedience of photo-taking for women. The handheld preloaded camera manufactured by Kodak beginning in 1889—advertised widely in women's magazines, including *The Farmer's Wife*—allowed for a broader and deeper range of photographic expression, as well as a more feminine one, since its ease of use encouraged the chronicling of domestic and informal moments that historically fell outside the purview of most camera work. And even professional photographic equipment became lighter and less cumbersome after the turn of the century, with the result that women turned increasingly to photography for financial support as well as for archival or expressive reasons. As the sheer weight, bulk, and fragility of older cameras and their accoutrements gave way to more versatile models and developing techniques, women found photography an increasingly congenial activity in both amateur and commercial contexts.

Certain aspects of the modern artistic and social landscapes proved propitious as well. The newness of photography as a medium meant that its aesthetic parameters, as well as its uses within the culture, were still largely uncodified, allowing a latitude—of subject, style, a/vocational posture, and so on—not available within the more established arts. And, as Melissa McEuen has pointed out, photography's relative infancy almost certainly enhanced its specific availability to women, who could hardly pose a serious threat to a fledgling occupation. The new social freedoms accorded to females, such as the ability to travel more widely without male chaperones, also helped to make photography an attractive endeavor, underscoring the professed modernism of women practitioners and enabling their gradual penetration into less mainstream social spaces, including distressed rural areas in the Deep South and Appalachia.[2]

The very notion of early twentieth-century women photographing inhabitants of such locales highlights intriguing issues of modernist representation and performativity, as suggested by recent work on early women photographers of Native Americans.[3] Merely brandishing the camera, of course, connected women to an exciting and powerful new technology, but their link to the modern was also enabled by their contrast with these subaltern subjects, who were aligned, either pejoratively or romantically, with a preindustrial, premodern society. As wielders of a gaze, then, as framers of an alternative space and place, these female photographers—generally white, educated, and reasonably secure in material terms, but often external to organized academic or professional circles—assumed potent roles as cultural interpreters, negotiating and shaping relations between modernity's centers and margins. In the process they positioned *themselves* as firmly modern and entered into developing discourses of ethnography and aesthetics, including controversies over the role of photography itself as either an evidentiary tool or an artistic medium. Those whose photographs were destined for publication in books, magazines, and advertising pamphlets also participated in the marketing and circulation of images that was fast becoming the central currency of modern life.

By the late 1930s, Roy Stryker's legendary photo-file for the Farm Security Administration (FSA), consisting of some 270,000 images documenting the effects of the Great Depression, would make several photographers of ruralism famous, creating a firm link between the rural and a particularly American modernist aesthetic—what critic Maren Stange has called the "new graphic rhetoric" that "conventionalized both currency and nostalgia."[4] Some of the FSA photographers were women, and, as we shall see, their visions could depart substantially from those of the men, and of Stryker himself. Long before the Depression, however, women evinced an interest in photographing rural life, perhaps due less to political or sociological impulses than to mere proximity. Several such women developed regional, national, and even international followings. Chansonetta Stanley Emmons (1858–1937), for example, photographed numerous rural scenes and activities around her native Kingfield, Maine, some including carefully costumed and posed figures. Though she exhibited sparingly, in the 1920s she augmented her income by traveling throughout Massachusetts and Maine presenting photographic slide shows of the glories of rural New England. Similarly, Ohio farm woman Nancy Ford Cones (1869–1962) created bucolic photographs of farm life that were published in such magazines as *Country Life in America* and *Woman's Home Companion* and were used in advertisements for Eastman Kodak. Marie Hartig Kendall (1854–1943) sold pastoral images taken from her Connecticut surroundings in postcard sets and as publicity pieces for the New Haven Railroad Company. Deaf sisters Frances Allen (1854–1941) and Mary Allen (1858–1941) of Deerfield, Massachusetts, earned international acclaim with their idealized rural scenes and managed largely to support themselves through their work. Though more privately motivated, Mattie Gunterman (1872–1945), an American who relocated to southern British Columbia for health reasons, created surprisingly playful photographs of the social and occupational experiences of her ranching neighbors, while Evelyn Cameron, a young English bride transplanted to a Montana homestead, took hundreds of photographs of shearing, threshing, and other ways of American farm life between 1889 and her death in 1928; both were well known locally, and their images now have substantial historical value.[5]

These largely forgotten women helped to establish the literal visibility of rurality within modern American culture, contributing to the vernacular visual archive within and against which further representations of the rural would find meaning. Hence they also suggest a web of relations that contextualizes rather differently the work of such renowned photographers of rurality as Dorothea Lange. Lange's FSA images are often considered in light of works by female contemporaries such as Berenice Abbott and Margaret Bourke-White, who were known for their preoccupations with the more avowedly modern arena of urban industrialism.[6] But a different pattern of emphasis might link Lange and other women photographers of the FSA to earlier women such as Emmons, Cones, or the Allen sisters, positioning all of them within attitudes about modernity that hinge on the rural as a primary signifier. As we have seen, the consideration of women and rurality within a broad range of representational concerns and practices—in fiction, in periodical publications, in reform rhetorics—sets up an alternative historical lens, an alternative set of social and aesthetic relations, an alternative way of tracing a trajectory through and about modernity. In photography, too, a consideration of women's relations to the rural generates a space for new interpretive resonances.

Not surprisingly, most women photographing rural life in the early decades of the century, those predating the FSA years, have been historically overlooked, perceived perhaps as simplistically sentimental or unrigorous in their visual sensibilities—attitudes similar to those assumed in reference to women writers of rural fiction. While the long absence of some of these photographers from the historical record may reflect prejudices regarding gender, subject matter, or both, late twentieth-century recovery studies nonetheless insist on the importance of women's camera work to an understanding of the general history of photography as well as the history of women in the professions, and hence to an understanding of women and the modern.[7] To be sure, many early female photographers of rurality eliminated overt references to modernity in their images, preferring instead to isolate rural individuals and landscapes in ways that make them seem entirely removed from urban-industrial society. Yet even the most conspicuously nostalgic of these works, those evoking an idyllic and emphatically precommercial pastoral America, necessarily constituted a response to modernist preoccupations with technology and commodification, and exploited modernist concerns with the "natural" and with American nativism. For an urban audience still mindful of its agrarian past (in many cases, only a generation or two removed from it), rural scenes in advertising or other venues tapped into the urban-rural tension that informed American perceptions of progress. As Lawrence Levine has argued, the widespread cultural interest in a "self-contained folk" in photography and other media of the early twentieth century betrayed a fixation with modern cultural forces through an exploration of "primitive" groups, who were envied for their presumably more authentic lives but also pitied for their exclusion from "the wondrous fruits of modernity."[8]

The combination of romantic conventions and ethnographic impulses that structured much photography of rurality through the 1930s may also be understood as part of a particularly modernist enterprise, namely, the creation of a broad visual lexicon by which Americans were publicly conditioned to see subalterns in ways that perpetuated hegemonic values.[9] Rural imagery, however, both furthered and complicated this project. Since rurality was at once marginal (to a valorized urban industrialism) and central (to American history and identity), its cultural position was, as I have already noted, particularly unstable, and its representation, visual or otherwise, carried connotations that were overdetermined. The conflicting impulses to document a degraded rural "reality" and render a valorized rural ideal were hypercharged, especially when the farmers in question were white. Furthermore, photographs of rural society, particularly in straitened areas, troubled the boundaries between self and other, between the native and the foreign. While white rural citizens seemed familiar (they were less exotic, for instance, than urban immigrants), they were nonetheless culturally bracketed by a nation that was distancing itself from its agrarian past. And indigent farmers, in particular, seemed external to the concerns of a thriving commercial populace, even as the farmer-as-icon retained considerable symbolic power. The situation of rural culture relative to the mainstream and the periphery, then, and to the real and the figurative, seemed especially vexed. Photography's ability to both inscribe and mold perception played into the resulting ambiguities in ways that other forms of visual imagery, such as painting, could not.

Indeed, the camera's simultaneous registering of evidence and perspective has particularly loaded ramifications regarding photography of nonmainstream peoples, a problem that, significantly, aligns openly romantic photographers of rurality with the later and more expressly documentary work of the FSA. If the camera always both reveals *and* constructs, then the disenfranchised who are caught in its gaze are necessarily manipulated, "captured," in new ways, notwithstanding protestations of journalistic neutrality. Michael North has recently argued that the productive tension between photography's expositional and aesthetic dimensions is precisely what made it a fundamentally modern medium, one that "could not be easily inserted into the traditional economy of the arts." Photography, North notes, rather than furthering an ideal of transparency, ended up destabilizing perception altogether; hence "the camera, celebrated from the first as objectivity incarnate, also came to serve as one of modernity's most powerful emblems of the subjectivity of perception and of knowledge." To submit liminal people and landscapes to the exposure of the camera was thus to enter especially deeply into modern dilemmas of representation, expression, and social power. This was precisely the point of James Agee when he asserted, in his discourse on representation and responsibility in *Let Us Now Praise Famous Men*—which, not coincidentally, concerned itself with a neglected rural tenant culture—that the camera was "the central instrument of [the] time." Its role in the mediation of rurality for a modern industrial society is necessarily of interest here.[10]

Since I am concerned, of course, with tensions between the real and the represented, between "objective" and "subjective" modes of filtering and ordering a rural arena in ways that allow it to bespeak the modern, photography is an intriguing medium, particularly when we consider those women whose photographic engagement with rurality was long and deep. This is not to deny or diminish a male canon of rural photography but to highlight, once more, the insistent relations between women and rurality—specifically, to situate women photographers of rurality within a larger body of women's representational effort that links them, through an exploration of rural spaces and ideologies, to particular negotiations of modernity. Of special concern is the manner in which framing rural life through the lens of a camera allowed them to exhibit their own modernness. Also important, however, is their visual construction of rurality as a means of intervening into contemporary debates about labor, gender, poverty, and even representation itself. For the most intriguing of these women, the decision to photograph rural life was not a retreat into sentimental sites and postures; on the contrary, it was an activist gesture of exploration, confrontation, interpretation, and self-determination. It also involved an intuitive awareness of the dynamics of the gaze and of the possibilities for photography both to reproduce and potentially to redress them.

This chapter takes up two women, Doris Ulmann (1882–1934) and Marion Post (1910–1990), whose differences help to elucidate the spectrum of women's photographic approaches to rurality. On the surface they appear to have little in common. Ulmann worked in a romantic, pictorialist tradition while Post practiced a "straightforward" documentary style; Ulmann was of independent means and operated outside of official channels while Post was a paid photographer in Roy Stryker's FSA corps; Ulmann was interested in insulated agrarian folk cultures while Post's work necessarily ranged across a wider variety of farm settings and groups. Yet both had ideologically progressive backgrounds and educations, both participated in organizations advocating for the socially disadvantaged, and both displayed a keen interest in racial dynamics, expanding the racial diversity of the visual rural record to an extent unusual in the work of other rural photographers, male or female. These similarities point to a shared engagement in contemporary social questions that was reflected in, but also transcended, their photographic work. While discussed less frequently than other female photographers of the rural (notably Lange, about whom much has been written), Ulmann and Post are of special relevance to this project because their engagement with rurality was unusually textured, and its parameters generally are not perceptible merely through looking at their most frequently reproduced photographs. These women took up the rural not merely as another subject for their photographic work but as a kind of social crusade,[11] and as a means of resisting many of the conforming forces—imagistic, political, gendered, class-oriented—of modern life. Together, they stand in for a large body of female photographers of rurality while also demonstrating the vitality and particularity of individual approaches to a subject matter often dismissed as trite, or considered less important than questions of photographic technique or compositional style.

Levine has pointed out that "the only culture the poor are supposed to have is the culture of poverty."[12] Ulmann represented the rural poor as culturally rich—a capitulation to romantic notions of American rurality, perhaps, but an idea that she used fruitfully to challenge prevailing assumptions about rural people's social roles and about the place of modern technology in our representations of them. In contrast, Post concerned herself with the ways in which poverty obliterates culture, at least insofar as long-standing notions of organicism that have structured our ideals of rurality become irrelevant in light of acute rural poverty. Yet both photographers approached rurality in the belief that representation itself serves as a form of social activism, even as they attempted in various subtle and unsubtle ways to correct for the imposition of power that their camera work enacted. As much as the discourse of rural reformers, as much as the varied registers of the agricultural press, as much as writers of rural fiction, their work contributes to an understanding of the imbrication of women, modernity, and rurality. Their rural photographs are, indeed, an integral aspect of American modernism.

Doris Ulmann and the Politics of Integration

An initial glance at Doris Ulmann's most recognized portraits, those of Appalachian craftspeople, would hardly evoke thoughts of the modern. Her pictorialist technique, which utilized soft lighting and an artfully blurred focus to approximate a painterly effect, was already dated by the 1920s and seemed to reinforce through formal compositional means the "backward" qualities of her sitters, who appeared to cling to ways of life fast disappearing in the new century. But Ulmann's relations to modernity are considerably more complicated than these romantic images first suggest. And while some have pegged her as "premodernist," others have linked her best work to that of Paul Strand and the photographers of the FSA, suggesting that "Pictorialism and Modernism were not so far apart."[13] Certainly her wide-ranging efforts to compile a visual catalogue of those she perceived as culturally marginal—including not just Appalachians but also Gullahs, Creoles, and even Shakers—align her with the modern urgency to survey and classify the social field. And her passion for documenting these technologically and geographically isolated communities seems all the more astonishing in a woman of genteel background and urbane tastes who was independently wealthy.

Of course, Ulmann did not begin her photographic career with such preoccupations. She first made a name for herself through photographing educated urban professionals, creating book-length compilations of individual portraits of the physicians of Columbia University and Johns Hopkins University, and of influential American editors.[14] These projects were modestly successful, and gradually, through her New York City contacts and her avid interest in books and the arts, Ulmann developed an avocation taking photographs of prominent intellectuals and, especially, famous writers. She was well known for all-day sittings, usually conducted in her Park Avenue apartment, in which she attempted gradually to "draw out" her subject through conversation and a steady supply of tea and cocktails; her only fee was an occasional request for the sitter's latest book. Her subjects included such period luminaries as H. L. Mencken, Albert Einstein, Carl Van Vechten, Ellen Glasgow, Edna St. Vincent Millay, James Weldon Johnson, Thornton Wilder, and Waldo Frank. One distinctive feature of many of Ulmann's portraits of these renowned individuals was their double signatures: the sitters' autographs, alongside hers, suggested through apposition a complementarity of vision and aesthetic endeavor.[15]

Thus in the early 1920s Ulmann was deeply enmeshed in an upper-crust urban-intellectual society. Exhibiting occasionally in the venues inspired and moderated by photographer Clarence H. White, her mentor and fellow pictorialist, and enjoying the cultural offerings of the city, she might have remained protected from the ugliness of poverty and race prejudice for her entire life. Yet her high-styled acquaintances and the gravitational pull of New York proved insufficient to prevent Ulmann from seeking out new and culturally remote subjects for her art, a tendency that may be explained in part by her rather unconventional education and her resulting iconoclasm. Raised in a sophisticated, well-to-do Jewish family, Ulmann was a graduate of the Ethical Culture School, part of Felix Adler's Ethical Culture Society of Manhattan. A liberal educator and a social reformer, Adler believed that "differences in type contribute importantly to a democratic society," and Ulmann readily adopted his attitudes, including his commitment to help the less fortunate, a stance that she maintained throughout her life and that resulted in her eventual bestowal of substantial financial bequests. Ulmann's early adult years—during which she was married to Dr. Charles Jaeger, who, among other endeavors, founded a trade school for crippled men—were marked by her links to various social reform causes and organizations, including the Russell Sage Foundation, created for "the improvement of social and living conditions in the United States of America."[16] Her participation in circles of affluence and privilege, then, was offset from the beginning by liberal social sympathies.

Significantly, Lewis Hine was also involved in the Ethical Culture Society, and though it seems unlikely that Ulmann knew him personally, she surely came to know his work; as Melissa McEuen argues, the influence of reform photographers such as Hine can be seen in Ulmann's eventual choice of subject matter.[17] Following the death of Clarence White and her divorce from Jaeger, Ulmann gradually changed the direction of her work, focusing less on the socially powerful and more on the socially disfranchised, notably laborers, folk types, Native Americans, and other groups representative of an older, preindustrial America. After 1925, she concentrated largely on field portraits, embarking on a years-long crusade to locate and photograph isolated backwoods and rural-coastal communities, a project that she found deeply gratifying and that linked her to other White-influenced female photographers, such as Laura Gilpin and Clara Sipprell, who were similarly interested in American subcultures.[18]

Though Ulmann clung to her old-fashioned pictorialist style, she apparently saw no disjuncture between her impressionistic approach and her urge to uplift a debased citizenry: while social reform had come to be associated with "straight" photographic modes such as Hine's (including flat lighting, sharp focus, and a disdain for darkroom manipulations), the link was not yet so absolute as to discount alternatives. As Ulmann herself put it, she hoped through her artistic effects to reveal the "great and deep humanity" of her subjects; in 1930 she commented to Allen Eaton of the Russell Sage Foundation that she wished her photographs to "serve some social purpose" rather than being appreciated merely as examples of art.[19] In some cases, Ulmann's picturesque images were created specifically to illustrate texts centering on vastly underprivileged populations, situating her apparent idealization of individuals within a larger context in which their poverty and disadvantage were fully acknowledged.

It would be misleading, therefore, to consider any individual Ulmann photograph without reference to its originating circumstances, or to the photographer's social attitudes. Nor would it be appropriate to ignore the context of Ulmann's oeuvre as a whole, which frequently relies on collective effects. Another aspect of her work that makes broader contextualization essential, for instance, is her investment in photographic series, which deliberately create dimension through multiplicity.

For example, virtually all of Ulmann's portrait studies, for which she is deservedly best known, consist of a range of distinct images. In her series of Aunt Sophie photographs, for instance, taken in Gatlinburg, Tennessee, Ulmann clearly attempts, in a succession of tight shots, to reveal disparate moods and attitudes of an elderly Appalachian woman (e.g., figs. 5.1–5.3). Of course, some of the images seem today to evoke rather too heavily the stereotypical resonances of the highland "cracker," notably those in which Sophie appears to smoke her pipe. (Sophie Campbell was, in fact, a pipemaker. In accordance with nineteenth-century conventions of portraiture, Ulmann liked to include objects that conveyed the social role of her sitter.) But Ulmann's focus on the face and, especially, the hands relays a venerability that transcends external trappings, including Sophie's worn clothing. And the more striking and poignant shots manage to juxtapose the harsh lines of Sophie's hard-worked body with a hint of gentleness—in one case, through a composition that counters the long, thin face with the surprisingly tender position of the large, gnarled hands, holding the pipe in a graceful, cradling curvature of repose (fig. 5.3). Above all, the accumulation of the images and the variety of moods evoked hint at the patience and tact with which Ulmann must have approached her sitter, a delicacy that belies what might be read as a condescending imposition of props or a pandering to the commercial appetite for southern "types."

Figure 5.1 Aunt Sophie—seated, with pipe in mouth. (Item No. PH038-07-0809, Doris Ulmann Collection, Special Collections and University Archives, University of Oregon Libraries.)

Figure 5.2 Aunt Sophie—standing, holding pipe. (Item No. PH038-07-0813, Doris Ulmann Collection, Special Collections and University Archives, University of Oregon Libraries.)

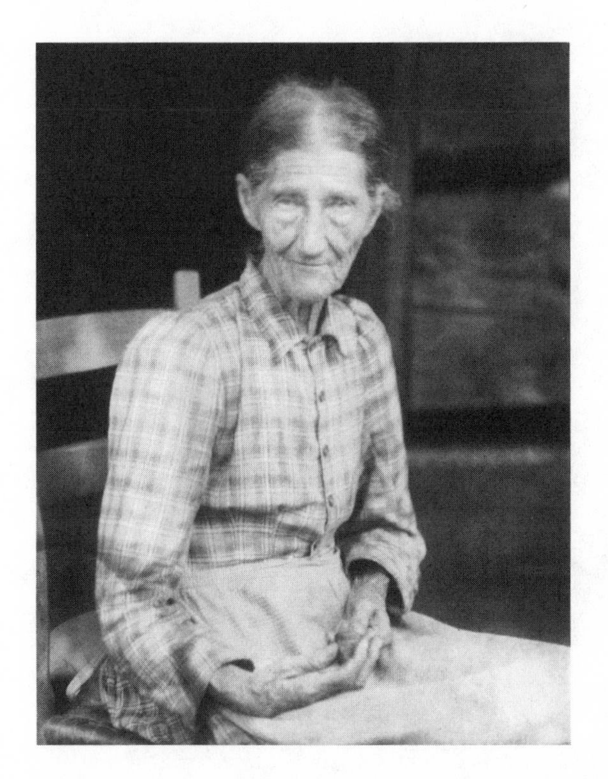

Figure 5.3 Aunt Sophie—seated, holding pipe in lap. (Item No. PH038-07-0807, Doris Ulmann Collection, Special Collections and University Archives, University of Oregon Libraries.)

A comparison of the Aunt Sophie photographs with Ulmann's portraits of contemporary writers and intellectuals, such as her portrait of Elizabeth Madox Roberts (fig. 5.4), also reveals the similarity with which she treated her glamorous subjects and her unsophisticated ones. In turning her deliberate, thoughtful approach from the privileged to the poor, Ulmann helped to revise the representational standards that had traditionally confined serious portraiture to the white middle and upper classes. In this sense she was hardly a passive imagemaker, but rather an artist with decided attitudes about the social implications of the visual. In elevating figures such as Aunt Sophie to new levels of distinction, Ulmann's portraits of the underclasses, despite their superficial romanticism, advance a progressive social attitude.

Significantly, Ulmann's photographs manage to lend hallowedness not merely to an individual subject but to the singular image itself, reinvesting both with a sense of seriousness and cultural value. Indeed, Ulmann implicitly challenged the modern tendency to treat images as cheapened commodities, increasingly plentiful and therefore readily consumed and discarded. For instance, due to her photographic techniques, her images could not be easily reproduced for mass-market

Figure 5.4 Ulmann portrait of Elizabeth Madox Roberts, with dual signatures. (78PA101 No. 4, Doris Ulmann Collection, University of Kentucky Archives.)

venues, suggesting her relative indifference to their wide circulation.[20] Those same techniques also made it impossible to capture movement or spontaneity: Ulmann remained dedicated to outmoded photographic equipment that required slow, careful preparation and still subjects. She considered snapshot photography, made possible by faster films and smaller cameras, "the end of vulgarities." Instead, she continued to use an awkward tripod and refused even a shutter, displacing the lens cap with her hand to admit light.[21] This outright rejection of the newest technology underscores her considered relation to modern advancements: though clearly devoted to photography as a medium, she resisted the unexamined appetite for its constant innovation. Hence while her pictorialism can be and has been read as flatly retrogressive and as evidence of a misplaced gentility (like the long, filmy dresses she wore even while combing remote areas for likely subjects), such a reading appears to oversimplify her photographic sensibility, which relied on an ethic of representation that demanded an attenuation of, rather than a wholesale capitulation to, photography's technological potential.

This deliberate restraint helped to obscure the radical dimensions of her work. There is no question that Ulmann's reported soft-spokennesss and frail demeanor, together with her opaque, softly blurred images, deflected attention from the unorthodox role she adopted for herself as an aesthetic champion of forgotten cultures and impoverished communities. While being a female photographer was unconventional enough, Ulmann's particular enterprise, often characterized by grueling travel through miles of wilderness, called for unusual pluck. It was not always easy to approach or even locate her desired subjects, who could not be further removed from Ulmann's personal range of experience; her sympathetic but also active interest in groups that others seemed to overlook—African Americans in isolated enclaves, poor white mountaineers, rural laborers of mixed race—was quite uncommon. Ulmann's singular artistic crusade was also matched by her curious personal circumstances. She suffered from ill health and eventually adopted as her companion and helpmate a younger single man, folklorist and balladeer John Jacob Niles, who carried her heavy glass plates and equipment; on a few notable occasions over rough terrain, he even carried Ulmann herself. Upon her death Ulmann left Niles a comfortable inheritance. Though the precise nature of their relationship remains somewhat obscure, all accounts maintain that this quiet, middle-aged divorcée and her charmingly effusive but arrogant male companion made a highly irregular traveling pair.[22]

All this tends to suggest that, despite certain incongruities,[23] Doris Ulmann was a freethinker with an independent spirit—something of a "New Woman." This necessitates an understanding of the underlying attitudes resulting in photographs that might appear to us conservative and even reactionary. Holding to a course that privileged substance over surface and deliberateness over speed, she rejected technical developments that diminished the relationship between photographer and sitter, including those that made the entire photographic process shorter and therefore less relational. Moreover, the importance Ulmann ascribed to the individual—she rarely photographed groups or places, as many have noted—was only enhanced by her extensive preparation, long exposure times, and serial approach. If photography were to lend dignity to her often maligned subjects, if it were to capture the essence of the individual rather than merely recording a fleeting and perhaps anomalous moment, then she felt that it would and should take time. Thus Ulmann invested in the "modernness" of photography only insofar as it enhanced her own philosophical attitudes about the appropriate role of pictures, *her* pictures, in modern culture. While she wanted to reveal to outsiders the beauty and nobility of the people she encountered, she was not interested in an unreflective circulation of images, especially those "stolen" without the full cooperation and consent of their subjects: such practices seemed to her to be morally reprehensible, as did excessive attention to details that highlighted a subject's material humiliation over personal bearing. Instead, her portraits are almost always taken at close range, proffering intimacy even in cases when the sitter seems emotionally distant; they also engage an artful use of light and focus to direct the viewer's attention away from ancillary aspects of poverty that might encourage pity or condescension. Ulmann's photographs also strive for a sense of equality between viewer and sitter: she aspired to serious, deferential images that cemented the genuine emotional bond that she insisted on establishing with her subjects (and to which those subjects later attested). Her deep belief in this personal relationship even prompted her to leave provisions in her will so that anyone she photographed would receive a copy of the print, a practice that distinguished her from documentary photographers, for whom the image served official agencies and purposes and justified sweeping social outreach policies.[24]

Ulmann's philosophical posture as a photographer resonates with her efforts to dignify labor generally, to remove work from the unthinking realm of mass production and reinvest it with spiritual meaning. Her respectful, artistic portraits ironically align her own camera craft, based on modern technology, with the work of her sitter-laborers, whom she depicted as achieving an organic and even elegant union with the natural products shaped by their hands. Typically posed, as Sophie Campbell is, with the fruits of their labor, these rural workers are presented as accomplished, even masterly. This is especially the case in Ulmann's many photographs of Appalachian craftspeople, where the individual's domestic production is the primary identifying trait and a marker of status, as in photographs such as "Arlene McCarter, Basket and Fan Maker" (fig. 5.5), "Anthony Lord, Blacksmith, in Leather Apron with Tools" (fig. 5.6), "Clementine Douglas, Spinner, at the Wheel" (fig. 5.7), and "Bristol Taylor, Dulcimer Maker, Farmer, Poet" (fig. 5.8). Particularly striking among such photographs, especially those of female subjects, is the lack of familial signification: Ulmann's images collectively bestow a relative gender neutrality through which women, like men, are identified by their talents rather than their roles as mothers and wives. Naturally, this practice was partly dictated by the parameters of her most focused Appalachia project, a collaboration with sociologist Allen Eaton, who was preparing a book specifically on mountain handicrafts; it may also be related to Ulmann's personal status as an unmarried, childless professional. Yet it seems, too, to constitute an implicit critique of the gender conventions of genteel portraiture, and it certainly differs from documentarians' use of the family unit, especially joint images of mothers and children, to evoke pity.[25] Ulmann's many close-up photographs of working hands function similarly as an ennobling and gender-neutralizing device.[26]

Of course, many, if not most, of the Appalachians featured in Ulmann's portraits practiced subsistence agriculture; yet Ulmann's focus on their crafts work rather than their field work allowed for an alternative framing of rural society, one that, significantly, stressed delicacy and refinement rather than backbreaking menial labor. To be sure, sometimes Ulmann's practices seemed less than ennobling: for example, she also dabbled in hyperbole, notably when she asked her sitters, as she occasionally did, to don their grandparents' clothing or pose with traditional equipment retrieved from dusty cellars and attics.[27] The resulting photographs, once identified, seem to us overly contrived, and suggest a nostalgically motivated erasure of even those minimal modernizations that had, by the 1920s, reached the mountains. But our judgment of such images as lacking in authenticity has more to do with our assumptions about the limits of evidential propriety than with Ulmann's photographic purposes, which were not intended to mislead. As McEuen avers, these posings were not about falsifying mountain experience; rather, they were tableaux created in the spirit of the appreciation of the American rural past that was central to new settlement schools such as Berea College in Kentucky and the John C. Campbell Folk School in North Carolina. Ulmann was personally attached to both of these institutions, often using them as home bases in her travels; her admiration of their leaders, and of their educational mission to preserve mountain culture and educate mountain people, is well documented. Indeed, upon her death Ulmann bequeathed to Berea College an entire set of her Appalachian prints and money sufficient to build an exhibition gallery for them, and she left the bulk of her estate to the Campbell School, for which it continues to generate substantial income.[28] Ulmann's material support of mountain folk culture through these bequests suggestively counters the claim that her interest in the people she photographed was merely sentimental, that it served her own romantic vision rather than their needs.

Ulmann's mountaineer portraits have generated other misconceptions about her work as well. Specifically, it would be tempting to align her, as some did, with nativist sensibilities—the celebration of a white rural worker ideal—if it were not for her equally sensitive portrayals of nonwhite American cultures, which included Native Americans and those of mixed race.[29] By far her best-known work with nonwhites was with African Americans: most famously, she provided illustrations for her friend Julia Peterkin's nonfictional study of the seacoast Gullah culture, *Roll,*

Figure 5.5 "Arlene McCarter, Basket and Fan Maker." (Item No. PH038-08-0931, Doris Ulmann Collection, Special Collections and University Archives, University of Oregon Libraries.)

Figure 5.6 "Anthony Lord, Blacksmith, in Leather Apron with Tools." (Item No. PH038-02-0113, Doris Ulmann Collection, Special Collections and University Archives, University of Oregon Libraries.)

Figure 5.7 "Clementine Douglas, Spinner, at the Wheel." (Item No. Ph038-10-1210, Doris Ulmann Collection, Special Collections and University Archives, University of Oregon Libraries.)

Figure 5.8 "Bristol Taylor, Dulcimer Maker, Farmer, Poet." (Item No. PH038-10-1172, Doris Ulmann Collection, Special Collections and University Archives, University of Oregon Libraries.)

Jordan, Roll (1934). Centered around the Gullah-descended residents of Peterkin's family plantation, Lang Syne, located near Fort Motte, South Carolina, the book is an early example of the illustrated documentary volumes that became a standard genre in the later 1930s.[30]

Given the times, and Peterkin's personal investment in Lang Syne, it is not surprising that her text posits this rural African American community as wholly content in its preindustrialism, "hold[ing] fast to the old ways and beliefs acquired by their forefathers" and "deplor[ing] the foolishness of discarding" what is "gleaned through generations of experience." Without the distractions of machines, reading material, or radio and cinema, she writes, these rural laborers are able "to develop faculties of mind and heart and to acquire the ancient wisdom of their race."[31] Ulmann's accompanying photographs, many of which are hauntingly beautiful, depict the Lang Syne residents in their work and religious rituals as well as in more leisure moments; whether or not they primarily support Peterkin's perspective or offer an alternative one has been open to debate.

The publication of *Roll, Jordan, Roll* was greeted with enthusiasm by such prominent African Americans as Walter White, secretary of the National Association for the Advancement of Colored People, and poet and novelist James Weldon Johnson, though subsequent critical responses have been mixed.[32] Recently, Nicholas Natanson has dismissed both Peterkin's text and Ulmann's photographs as taking merely a "celebratory approach to black rustics" that has less to do with reality than with an imagined "agrarian idyll." Others, however, have argued that Ulmann's illustrations evade the "patronizing quality of Peterkin's text" and depict Gullah culture in a manner that resists both the iconography of noble savagery and Peterkin's tendency to validate "the psychological security of plantation existence."[33] Certainly Ulmann's several images of a chain gang, watched over by an armed white guard and suggesting invidious levels of surveillance and control, signify beyond Peterkin's breezy, one-line explanation that such convicts simply failed to pay their taxes. And Ulmann's portrait of an old man, whom Peterkin craftily presents as defeated not only by natural circumstances (boll weevils, the drowning of his children) but also by drink and voodoo, testifies not merely to dispossession but, given the state of his clothing, to abject poverty and even degradation (fig. 5.9), which only seems more pointed in comparison to Peterkin's attempted folksiness ("He would have died from pure worryation except for the little whiskey he drank now and then to cheer himself up").[34] The extended relation in this latter case between Peterkin's lengthy commentary and Ulmann's photograph is, however, unusual; more often than not, Ulmann's images serve as general illustrations that float relatively free of direct reference in the text. That they dovetail with Peterkin's narrative less precisely than they might tends to support the notion that Ulmann's photographs constitute

Figure 5.9 From *Roll, Jordan, Roll.* (Collections of the South Carolina Historical Society. Image courtesy of the Snite Museum of Art, University of Notre Dame.)

a separate vision of this culture, one that is not always or necessarily a complement to Peterkin's.

But Ulmann's photographs of African Americans were not restricted to those at Lang Syne, and her race attitudes are perhaps better illuminated through broader comparisons of her white versus black imagery, especially where portraiture is concerned. Of course, some critics find Ulmann's portraits of African Americans quite distinct from those, for instance, of her white mountaineers. Judith Fryer Davidov argues that Ulmann's Gullah subjects, unlike her Appalachian ones, appear subtly to resist Ulmann's efforts at intimacy: the resulting portraits are "disquieting," Davidov argues, testifying to a "compelling and disturbing" tension between the photographer and her subjects.[35] If this is true, then at the very least it reaffirms the significance of Ulmann's presentness while in the act of taking pictures. I would argue, however, that Ulmann's portraits of African Americans and those of poor whites seem more noteworthy for their similarities than their differences. Specifically, most of them are framed relatively tightly, minimizing telltale background aspects and directing the viewer's vision to the expressiveness of the individual body, and especially the face. The shot is never taken from above or below (angles that manipulate the viewer's perspective, and that were used famously in rural photography by Dorothea

Figure 5.10 "Elderly woman with bowl." (Item No. PH038-09-1134, Doris Ulmann Collection, Special Collections and University Archives, University of Oregon Libraries.)

Figure 5.11 "African-American woman in big straw hat." (Item No. PH038-13-1606, Doris Ulmann Collection, Special Collections and University Archives, University of Oregon Libraries.)

Lange and Margaret Bourke-White); rather, the camera meets its subject straight on, at medium height, imparting quiet regard. The consistency of Ulmann's approach is striking, and side-by-side examples point toward a respectful equality of status among blacks and whites in Ulmann's vision (figs. 5.10 and 5.11). This is true even in Ulmann's most artfully rendered images: figures 5.12 and 5.13, for example, strive through luminous lighting and compositional balance to reveal the grace of their respective subjects. It would appear that Ulmann, whom some have impugned for failing to account for the realities of modern industrialism, also failed to register prevailing racial hierarchies, preferring to photograph her racially diverse subjects in ways that suggested their deep similarities as dignified human beings.

Ulmann's photographic style is not documentary, if by that term we acknowledge an ultimately pragmatic motive to move individuals, and hence institutions, to effect material change in the lives of those represented. Yet Ulmann shared with overt documentarians a desire to depict those on the very fringes of American modernity, even if she did so with the deliberate intention of elevating them rather than

Figure 5.12 From *Roll, Jordan, Roll.* (Collections of the South Carolina Historical Society. Image courtesy of the Snite Museum of Art, University of Notre Dame.)

Figure 5.13 Girl carrying a crock, published in *Handicrafts of the Southern Highlands*. (LC-USZ62–53627, Library of Congress Prints and Photographs Division.)

attempting to substantiate their full "realities." And while her photographs were not conducive to mass-market reproduction, they were nonetheless exhibited broadly in pictorialist and settlement school circles and reached the public through influential books such as *Roll, Jordan, Roll* and Allen Eaton's *Handicrafts of the Southern Highlands* (published after Ulmann's death). Thus Ulmann was an instrumental figure in establishing and sustaining rurality as part of the modern visual-cultural chronicle of America, a role that required her to travel far in both literal and figurative terms. The photographs themselves testify to the success of this stylish urbanite's improbable social transactions with the remote, the inconspicuous, and the poor; they also memorialize a sensitive, often exquisite vision.

Marion Post and the Alienated Rural Body

By the time Marion Post died in 1990, having returned to serious photography in her later years, her Depression-era work had begun to attract long-overdue attention. Several critics reconsidered not only her three-year stint as principal photographer in the Historical Section of the Farm Security Administration but also her abrupt withdrawal from the professional realm following her marriage in 1941 to Lee Wolcott, assistant to the secretary of agriculture. (Not incidentally, the couple farmed for the first ten years of their marriage.) Two insistent questions haunt these recovery projects: First, why was Post's work largely overshadowed by that of her FSA colleagues, and second, why did this modern young woman, who clearly had an adventurous streak and a discerning eye, abandon her vocation to follow her husband's career? Apologists for Post seem compelled to redeem her for modernism in both personal and professional terms, as if in marrying Wolcott she somehow repudiated not just her photography but her "feminist" self.[36] Yet her brief Depression-era career offers insight into the pressures faced by female photographers of the time, as well as the internal conflicts generated by the demands of accommodating one's own perceptions to the requirements of a government agency. Moreover, Post's life following her FSA involvement hardly invalidates this high point of her photographic vision: regardless of her subsequent choices—which may partly explain her relative anonymity when compared with Lange, Walker Evans, or Arthur Rothstein, who remained active photographers—Post's participation in what might be called the national documentation of rurality stands the test of time.[37]

When Post first joined the FSA in 1938—the only woman granted a full-time appointment—she was twenty-eight years old and relatively untested professionally; she soon proved her mettle, however, by taking on long, arduous research trips through regions that were unfamiliar and occasionally unfriendly. In some cases, Post traversed the exact same isolated country roads that Doris Ulmann had traveled several years earlier.[38] But unlike Ulmann's, Post's aesthetic seems fresh and forward-looking for the time: the more than 5,000 photos that Post took for the FSA showcase not only a classic documentary style, featuring candid shots and unmanipulated lighting, but also an edgy, intelligent, sharp-witted perspective. And this perspective was clearly her own. Despite continuing controversy over the extent to which FSA director Roy Stryker controlled his photographers by, for instance, distributing shooting agendas, which some claim resulted in a uniformity of vision within the FSA archive, there seems little question that individual photographers maintained their distinctive outlooks. What makes Post especially noteworthy is the extent to which she veered from, rather than fully complied with, Stryker's directives. While critics have argued that Lange, for instance, shared fully in Stryker's vision,[39] Post evinced a more oblique relation to official mandates, never wholly refuting them but always supplementing them with angles decidedly her own. Her unique response to the plight of Depression-era rural citizens is inscribed not only through her choice of shots, but also through her letters to Stryker and such details as her captioning practices.

Post was well prepared philosophically for the FSA project: her education had encouraged both social conscience and independence of mind. She was heavily influenced by her mother, Nan Post, a registered nurse who worked with Margaret Sanger to establish birth control clinics throughout the country. The young Marion Post spent her teenage years with her divorced mother in Greenwich Village, immersed in progressive politics and avant-garde aesthetics, and was for a while a serious student of dance with pioneering movement specialists Ruth St. Denis and Doris Humphreys. She came to photography accidentally, while in Germany studying child psychology and education, and was initially drawn to the workers' photography movement, which focused on quotidian concerns and subjects. Back in the United States, she combined her new interest in photography with her radical sensibilities by photographing, among other things, the activities of the Group Theatre, dedicated to a collective acting approach and a direct response to the times. An auspicious introduction to Ralph Steiner and participation in his informal photo workshops led to Post's involvement with *People of the Cumberlands,* a pro-union documentary film project spearheaded by Steiner and Elia Kazan, for which Post created promotional photographs. Post's talent, nurtured by Steiner, was also noted by his colleague Paul Strand: both photographers recommended Post to Roy Stryker.

With this background, it is not surprising that Post became, according to one critic, "as partisan a documentarian as anyone who claimed the title in the 1930s."[40] Initially, she was assigned to broaden and deepen the FSA file by documenting New Deal successes, which would balance out the images of rural indigence created by Lange, Evans, and Rothstein (all of whom had preceded Post in the agency) and help to justify a continued flow of resources into New Deal social programs. But Stryker had also expanded his documentary vision to include the creation of, more generally, an "intellectually respectable" chronicle of 1930s America; hence he also wanted photographs that moved beyond poverty, and even beyond rurality.[41] Post readily conformed to these prescripts, as her personal file demonstrates. Her FSA images include large numbers of workmanlike responses to Stryker's pro–New Deal injunctions, including, for example, serial shots of rural agents teaching locals how to make and install screen doors, and of smiling resettlement families in front of their newly built, sanitary homes. Her images of small-town New England and of middle- and upper-class vacationers on the Florida coast, as well as her landscapes, also helped to fulfill Stryker's dream of creating a national photographic record of the era. Thus much of Post's FSA work is upbeat, reinforcing government perspectives, generating enthusiasm for already existing programs, and, as Post herself later recalled, "documenting America [as] the land of fertility, abundance, beauty."[42]

But Post did not confine herself to these assignments. On the contrary, she departed from them freely and productively, generally with Stryker's blessing, and it is in her digressions that we see most fully her unique aesthetic sensibility and her sharp social criticism. One prominent feature of Post's less scripted FSA work is its emphasis on corporeality: her most arresting photographs hinge on a hyperawareness of the body as a sign of social dislocation—broken, excessive, disaffected. This aspect was largely dependent, of course, on a manufactured distance from her subjects that allowed her to focus on surface details—the precise opposite of Ulmann's relational emphasis. Hence Post's perspective on rurality was fundamentally at odds with Ulmann's, and far less vulnerable to charges of sentimentality. If Ulmann was primarily concerned with depicting rural dignity through a symbolism of integration (of the body and the products of its labor, for example, or of body and setting), then Post's preoccupation was with the rural body's estrangement: in many of her works, the rural corpus is fractured, isolated, or somehow made foreign, a sign of not only its difference but also its alienation from mainstream American culture.

A favorite site for Post was the regional fair or festival, where carnivalesque attractions show up the body as cultural display. More than a hundred photographs taken on midways at county fairs in Florida, Tennessee, Kentucky, and West Virginia evidence Post's sly wit and her knack for condensed cultural commentary. The stale fascinations of physical grotesquerie create a fruitful tension in many of these images. For instance, Post highlights oversized banners advertising the "Double Sex Person," the "Kentucky Cave Man," or "Dolly Dimples," the fat lady, while comparatively diminutive hucksters or patrons occupy her photographs' foregrounds, implicitly challenging the extremity of the banners' claims while also testifying to the apparent allure of the specimens enshrined beyond, and hence to a subtle link between the attractions and their audiences (see, e.g., fig. 5.14). In one image, a banner promising to "Expos[e] Birth Control" hangs beside another promoting "The Man without a Skull—ALIVE," intimating that real-life bodily concerns become distorted in the carnival context, trivialized or sensationalized in humorous and not-so-humorous ways (fig. 5.15). Some carnival photographs enlarge upon their own inherent specularity: as we stare, for instance, at the upturned faces of coal miners who are in turn gazing at trapeze artists or posters of scantily clothed women, our own voyeurism—urban, middle-class, sophisticated—is necessarily underscored (fig. 5.16). In the aggregate, these images resonate with the work of other Depression-era artists such as Reginald Marsh, whose paintings of Coney Island and New York's burlesque houses are similarly concerned with materiality, commodification, and the power of the gaze.

Figure 5.14 "Plant City, Florida, strawberry festival and carnival." (LC USF33-030477-M4, Library of Congress Prints and Photographs Division.)

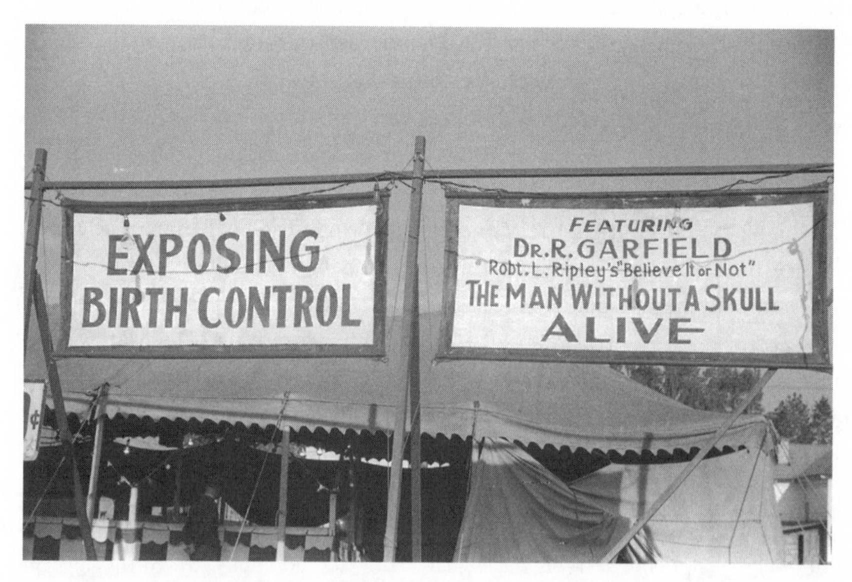

Figure 5.15 "Plant City, Florida, strawberry festival and carnival." (LC-USF33-030474-M2, Library of Congress Prints and Photographs Division.)

Figure 5.16 "Coal miner's sons watch aerial trapeze artists at outdoor carnival. Large event and only outdoor amusement during year. Granville, West Virginia." (LC USF34-050280-E, Library of Congress Prints and Photographs Division.)

Like Marsh's, virtually all of Post's carnival or festival images, even those that merely capture the absurdity of middle-class amusement seekers posing in outlandish costumes, achieve a heightened sense of the physical body as cultural spectacle.

Post's deep and often ironic awareness of the body's power to signify comes into play most effectively, however, in her photographs of rural destitution. To be sure, her FSA file contains dozens of prints in which people are entirely absent, though their absence is often made oddly palpable: in particular, her numerous images of tumbledown houses and shacks are especially poignant, gesturing as they do to the stunted lives, and bodies, of those who live in them (fig. 5.17).[43] But her photos of desperately deprived individuals—often uncentered, and frequently unposed—are generally more startling, suggesting a populace caught off guard. They feature bodies heavily marked in various ways: by overwork, by malnutrition, or by racial imprints that help to sustain segregation and economic marginalization. At times the role of the camera in capturing these bodies is visibly called into question. One of her more frequently reproduced photographs, for example, is of the torso of an African American tenant farmer tilted back on a rickety chair, gesturing with a hand that is missing two fingers. The skewed angle of the image, and the way the subject's head is cut off by the photograph's frame, make the camera complicit in his dismemberment (fig. 5.18). Other images exploit multiple dimensions of social-corporeal containment. Post's complementary photographs of white and black farmers sleeping in separate "camp rooms" as they await the selling of their tobacco, for instance, offer a doubled sense of restriction through first, the contours of cramped bodies and second, the politics of segregation. That we have stolen upon these figures, unaware, implicates us in their deprivations as well (figs. 5.19 and 5.20).

Perhaps most penetrating are Post's photographs of afflicted children, whom she often depicts alone, without adults, as if to underscore their assailability. In one photograph, two African American children, one obviously with rickets, seem swallowed by a dry, tired landscape, including a house that appears to be empty; these figures, the photo seems to say, are besieged by their circumstances, which they battle without guidance or protection (fig. 5.21). In other images the play of children among garbage, or in dirty creeks, or on sets of ravaged stairs reiterates the vulnerability of their thinly clad bodies, already compromised by poverty, and suggests that they inhabit a physically dangerous world, largely apart from their parents. In photos of children, too, Post's grim irony often emerges, as when she captures a filthy young girl on a bed, symbolically overshadowed by the image of a chubby baby on a calendar pinned to the bare wall behind her, or when a toddler is shown forcing his way into his dilapidated home through the "cat hole," toy gun in hand (figs. 5.22, 5.23).

Like Post's images of broken or contorted adults, these photographs contribute to a comprehensive vision of the poor rural-southern body as damaged, demeaned, or threatened. While more famous FSA photographs, such as Dorothea Lange's Madonna-like "Migrant Mother," may mute immediate physical circumstances in favor of universalizing effects,[44] Post's photographs of rural privation force an insistent and continuous awareness of corporeal abasement. They emphasize the inescapable singularity of the material body, refusing to allow the represented to take on the metaphoric contours of Everyman. And if the photographs themselves are newly consumable commodities, they nonetheless challenge any sense of the bodies depicted as expendable, since they so often refuse containment by their own frames. Those that gesture beyond themselves—to other images or contexts, or to us as viewers—are particularly powerful, as they indict a larger world that must be understood as collaborating in their subjects' degradation.

Figure 5.17 "Typical old tenant's house with bedding being aired and sunned. Coffee County, Alabama." (LC-USF34-051394-D, Library of Congress Prints and Photographs Division.)

Figure 5.18 "Old Negro, near Camden, Alabama, clothes and shoes badly worn." (LC-USF33-030350-M4, Library of Congress Prints and Photographs Division.)

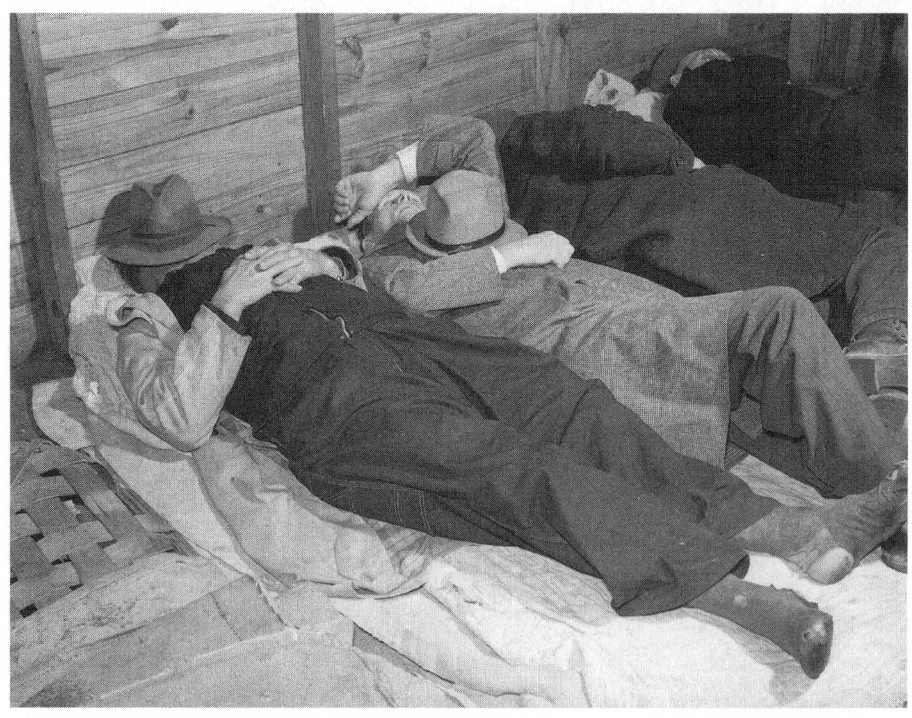

Significantly, Post's own body—female, attractive, young—was at issue in her work for the FSA, which suggestively extends for us her photographic preoccupations and may indeed have played a part in forming them. Post's professional situation as a single woman traveling without a male companion (the only one in the agency to do so) raised questions of propriety to which Roy Stryker, as her boss, was constantly attuned. Her demeanor while in the field was a regular topic of Stryker's letters, in which he urged Post not to roam alone after dark, cautioned her against drawing too much attention to herself, and even chided her for dressing inappropriately. ("The closer you keep to what the great back-country recognizes as the normal dress for women," Stryker insisted, "the better you are going to succeed as a photographer.")[45] Post viewed Stryker's strict standards for her behavior as chauvinistic, but she also knew that society was on Stryker's side; this was made abundantly clear in press accounts that described her as a "comely young girl photographer" and suggested that "her looks are against her. She is too pretty and young looking to be taken seriously."[46] Hence Post generally abided by Stryker's rules, recognizing that her professional opportunities, especially in the conservative South, frequently depended on her inconspicuousness, including her conformity to certain gendered norms.

But she did not accept such strictures in silence. On the contrary, her return letters to Stryker contain irreverent and forthright responses to his directives. When Stryker suggested that she wear only skirts, she insisted on the practicality of pants, writing, "My slacks are dark blue, old, dirty, and not too tight—OK? To be worn with great discrimination, sir."[47] She also used her wit to deflect Stryker's anxieties, revealing her astute grasp of his particular apprehensions where she was concerned:

> Chief Stryker! Calling all cars. Caution all photogs! Never take picture of pregnant woman sitting in rocking chair on sloping lawn while visiting family on Sunday afternoon! Consequences are—lady doesn't want photograph taken in present state, starts hurriedly to get up & run in house, but chair tips over backwards dumping (& embarrassing, not seriously damaging) her. Photog is surprised, sorry, tries to apologize, inquire after victim's health, etc., etc., & succeeds only in

Figure 5.19 (***opposite, top***) "Farmers sleeping in Negro camp room in warehouse. They often must remain overnight or several days before their tobacco is auctioned. Several of them are using an old tobacco basket for a pillow. Durham, North Carolina." (LC-USF34-052830-D, Library of Congress Prints and Photographs Division.)

Figure 5.20 (***opposite, bottom***) "Farmers sleeping in white camp room in warehouse. They often must remain overnight or several days before their tobacco is auctioned. Durham, North Carolina." (LC-USF34- 052784-D, Library of Congress Prints and Photographs Division.)

Figure 5.21 "Negro children and old home on badly eroded land near Wadesboro, North Carolina." (LC-USF34-050720-E, Library of Congress Prints and Photographs Division.)

> almost being mobbed & beaten & driven off by irate & resentful & peace loving members of family—DOZENS of them. (P.S.—Camera was saved.)[48]

Post repeatedly used her letters to Stryker as an outlet for some of her frustrations in the field, many of which were created or exacerbated by her age and gender, and as a means of nudging him to see things a little more her way, to expand his outlook to include sympathy for a modern professional woman forced to observe genteel standards. Though she found Stryker an excellent boss in many respects,[49] Post chafed at his gendered perspectives throughout her tenure with the FSA.

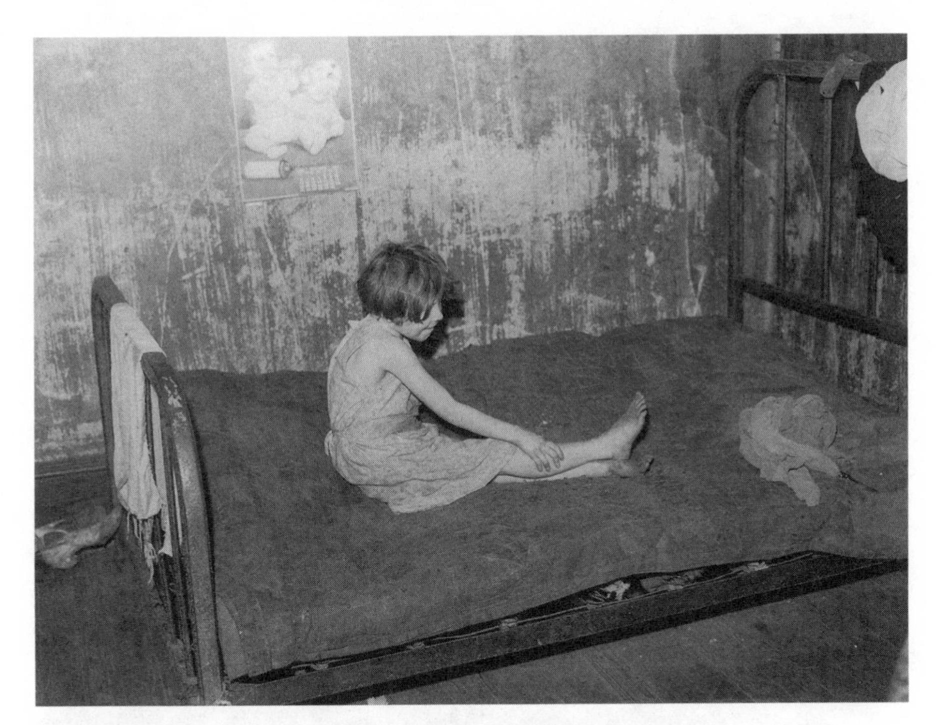

Figure 5.22 "Child in miners boarding house. Mohegan, West Virginia." (LC-USF34-050112-D, Library of Congress Prints and Photographs Division.)

Perhaps this explains some of her more unexpected shots. Post's photography offered another, more oblique outlet through which to challenge Stryker's emphasis on seemliness, and she fully exploited her opportunities to do so: certain images point to her willingness to violate social boundaries, even as they continue to demonstrate her interest in the materiality of the body. Post's up-close photographs of couples dancing in African American juke joints, for example, reveal her eagerness to venture beyond the predictable settings; they also record her success in gaining entry to sequestered spaces and access to moments of physical release. Even more transgressive is Post's photograph of a fully naked miner in a makeshift shower, an image that evidences Post's daring and obviously challenges the parameters of acceptable behavior for Post set by Stryker—who, as McEuen points out, must have been shocked by it (fig. 5.24).[50] Post's straightforward caption—"Miner takes shower, which he built in the cellar of his home"—offers no sense of irony or of the unexpected, though it tantalizes with its lack of information as to how Post managed to get such a shot. (A related image, less extraordinary but still surprisingly intimate, shows a miner on his knees, washing his head in a tub.)[51] Critics have also pointed

Figure 5.23 "Why open the door, coal miner's child uses the 'cat hole.' Bertha Hill, West Virginia. (Note pipe in one hand, gun in other)." (LC-USF34-050348-E, Library of Congress Prints and Photographs Division.)

out Post's tendency to lend an erotic dimension to some of her female subjects, in contrast to the emphasis on women's maternity stressed by other FSA photographers.[52] If Stryker wanted an expansion of the FSA file, Post certainly gave it to him, but perhaps in ways that he may not have anticipated.

Post also created images that, while continuing to focus on grinding rural poverty and on the signification of the body, appear to comment specifically on the hazards of femininity. This particular strain of Post's vision reveals how her photography could transcend its immediate settings to encompass larger social issues; it may also constitute another response to that hyperawareness of her womanhood evinced by Stryker and the public in general. One of Post's most unsettling photographs in this regard is of a pair of shabbily dressed little girls sitting on a dirty

Figure 5.24 "Miner takes shower, which he built in the cellar of his home. Westover, West Virginia." (LC-USF34-050289-E, Library of Congress Prints and Photographs Division.)

bed, the surrounding walls of the room papered with Corn Flakes wrappers; two dolls, hanging directly above them, are almost completely decapitated by the photograph's frame, and their feet are tied together with string. In this image, the common practice of hanging treasured items from the ceiling or walls so as to protect them from the filth of the main living space becomes a suggestive commentary on the thwarted lives of these two female children, who seem to share metaphorically in the dolls' abasement (fig. 5.25). Yet the photograph is also richly layered, for this overtly progressive symbolism is subtly undercut: one of the girls defies us with her forthright gaze, as if to suggest that Post's photograph, and our readings of it, cannot hem her in. Like Post herself, perhaps, this child seems to tell us that she is no fragile doll.

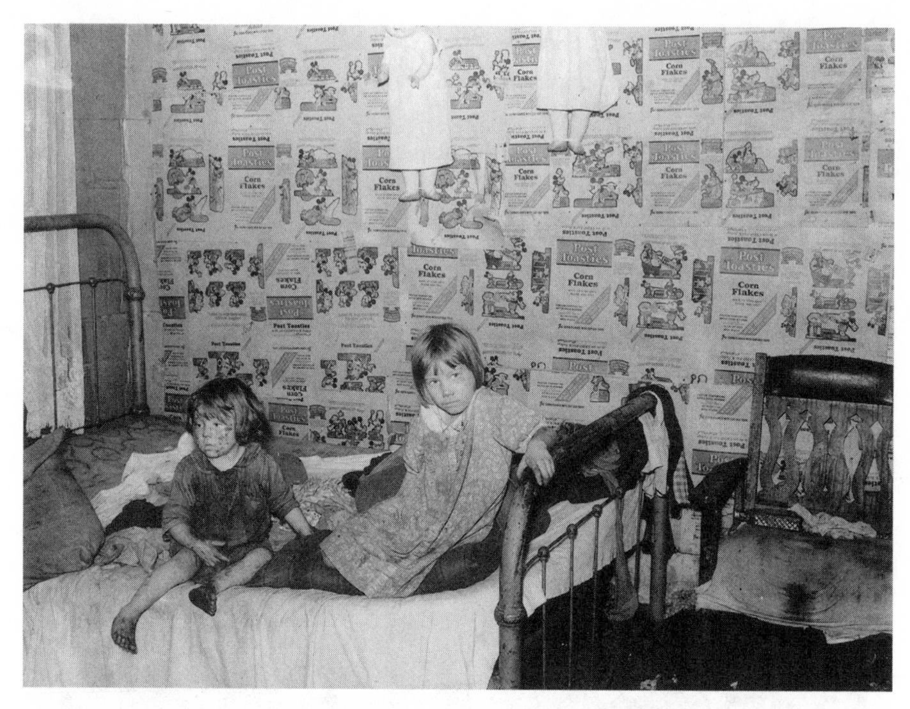

Figure 5.25 "Children in bedroom of their home, Charleston, West Virginia. Their mother has TB. Father works on WPA (Works Progress Administration)." (LC-USF34-050119-D, Library of Congress Prints and Photographs Division.)

As with the corporeal grotesquerie of the carnival scene, dolls seem provocative to Post, perhaps for their figurative potential as models of human physicality and because of their apparent incongruity in poor rural settings, where the concept of a toy, or of imitative domesticity, seems almost absurd. And of course, dolls call forth an entire semiotics of femininity. Hence Post's image of Kewpie dolls for sale alongside a rural highway, overshadowed by a billboard advertisement that uses the male physique as a symbol for Gulf No-Nox Ethyl (fig. 5.26), is at once humorous and sarcastic, a play on gendered de/constructions of power. And her photograph of a child bathing her doll, face down, in a battered tub, both figures filthy, mocks the notions of homemaking that structure expectations of family life, especially of womanhood, and yet are impossible to attain in the context of rural destitution (fig. 5.27). Similarly, in a haunting image, a clean and carefully made bed with a doll placed neatly upon it seems out of place in a room of mud walls partially obscured by a mismatched assortment of fashion advertisements, calendars, a Coca-Cola sign, and a single framed image of a woman (presumably a relative of the French mulattoes to whom the home belongs). The artificiality of the doll and the desperate attempts at

Figure 5.26 "Kewpie dolls bathing girls for sale along main highway near Charleston, West Virginia." (LC-USF33-030270-M2, Library of Congress Prints and Photographs Division.)

Figure 5.27 "Child of migratory packinghouse workers. Belle Glade, Florida." (LC-USF33-030480-M3, Library of Congress Prints and Photographs Division.)

decoration indicated by the surrounding pictures and cultural icons make us even more painfully cognizant of the human hands, almost certainly female, that lavish attention on this meager but affecting domestic space (fig. 5.28).

Yet another doll, in another image, is clutched by a child whom the caption tells us is "of mixed-breed Indian, white, Negro." While this particular photograph is rather blurred and not well composed, it nonetheless reminds us of the normativizing role of dolls in setting physical standards, which can be met neither by the desperately poor nor by those whose racial markings make them cultural outsiders. What opens up the photograph's interpretive intricacies is the caption, informing us of the child's racial heritage (otherwise unclear) and thus contrasting her with the white doll, which appears to be commercially made. This raises the importance of Post's captioning practices, which sometimes evidence her irony or outrage,[53] and which frequently draw attention to racial or ethnic categories that enhance the resonances of her images. In addition to "Negroes," Post's captions frequently mention "mulattoes," "mixed breeds," and "Indians," as well as using descriptors such as

Figure 5.28 "Melrose, Natchitoches Parish, Louisiana. Bedroom of home built by old French mulatto family. The walls of the house are of mud, the floors bare ground, dirt and a few bricks. Belongs to Zeline and Joe Rocque." (LC-USF34-054677-D, Library of Congress Prints and Photographs Division.)

"Bohemian," "Spanish," "Mexican," and "French"—classifications that are not always visually obvious. While Post's descriptive precision may be partly ascribed to the documentary ethos of the FSA photography project, Stryker appears to have given few directions about photographing social diversity; rather, it seems that Post herself was interested in these categorizations, perhaps because they lend dimension to the circumstances of her pictured subject(s).[54] Specifically, since the vast majority of photographs bearing such descriptors also evidence rural poverty, Post seems subtly to underscore the link between deprivation and racial or ethnic marginalization. Some of the poorest rural bodies, she seems to suggest, may be doubly marked: first by their cultural otherness, and then by the hardship resulting from lives lived on the social and economic periphery.

The many ways that Post interested herself in materiality, in the physical body and its circumstances, offer a distinct contrast to Ulmann's works, as well as to the works of other FSA photographers. Her rural subjects are not idealized, but neither are they presented as pathetic or depraved; indeed, Post's photography appears to eschew such ideational concepts altogether and instead focuses on a rurality that is profoundly, adamantly embodied. Uninterested in agrarianism as an imagined escape from the brutalities of industrialism, Post was determined to show that rural life in the poorer sectors inflicts a brutality of its own. And her genuine concern for those wounded by it extended beyond the specular: she did not fail, for instance, to register her criticisms of ineffective New Deal programs to Stryker or other government administrators. In Post's vision, the rural South and its "primitiveness" could not be construed as a recaptured realm of integrity and authenticity; rather, it marked a tragic failure to bring the disadvantaged into the fold of modernity and progress.

Yet the differences between Post and Ulmann should not blind us to their similarities, and hence to the reasons for their inclusion in this study. Though taking very different tacks, and operating within quite different generational and aesthetic contexts, they both approached rurality with activist purpose and a compassionate eye. Moreover, they enacted their own modernism through their engagement with the rural other. That other, once familiar, had begun to take on the qualities of something exotic in the swiftly developing urban-commercial culture of the early twentieth century, and Post and Ulmann took seriously the responsibilities associated with, in John Tagg's phrase, the burden of photographic representation.[55] They recognized the power they wielded through the production and dissemination of images, even as they remained fascinated by the rural subjects who helped them to create their finest work. As Marion Post once wrote from the field to Roy Stryker: "I continue to be startled and shocked and amazed, no matter what I've expected."[56] Both Post's and Ulmann's photographs might prompt us to say the same.

Epilogue
On Heartlands and Borderlands

In 1935 The painter Grant Wood published a tract entitled *Revolt against the City*, in which he identified a "new regionalism" in the arts. (A celebrated regionalist himself, Wood was already famous for his painting *American Gothic* [1930], an ironic image of a farm couple that was destined to become iconic as well.) Citing fellow painter Thomas Hart Benton and dramatists Paul Green and Jack Kirkland, among others, Wood pointed out that the "distinctively rural districts" of the Midwest and the southern "provinces" were being increasingly mined for their source material. According to Wood, this aesthetic shift was owing to the Depression, which prompted Americans to turn from the disillusioning urban-commercial realm toward that which is "true and fundamental" as well as "distinctively ours to use and exploit." The "old frontier virtues," representing an authentic American spirit, he argued, were being newly invoked as an antidote to the imitative aspects of the "colonial" (i.e., urban eastern) mind-set, with the result that "American village and country life" was providing the inspiration for an "indigenous art" that was not merely picturesque but rigorously native. Wood even went so far as to imply that the farmer, that quintessential American figure whose struggle with natural forces is the very stuff of art, should be grateful for this turn of events: being naturally inexpressive, Wood claimed, "the farmer *needs* interpretation" (my emphasis).[1]

Patronizing attitudes aside, Wood's rhetorical manipulation of the rural-urban binary is, of course, familiar: even if the particular forms of regionalism he describes were in some ways new (a dubious point), then the artists' "revolt" against urbanity certainly was not. To be sure, in *The Country and the City* (1973), Marxist critic Raymond Williams traces the persistence of rural nostalgia as a cultural mode, one that originated in ancient times and remains vital today. But Williams argues that the "backward reference" of a frequently unlocalized literary pastoralism is not primarily about a lost history. "What is really significant," he asserts, "is this particular kind of reaction to the fact of change." In other words, the details of the rural evocation matter less than the act itself, the imaginative re/turn to a "natural" social order that appears to counter a more unpredictable present. For Williams, focusing on English tradition, the broadly feudal and postfeudal values idealized in the pastoral, representing "settled and reciprocal social and economic relations," frequently operate as a critique of a burgeoning capitalism, of "the utilitarian reduction of all social relationships to a crude moneyed order."[2] Writing forty years earlier and in an American context, Wood exemplifies Williams's point, for he, too, is invested in a retreat from the corruptions of an urban market economy, the dangers of which are symbolized for him by the crash of 1929. His "new regionalism," then—another version of Williams's pastoralism—is hardly original, nor is it fundamentally about the past.

But Wood's comments are noteworthy for other reasons. For example, in articulating a recentering of what was formerly the center of American life—"values" that are "chiefly non-urban"[3]—Wood acknowledges the reshuffling of centers and margins that makes for ongoing cultural renewal. This study has concerned itself largely with that reshuffling, and with the related idea that American rurality in the period between 1900 and 1940 could occupy two locations at once. Pushed to the borderlands of consideration by a modern urban-industrial hegemony, rurality nonetheless retained its status as a kind of heartland of the cultural imaginary. Its simultaneous marginality and centrality, I have argued, offered rich opportunities for strategic responses to the modern condition. This was especially true for women, whose shifting patterns of labor and leisure inspired an exploitation of country settings and concerns that was decidedly modern-minded, and not limited to a romantic agrarianism.

Perhaps this is why they are not mentioned by Wood. It hardly needs saying that Wood's 1930s celebration of a "new" regional inclination in American arts and letters largely ignores the earlier achievements of numerous women (and some men) whose works apparently did not suit Wood's notion of regionalism, or of art. (For that matter, Williams's critical analysis of pastoralism is not much different, as it draws on a canon that is exclusively male.) Perhaps Wood dismissed the aesthetic expressions of many rural-oriented women in the early twentieth century as cloyingly sentimental, assuming that they reduced the rugged potential of the heartland to hackneyed affairs of the heart. Or perhaps they were deemed unworthy because they embodied social critiques that obscured or challenged the fundamentally affectionate agrarian vision that defined the work of Wood himself and the male cohorts he extolled.[4] We can only guess. What is certain, though, is that the regionalist "heart" with which Wood is concerned is not merely about geography; it is also about artistic status.

As a concept, then, "heartland" is useful because it helps to structure issues of canonicity, even as it also limns a complex of ideas related to rurality and agrarianism. The heartlands and borderlands of representation, the centers and margins of culture, have been at issue in this study, which calls into question, among other things, rhetorical uses of rurality that have misrepresented the roles and attitudes of rural women; literary-critical histories that have overlooked certain types of texts; and notions of modernism/modernity that have privileged the city. My preoccupation with the noncanonical, the less familiar texts and contexts, therefore, reflects a desire to illuminate the received periphery in order to reimagine various centers. But it is also to acknowledge that the centers can shift, and that the key questions—who speaks? who represents? who interprets?—are always subject to renewed scrutiny from a variety of vantage points. Further consideration of women, modernity, and rurality will, I hope, result in responsive future projects that are beyond the scope of my work here, in which others may offer new and different answers to those queries.

Raymond Williams reminds us of the importance of historicizing rural nostalgia, which, he asserts, is the result in different ages of different problems and motivations. In thinking through the relations among women, an American agrarian ideal, and the onset of modern urban industrialism, I have tried to keep his injunction in mind. But of course I have been far less interested than Williams is in pastoralism per se—if by that we mean, as he does, a romanticized evocation of a lost rural innocence. Instead, I have found more intriguing Patricia Yaeger's reminder that "[p]astoral always happens at someone's expense."[5] The women discussed herein—real and imaginary—are *modern* precisely insofar as they refuse to accept the containment of the pastoral category, of the agrarian ideal. To historicize them properly is necessarily to interrogate the ideal itself.

NOTES

Introduction

1. Two recent and excellent examples are Harding's *Writing the City* and Yablon's "The Metropolitan Life in Ruins."

2. North offers a superb discussion of gendered responses to Cather's *One of Ours* in chapter 5 of *Reading 1922;* the quotation is from p. 179. See also North's introduction, p. 3, for Gilbert Seldes's explanation of the "modern spirit" that was constructed as antithetical to Cather's work.

3. Discussions of Cather's oblique relation to modernism include Rose, "Modernism: The Case of Willa Cather," and Thompson, *Influencing America's Tastes* (especially chap. 5, which provides a brief overview of similar critical contexts).

4. The word is Cather's own. See her *Not under Forty,* v.

5. Strauss, "Ideas of a Plain Country Woman," *Ladies' Home Journal* 24 (Dec. 1907): 38; 27 (Feb. 1910): 30; and 26 (Dec. 1909): 36. Some of Strauss's early columns were collected in a 1908 book entitled *The Ideas of a Plain Country Woman.* For more on Strauss's life and writings, see Boomhower, *The Country Contributor.*

6. On Curtis's efforts to market the *Ladies' Home Journal* as a middle-class magazine, see the first chapter of Steinberg's *Reformer in the Marketplace.* On the Curtis building in Philadelphia, see *A Short History of the* Ladies' Home Journal. When *Progressive Farmer* polled its readers concerning their favorite magazines, *Ladies' Home Journal* was third out of the twelve periodicals most frequently mentioned (14 Jan. 1919). Margaret Jarman Hagood reported that in the late 1930s, *Ladies' Home Journal* was one of the very few mainstream magazines occasionally seen in the homes of the poorest tenant farmers (*Mothers of the South,* 70).

7. Scanlon, *Inarticulate Longings,* 98–103.

8. On the *Ladies' Home Journal*'s efforts to position itself in response to modernity, and especially to the shifting gender paradigms of modern consumer culture, see Scanlon's introduction.

9. See especially the six-month period between January and June 1915, when "The Ideas of a Plain Country Woman" was suggestively appositioned to a column entitled "A Daughter of Today"—both appearing under the overall banner "The Ideas of Two Women." That the Country Contributor's voice and perspectives are rather contrived is similarly suggested in remarks about her job: "I do my work as those who hire me to do it wish it done—or they get somebody else. It is just business, pure and simple, as all transactions of work and wage should be" (July 1915, 22).

10. Santmyer, "A Pageant of Sisterhood." This was reprinted in *Rural Manhood* with an accompanying note stating its availability as a separate pamphlet disseminated by the Young Women's Christian Association.

11. Michael Denning suggests that the success of *Grapes* hinged on its dual exploitation of documentary and sentimentality, and on its symbolic deployment of narrative motion and implied resolution—especially appealing for a culture immobilized by the Depression. See *The Cultural Front,* chap. 7. On the tension between stasis and change as a characteristic concern of Depression-era literature and art, see my "(Left) Contexts and Considerations."

12. Classic formulations of the relations between nature and American identity include Miller, *Nature's Nation;* Smith, *Virgin Land;* and Marx, *The Machine in the Garden.* Annette Kolodny's *The Lay of the Land* is the standard study of the connection of these tropes to the oppression of women. Other books that link romanticization of nature in the United States to the effacement of marginal groups include Slotkin's *Regeneration through Violence* and Norwood's *Made from This Earth.*

13. Jardine, *Gynesis;* Gilbert and Gubar, *No Man's Land;* Huyssen, *After the Great Divide.* Recent studies that pluralize approaches to the modern by resisting previously posited historical narratives of its development and/or by incorporating "nonaesthetic" disciplinary perspectives are too numerous to be mentioned here but include the following examples, many of which have influenced this study, conceptually or otherwise: Ardis, *Modernism and Cultural Conflict;* Clark, *Farewell to an Idea;* Rainey, *Institutions of Modernism;* Felski, *The Gender of Modernity;* Williams, *The Politics of Modernism;* Strychacz, *Modernism, Mass Culture, and Professionalism;* Rado, *Modernism, Gender, and Culture;* Szalay, *New Deal Modernism;* Dettmar and Watt, *Marketing Modernisms;* Bhaba, "'Race,' Time, and the Revision of Modernity"; Gilroy, *The Black Atlantic;* and Ardis and Lewis, *Women's Experience of Modernity.*

14. On modernity as "a constantly shifting set of temporal coordinates," see Felski, *The Gender of Modernity,* 12. At the risk of appearing to overlook the complexities involved in establishing a historical time frame for modernity, I am following recent practice in literature and the visual arts in aligning the modern not merely with the emergence of highly experimental modes of expression—the hegemony of which, especially in terms of its claim to a privileged radicalism, is challenged here—but also with other, temporally correspondent, notions of modernity, especially those that relate specifically to rurality. These include the rapid growth of a consumer culture, legislative efforts to revivify farming in the face of rural flight, and the controversy over technological advances in agriculture.

15. Conlogue, *Working the Garden*, 19.

16. Felski, *The Gender of Modernity*, 36, 41, 58–59.

17. For classic formulations of high modernism, see Bradbury and McFarlane, "The Name and Nature of Modernism," and Howe, "The Idea of the Modern." Both stress high modernism's formalist experimentation and extreme self-consciousness, as well as its inclination to render a world apparently drained of sociopolitical specificity. Writes Howe, "The [modernist] *avant-garde* scorns notions of responsibility toward the audience" (24). The contrast between this aesthetic vision and popular notions of rurality seems clear. If high modernism is esoteric, rurality is populist; if high modernism locates meaning in psychological interiority, rurality is mired in materiality; if high modernism treats the natural world as an abstraction, rurality is literally shaped by nature's rhythms. Above all, if high modernism is, as one critic has recently argued, about contingency ("the omnipresence of change" [Clark, *Farewell to an Idea*, 7]), then rurality calls to mind tradition and social stability. For a recent and provocative exchange concerning new ways of thinking through the (high) modernist project, see Clark, *Farewell to an Idea*, and Altieri, "Can Modernism Have a Future?" According to Altieri, despite their differences both he and Clark agree that (high) modernism represented a "resist[ance to] the philosophical and psychological economies put in place by modernity" (141); thus they deny high modernism's often-presumed *complicity* with modernity, effectively undermining its privileged status as aesthetic expression vis-à-vis the modern.

18. For example, "progressive" referred more specifically to the new political party, descended from the agrarian Populists, that split off from the Republicans around 1912 and endorsed Theodore Roosevelt for president, and later to followers of Henry A. Wallace in the presidential campaign of 1948. (Wallace was secretary of agriculture and a member of the prestigious midwestern farm family that published the periodical *Wallace's Farmer*.)

19. Kaplan, *The Social Construction of American Realism*, 7, 11, 13.

20. The anecdote about Meredith is told in Manchester, "The Farm Magazines," 58. See Shortridge's *The Middle West* for a discussion of the conflation of the two concepts of "pastoralism" and "Middle West," which he dates to the years around 1900 (27–28).

21. On the conflation of these concepts, and on the association of the Middle West with "heartland," see Shortridge's exhaustive study, *The Middle West*.

22. The single major exception is Conlogue's insightful *Working the Garden*, which reads selected twentieth-century farm novels as responses to the industrialization of agriculture. Most farm novels, however, are folded for the purposes of critical analysis into the broader categories of nature writing or landscape representation and are considered within studies that organize themselves along regionalist lines. Recent examples have distinguished themselves by focusing on writing by women. See, for example, Yaeger, *Dirt and Desire;* Harrison, *Female Pastoral;* and Manning, *The Female Tradition in Southern Literature.* Sylvia Jenkins Cook's *From Tobacco Road to Route 66* is also an important early study. Controversies over what constitutes southern literature have continued to animate this genre, thus maintaining its integrity *as* a genre. Yaeger is a useful source for articulating the standard critical conception of southern writing, which her study

ultimately challenges (*Dirt and Desire,* ix–xvi). General studies of midwestern or "prairie" literature—as opposed to single-author studies of, for instance, Willa Cather—have been far fewer but include Meyer, *The Middle Western Farm Novel in the Twentieth Century,* and Fairbanks, *Prairie Women.* Also important to considerations of southern and midwestern writing is the "new regionalism," which reinscribes regionalist categories but also seeks to recoup regionalist fiction, long devalued as a "minor" women's genre. See, for example, Inness and Royer, *Breaking Boundaries.*

23. On regionalism and marginal voices, see Inness and Royer's introduction to *Breaking Boundaries* and Fetterley and Pryse's *Writing Out of Place;* Kaplan, *The Social Construction of American Realism,* 1–5; Baym, "Melodramas of Beset Manhood."

24. This despite the strong agrarian tradition of rebellion against the encroachments of industrial capitalism, especially through organizations such as the Grange. For a general overview, see McMath, *American Populism.* On women and the Grange, see Marti, *Women of the Grange.*

25. In addition to Norwood's *Made from This Earth,* other recent studies in this category include Alaimo's *Undomesticated Ground* and Stein's *Shifting the Ground.* Of course, the entire field of ecofeminist criticism has evolved in response to the perceived need to articulate women's relation to the natural world, both as historically constituted by men and as theorized through alternative constructs. For an overview of the field viewed through the lens of the nature/culture divide, see Alaimo's introduction.

26. In *The Wages of Whiteness,* Roediger argues that "working class formation and the systematic development of a sense of whiteness went hand in hand for the US white working class" (8). While Roediger's study focuses on eighteenth- and nineteenth-century race relations and class consciousness, the dynamics he describes extended well into the twentieth century and, as this study will show, animated Progressive Era attitudes toward farm culture.

27. Clark, *Farewell to an Idea,* 7.

28. Jellison, *Entitled to Power;* Neth, *Preserving the Family Farm;* Walker, *All We Knew Was to Farm;* Fink, *Agrarian Women.*

29. Kocks, *Dream a Little,* chapter 1; Yaeger, *Dirt and Desire,* xiii.

30. Vera Norwood explains why farm women were excluded from her sweeping study of American women and nature: "The selection here was informed by my sense that . . . women's work in landscape architecture and ornamental gardening offered more information on the values driving popular ideas about nature than did the lives of farm women" (*Made from this Earth,* xx). Conlogue argues that ecocriticism generally has been more interested in "wild nature" than in "farm landscapes" but suggests that the latter are more essential to thinking through relations between humans and the land (*Working the Garden,* 9).

31. The reader will note, for instance, that the aesthetic texts I discuss are primarily by and about white women. This is not because modernist works by minority women eschewed rural settings—Zora Neale Hurston's *Their Eyes Were Watching God* is an obvious example to the contrary—but because, in my estimation, such works do not grapple primarily or even largely with the masculinist discourses concerning the (white)

Farm Woman as cultural trope that are a key aspect of this study, and that were central to considerations of modernity and agriculture. Nonetheless, as I will demonstrate, rural novels by white women occasionally interest themselves in minorities and rurality, which distinguishes them from many men's novels. Moreover, this study sheds light on minorities and agriculture, however indirectly, by evidencing the lack of attention they received in public debates.

32. Felski, *The Gender of Modernity,* 212.

Chapter 1

1. Quotations are from Atkeson's foreword, vii–viii. As she explains, the letters she read included "hundreds" written to *Farm and Home* in 1920, and 7,000 letters written to *The Farmer's Wife* in 1922. The latter were in response to that magazine's contest, "Would You Want Your Daughter to Marry a Farmer?" discussed in chapter 2.

2. For example, Tugwell characterizes the farm woman of yesteryear as "wealthy with the richest experience common to the race, both gay and grinding"; he argues that she "shaped" the "ends" and "virtues" of rural life, and that in executing her tasks she embodied the "abandoned devotion of a master craftsman." See Tugwell, "The Woman in the Sunbonnet." Tugwell, of course, became administrator of the New Deal's Resettlement Administration in 1935 and famously hired Roy Stryker to coordinate what became the Farm Security Administration's documentary photo-file. Chapter 5 takes up FSA photographer Marion Post Wolcott.

3. Butterfield, "The Outlook from the Farm Home." Atkeson's awareness of recent agricultural reform movements and their uncertain results is clear: she relays, for instance, with tongue in cheek, how country people have been "forced to look on" while city folks, and those country people lacking in backbone, have been swayed by the shifting extremes of public opinion regarding rural life. See chap. 14, "The Truth about Country Life."

4. As a point of comparison, and for a less restrained celebration of country women that draws heavily on stereotype, see Crowe's *The American Country Girl.*

5. Galpin, *Rural Social Problems,* 51–57.

6. See Heath, "The New Kind of Housekeeping."

7. In *Farm Women,* Rachel Ann Rosenfeld argues that, among other things, regionalist preoccupations, masculinist biases in census-taking procedures, and attitudes of social scientists on the division between family and work in industrialized societies have prevented, until recently, sustained studies of women and agriculture. Similarly, a special section of the November 1981 issue of *Rural Sociologist* discusses the challenges to scholarship on farm women due to lack of data ("Counterpoint"). Carolyn E. Sachs points out, somewhat less concretely, that "rural women's experiences" have been "largely overlooked by feminist and rural scholars alike," and that studies of rural women were "few and far between" until the late 1970s (*Gendered Fields,* 177, 11).

8. On this topic see Strychacz, *Modernism, Mass Culture, and Professionalism;* Ardis, *Modernism and Cultural Conflict;* Rainey, *Institutions of Modernism;* Felski, *The Gender of Modernity.*

9. Bailey, *The Country Life Movement in America.* For a compact history of Jeffersonian agrarianism and its dependence on the "subordination of women," see Fink, *Agrarian Women,* chap. 2.

10. Deborah Fink argues that farm women never really utilized their Granges to challenge patriarchal structures (*Agrarian Women,* 23); for more on women and the Grange generally, see Marti, *Women of the Grange.* Karen Blair's *The Clubwoman as Feminist* reveals women's clubs of the late nineteenth and early twentieth centuries to be mainly located in urban centers and to be largely concerned with urban social ills or with members' intellectual self-growth. See also Rothman, who points out that clubs "structured [middle-class women's] leisure in a pleasant way," making the city their "ideal breeding-ground" (*Woman's Proper Place,* 65, 69). Rothman also discusses how women's clubs often focused specifically on the social "problem" of unprotected country girls coming to the city, sometimes going so far as to scout train stations in an effort to identify and assist such girls before their virtue could be compromised; the club women's concern, then, was not with rurality per se but rather with helping rural women adapt to the pace and conditions of urban life (*Woman's Proper Place,* 74–81).

11. On the agricultural situation in the United States in the first two decades of the twentieth century, see especially Bowers, *The Country Life Movement in America,* chap. 1, and Danbom, *The Resisted Revolution,* chap. 1.

12. Danbom, *The Resisted Revolution,* viii.

13. These ideological contradictions included, according to Rebecca Edwards, "nativism and racial tolerance, socialist influences and anti-statism." See her "Recent Literature on American Populism" for an overview of recent scholarly debates. Classic studies of the movement include Hicks, *The Populist Revolt,* and Goodwyn, *Democratic Promise.*

14. See Danbom, *The Resisted Revolution,* chapter 2, for the argument about rurality seen through a persistently urban lens. David Shi also sees the Progressive Era longing for the "simple life" as a reaction to industrial dominance and traces it more broadly through cultural impulses such as the Arts and Crafts Movement and the establishment of the Boy Scouts of America; see *The Simple Life,* chap. 8. On antimodernism generally, see Lears, *No Place of Grace.*

15. *Annals,* March 1912. This special edition consisted of twenty-eight essays by prominent country life analysts. The quotation is from Butterfield, "Rural Sociology as a College Discipline," 16. The discussion of industrialism is also especially prominent in Wilson, "Social Life in the Country."

16. Danbom, "Romantic Agrarianism in Twentieth-Century America," 5.

17. Borsodi, *This Ugly Civilization;* see especially chap. 7, "The Factory's Customers." Borsodi is discussed substantially in Shi, *The Simple Life,* 226–30, and briefly in Danbom, "Romantic Agrarianism in Twentieth-Century America."

18. F.E.B., "Mr. Borsodi's Way Out." Significantly, Borsodi did not oppose machinery in the home and professed a desire to bring the best of mechanization to the country in order to allow for more leisure. Yet, as F.E.B. notes, "as far as I know, there is no

machine for making beds and washing the children's faces," suggesting that laborsaving devices generally help men more than women. "If you think all that work can be done [by women], come out to my place and try it," she adds. "Not with all the machines in kingdom come."

19. As Shi notes, the Nashville Agrarians were prominently linked to Borsodi in critical discussions of the period (*The Simple Life,* 276–77), although Borsodi has received little attention since then. For a recent overview of the numerous books, articles, and dissertations written on the Nashville Agrarians, see Murphy's introduction to *The Rebuke of History,* especially 6–10.

20. Murphy, *The Rebuke of History,* 21.

21. Ransom, "Reconstructed but Unregenerate," 1. See Shi, *The Simple Life,* chap. 8, on other attempts in the period to recover a nature-based sensibility.

22. Roosevelt added, "It is at least as important that the farmer should get the largest possible return in money, comfort, and social advantages from the crop he grows, as that he should get the largest possible return in crops from the land he farms. Agriculture is not the whole of country life. The great rural interests are human interests, and good crops are of little value to the farmer unless they open the door to a good kind of life on the farm" (letter from Theodore Roosevelt to Liberty Hyde Bailey, 10 August 1908, courtesy of the Division of Rare and Manuscript Collections, Cornell University Library).

23. Roosevelt, quoted in Nash, *Wilderness and the American Mind,* 151; Introduction to the *Report of the Commission on Country Life,* 10. For more on Roosevelt and gendered ideals of the strenuous life, see Bederman, *Manliness and Civilization,* chap. 5, and Watts, *Rough Rider in the White House.*

24. See, for instance, Bowers, *The Country Life Movement in America,* 27–28, 65; Danbom, *The Resisted Revolution,* 46.

25. *Report of the Commission on Country Life,* 44.

26. Quotations from Gilman, "That Rural Home Inquiry." On Gilman's assertions and the resulting survey conducted by *Good Housekeeping,* see Knowles, "'It's Our Turn Now,'" 305–6. Later in her career, Gilman proposed a realignment of farm land to create pie-shaped lots that would radiate from a community center, thereby easing rural isolation. See Gilman, "Applepieville."

27. Knowles argues that, since surveys were virtually the only means rural women had of expressing themselves, they seized on them; their impact, however, was limited. In addition to Knowles, who points out that *Good Housekeeping*'s summation of its survey responses was inaccurate, see Elbert, "Women and Farming," on female correspondents to the Cornell Extension Program; "Is This the Trouble with the Farmer's Wife?" on a woman-authored survey of 956 farm women; and Jellison on the letters written to Houston (*Entitled to Power,* 10–15). The Houston letters generated a *New York Times* article, "Farm Women Find Life Hard." It is worth noting that farm women correspondents to the Extension Service at Cornell frequently apologized for their failure to complete surveys more thoroughly or promptly and consistently cited exhaustion or the perceived irrelevance of their own circumstances as the reason. See College of

Human Ecology Records, No. 23–2–749 (especially folders 48–50), Division of Rare and Manuscript Collections, Cornell University.

28. Jellison, *Entitled to Power,* 27–30. Neth also discusses briefly Emily Hoag's survey (*Preserving the Family Farm,* 237).

29. Brown, "Woman's Task." Discussions of women's overwork in the periodical press will be addressed more fully in chapter 2.

30. See "Feminism on the Farm." The perception that conditions for farm women had improved little by the 1920s is evidenced, for example, by comparing "Is This the Trouble with the Farmer's Wife?" (1909) and Winter's "They Starve for Beauty" (1925), both published in *Ladies' Home Journal.*

31. Kline, *Consumers in the Country,* 92–93.

32. For Fels-Naptha advertisements featuring Anty Drudge, see, for example, *The Syracuse* (NY) *Herald* 13 Oct. 1908: n.p.; and *The Progressive Farmer and Southern Farm Gazette* 29 March 1913: 13 and 26 April 1913: 10. The Fels-Naptha Company also published a cookbook by Anty Drudge in 1910. The quoted letter is from *Farm Journal* 39 (15 Nov. 1915): 18.

33. On the myth of insanity among farm women, see Kline, *Consumers in the Country,* 11–12, 35, 90. Kline also discusses the controversy about the farm woman's hardships, which raged in such venues as *Farm and Home* (88–93).

34. See Bowers, *The Country Life Movement in America,* chap. 7; Danbom, *The Resisted Revolution,* chap. 4.

35. Bowers and Danbom, for instance, largely avoid gender analysis; Shi discusses even the *Ladies' Home Journal* less in terms of its audience than its male editor. These studies are primarily concerned with the shaping influences of institutional voices; in contrast, recent work by female rural historians has recovered women's attitudes and opinions through archival work and interviews. Examples include Jellison, Neth, Fink, and Walker.

36. See Neth, *Preserving the Family Farm,* chap. 4 ("Social Policy and Agricultural Institutions"). Lowry Nelson's *Rural Sociology,* on the development of the discipline generally, has little to say about women. Letters in the Cornell University home economics archives document the struggles for professionalization by women teachers such as Martha Van Rensselaer and Flora Rose: not until April 1911, for instance, after organizing extension services and teaching home economics at the university for more than a decade, were they granted seats and votes in the faculty of the College of Agriculture. See Elbert, "Women and Farming," for more on the background of Van Rensselaer in particular.

37. Fink, *Agrarian Women,* 190.

38. On the Boy Scouts, see Shi, *The Simple Life,* 208–14. *Rural Manhood* was published monthly from 1910 to 1920; women's concerns were confined to the November issues.

39. "Do You Know a Master Farm Homemaker?" *The Farmer's Wife* April 1927: 215.

40. Felski, *The Gender of Modernity,* 19–20.

41. Felski suggests that the lesbian symbolized yet another "feminized modernity" in her magnification of transgressive desires (*The Gender of Modernity,* 20–21).

42. On women of color working beyond the confines of the farm home, see Fink, *Agrarian Women*, 23.

43. Felski discusses such shifts briefly (*The Gender of Modernity*, 18–19). On the role of the department store, see Benson, *Counter Cultures.* On women's magazine culture and the privacy/publicity divide, see my "Farm Women, Letters to the Editor, and the Limits of Autobiography Theory." Felski points out that the link between women and consumption was central to the dissolution of the separate spheres idea, since "consumption cut across the private/public distinction that was evoked to assign women to a premodern sphere" (*The Gender of Modernity*, 61). Alan Dawley argues that the gradual imbrication of work and leisure, profit and pleasure, weakened the proprietary role of the nuclear family as well, compromising its privacy (*Struggles for Justice*, chap. 2).

44. So many studies touch on these concerns that there is only room here to provide basic examples. On advertising invading the sanctity of the home, see Lears, "From Salvation to Self-Realization." For an example of the period's popular discourse on housekeeping and management principles, see Heath, "The New Kind of Housekeeping," and Rutherford's recent study of efficiency expert Christine Frederick (*Selling Mrs. Consumer*), which addresses the intersections between progressive reform and women's domestic labor. On the mixed legacy of home economics, see Stage and Vincenti, *Rethinking Home Economics.*

45. Melosh, *Engendering Culture*, chap. 3. On the ways that race operated more powerfully than gender in defining the work of African American farm women, sometimes with advantageous results, see Hilton, "'Both in the Field, Each with a Plow.'"

46. Letter from Katherine Russell to Martha Van Rensselaer, n.d., College of Human Ecology Records, No. 23/2/749, courtesy of the Division of Rare and Manuscript Collections, Cornell University Library.

47. According to Danbom, "growing unease [among sociologists] about immigrants in the countryside" led to the position that the city was "the best place for the assimilation and control of the immigrant" (*The Resisted Revolution*, 30).

48. This linkage was due in no small part to the class status of the reformers themselves, whose own patterns of labor and leisure, production and consumption, were assumed to be preferable. Dawley defines these members of the "helping professions" (such as social workers) as part of "the newer middle classes"; while he asserts that they mediated between the wealthy and the specifically *urban* poor, it is easy to see how agrarian reformers also fit this description. See Dawley, *Struggles for Justice*, 72. For a clear example of the tensions between farm women and agricultural reformers who promulgated urban standards of living, see Babbitt's "The Productive Farm Woman."

49. Fink, *Agrarian Women*, 61. On farm women being more firmly defined by their husbands' occupation, see Neth, *Preserving the Family Farm*, 18, and Hagood, *Mothers of the South*, 5.

50. Letter to Martha Van Rensselaer, College of Human Ecology Records, No. 23/2/749, courtesy of the Division of Rare and Manuscript Collections, Cornell University Library.

51. Jellison, *Entitled to Power,* chap. 2, especially 63–64; Elbert, "Women and Farming," especially 251. On women preferring field labor, see also Hagood, *Mothers of the South,* 90. Attempts by Extension Service agents to force farm women to take up work deemed more appropriate—studying food and nutrition, for instance, instead of making income-producing crafts products—were also met with resistance. See Babbitt, "The Productive Farm Woman," 90–91.

52. "My Everyday Problems," 25.

53. On the shame issue, see Melosh, *Engendering Culture,* 66. Discussions of women's labor in the farm press will be taken up more fully in chapter 2.

54. Examples can be found in virtually any farm journal in the years before the war. See, for instance, the early years of *The Farmer's Wife* (between 1906 and World War I) when numerous stories appear with "mother-love" or "mother-wisdom" in the subtitle. In 1913 the *Progressive Farmer and Southern Farm Gazette* quoted prominently and approvingly a description from William Dean Howells's novel *The Rise of Silas Lapham,* of an overworked and underappreciated farm mother. In the excerpt the protagonist recalls his "little frail" mother "with a lump in the throat" ("Silas Lapham's Wife and Mother").

55. L. H. Bailey declared, "So far as possible, the labor that is necessary to do the work of the open country, whether in-doors or out-doors, should be resident labor. The labor difficulty increases with reduction in the size of the family" (*The Country Life Movement in America,* 87). See Danbom, *The Resisted Revolution,* 28, on agrarian leaders' belief that the country would supply the city with an exceptional populace. As late as 1936, medical professionals fretted that a declining birthrate among rural women was detrimental to cities; see "How Many Babies?" (*The Farmer's Wife* October 1936: 16).

56. McNeill's "The White South" appeared in 1910.

57. "What May Happen Here After the War." This propaganda piece, illustrated with photographs of Ellis Island immigrants by Lewis Hine, warns readers of the inevitable "flood of immigration" that will threaten social stability in the United States.

58. Bederman, *Manliness and Civilization,* 170–215; Kline, *Building a Better Race.* For Edward A. Ross's views on race suicide, see his "The Causes of Race Superiority."

59. See Dyer, *Theodore Roosevelt and the Idea of Race,* 143–67. The quotations can be found on pp. 161 and 158.

60. All quotations are from Roosevelt's speech "On American Motherhood." Typically Roosevelt's call to reproduce has been understood as directed to middle-class white women, which some, such as Bederman, apparently take to include farm women. Yet Roosevelt seemed to perceive farmers and ranchers, and especially their wives, as a class unto themselves, removed from the excessive civilization of cities and combining the moral integrity of Roosevelt's own Victorian upbringing with the physical hardiness of the pioneers—this despite his aversion, according to Sarah Watts, to both racial miscegenation and class hybridization. See Watts, *Rough Rider in the White House,* especially 69 and 83, and Bederman, *Manliness and Civilization,* 200–206. In a related vein, Kline discusses the contrast in eugenics discourses between the positive pioneer-mother figure and the urban

working-class female who frequents dance halls and whose reproduction is in need of regulation (*Building a Better Race,* 1–31).

61. The Country Contributor, *Ladies' Home Journal* Dec. 1906: 36 and March 1908: 29; "Mothers' Council: Race Suicide vs. Mother Suicide," *The Farmer's Wife* Nov. 1906: n.p. For a reply to the second piece, see "Mothers' Council: From a Mother's Standpoint," *The Farmer's Wife* Dec. 1906: 151. A short story with feminist overtones published that same year features a female character in a rural village who complains that "the president is trying to make folks believe that there is only one thing which a woman ought to want to do" ("The Fads of Philancy's Friends," *The Farmer's Wife* March 1906: 203+).

62. Rural populations were especially affected by the Comstock Act, which prevented the mailing or importation of contraceptive devices or information. And James Reed shows that as late as the 1930s, efforts to extend birth control more fully in rural areas were thwarted by lack of funds and by race- and class-based assumptions that the rural poor either did not need or could not follow birth control instruction (*From Public Vice to Private Virtue,* 254–55, 266). According to Rosalind Rosenberg, the Farm Security Administration funded birth control "surreptitiously" by paying nurses to bring contraceptive information to women on farms and in migrant labor camps (*Divided Lives,* 118). For examples from the period of rural women lacking birth control, see Hagood, *Mothers of the South,* 23, 29, and Lind and Lind, *Middletown,* 123.

63. As an example of the currency of this notion, see the series of position pieces on the subject published in *Popular Science* and reprinted in Newman, *Men's Ideas/Women's Realities,* 105–55.

64. See "Fitter Families for Future Firesides" (chap. 6) in Lovett, *Conceiving the Future.* Lovett discusses at length the "Fitter Families" contests, arguing that they were "deeply rooted in nostalgia for the rural family." See also Holt, *Linoleum, Better Babies, and the Modern Farm Woman.* In chapter 2 of *World of Fairs,* Rydell describes eugenics exhibitions between the world wars, notably those attempting to bring "the message of eugenic reform to rural America" (49).

65. See Bowers, *The Country Life Movement in America,* 107, and, for example, "Editor's Page: The Future of Farm Life," *The Farmer's Wife* Feb. 1926: 64. One farm wife writing in 1928 declared, "[I]f all farmers could do big things in poultry the cry in a year's time would be 'overproduction' and we should be selling eggs for 5 cents a dozen and poultry accordingly" ("What Ails Agriculture?" in *The Farmer's Wife* July 1928: 14+, 23).

66. "Mothers' Council: Race Suicide vs. Mother Suicide," *The Farmer's Wife* Nov. 1906: n.p.

67. For examples of such agitation, see the following magazines and issues: *Farm Journal* May 1910; *The Farmer's Wife* Sept. 1910 and Aug. 1913. Anna L. Brown, M.D., suggested that the particular victimization of country girls made their informed awareness of sex and reproduction even more urgent ("Laws of Sex Education and Country Girls"). A broader study of the white slave narrative in Progressive Era culture can be found in Johnson, *Sisters in Sin;* on country girls as white slaves, see especially pp. 118–20.

68. See Passet, *Sex Radicals and the Quest for Women's Equality.*

69. Borsodi, *This Ugly Civilization*, 13–14; the Country Contributor, *Ladies' Home Journal* Feb. 1909: 38. On advertising and women, see Scanlon, for example, who argues that women's magazines "helped naturalize women's link to the marketplace through consumption" (*Inarticulate Longings*, 13).

70. Ronald R. Kline has explored this issue most fully, notably in reference to technological goods. See *Consumers in the Country*.

71. On farm women's preferences for communications technology, see Jellison, *Entitled to Power*. The *Farm Journal* letter is signed by E.P.G. and is entitled "Indoor Conveniences" (April 1910: 252). The letter to David Houston is quoted in "Farm Women Find Life Hard," 15.

72. Matt, "Frocks, Finery, and Feelings." On consumerism, rurality, and women, see Neth, *Preserving the Family Farm*, chap. 7; Jellison, *Entitled to Power*, chap. 2; Kline, *Consumers in the Country*.

73. Groves, "Suggestion and City-Drift," 49; Quick, "Women on the Farms," 313.

74. "I Glory in My Job!" *The Farmer's Wife* April 1932: 24+, 40.

75. Matt, "Frocks, Finery, and Feelings," 389–90.

76. Virtually any edition of *The Farmer's Wife* or *Ladies' Home Journal* (as mentioned in Scanlon, *Inarticulate Longings*, 52) exhibits this combination. On Bok's marketing of the "simple life," see Shi, *The Simple Life*, 181–89, and Scanlon, *Inarticulate Longings*, 51–54.

77. "What Ails Agriculture?" 14.

78. Conlogue, *Working the Garden*, 16. Mary Neth points out that portrayals of farm leisure reveal a shift from community images to those of the isolated farm family (*Preserving the Family Farm*, 191–92).

79. Quick, "Women on the Farms," 318.

80. In 1920, for instance, a female doctor answering medical questions posed by readers of a women's farm journal railed against their lack of reproductive choice, arguing that "[m]en have passed laws to punish those who interfere with the birth of children but they never touched the cause, and women have been ground between the upper millstone of the law of man and the nether millstone of the law of God" (Alexander, "The Welfare of the Home").

81. Lena Martin Smith, "I Like to Live on the Farm," *The Farmer's Wife* May 1921: 459.

82. Grosz, *Volatile Bodies*, 19.

Chapter 2

1. On rural reading of magazines generally, see Hays's introduction to *Early Stories from the Land*. Standard reference books on American periodicals by Mott and Wood devote substantial space to the enumeration of farm journals, of which there were probably, according to Mott, "well over a thousand" published between 1885 and 1905 alone (*A History of American Magazines*, 337); Wood suggests, more modestly, that "hundreds" have been published since the first appeared in 1831 (*Magazines in the United States*, 179). John J. Fry's recent book, *The Farm Press, Reform, and Rural Change*, considers a more targeted selection of midwestern farm papers that nonetheless allow him to make

some useful generalizations. On the farm press during the earliest years of the twentieth century, see Shulman, "The Progressive Era Farm Press." The consolidation by the 1930s of many of the smaller rural magazines into larger, national publications is described in Manchester, "The Farm Magazines." This source also touches on the role of advertising revenues through the 1920s and 1930s in determining these journals' fiscal health, and the ways in which they were increasingly pitched to a "better" class of farmers.

2. Scanlon, *Inarticulate Longings;* Garvey, *The Adman in the Parlor.*

3. Ohmann, *The Politics of Letters,* especially chaps. 9 ("Where Did Mass Culture Come From? The Case of Magazines") and 10 ("Advertising and the New Discourse of Mass Culture"). The point about the limited readership of mass magazines is made on p. 142. Other recent studies of mass-circulation periodicals in the period 1900–1940 include, of course, Scanlon, *Inarticulate Longings,* and Garvey, *The Adman in the Parlor.*

4. Fry's book, mentioned above, is an important addition to the historical literature. Evans and Salcedo's *Communications in Agriculture* is an older source that remains useful; it focuses primarily on advertising revenues, circulation statistics, and other quantifiable measures. Briefer considerations of the farm press have also been undertaken in the context of the new attention being paid to farm women. See Neth, *Preserving the Family Farm,* especially chap. 7; and Jellison, *Entitled to Power,,* which attends particularly to *Wallace's Farmer,* an important farming periodical of the Midwest. For a more focused study of women within an individual farm journal, see Tyler, "The Ideal Rural Woman as Seen by *Progressive Farmer* in the 1930s." General compilations of periodical pieces related to women and farming include Juster's *So Sweet to Labor* and Hays's *Early Stories from the Land.* The only study of specialized magazines in the United States is Ford's *Magazines for Millions,* which posits farm journals as among the most prominent of specialized magazines in the twentieth century (226–38).

5. To put this in perspective, the following circulation statistics are available for the year 1930: *Woman's Home Companion:* 2,400,344; *Good Housekeeping:* 1,741,640; *Ladies' Home Journal:* 2,555,996; *Farm Journal:* 1,412,523; *The Farmer and Farm* (predecessor of *The Farmer*): 262,099 (from *N. W. Ayer and Son's Directory of Newspapers and Periodicals, 1930–1969*). *Country Gentleman,* the farm magazine with the largest general circulation in 1930 (1,600,000), also achieved at that point the largest circulation ever for a farm periodical (Wood, *Magazines in the United States,* 170–72). In October 1911 a *TFW* publisher's note stated that circulation had reached 500,000 and estimated that five persons read each copy—admittedly an unverifiable number. Garvey, however, offers evidence that magazines at the turn of the century were often shared among multiple households, sometimes in highly organized ways (*The Adman in the Parlor,* 188–89).

6. For more background on organizational and business issues related to the Webb Company and *The Farmer's Wife,* including the magazine's eventual purchase by *Farm Journal,* see my "'This Is YOUR Magazine.'" Nora Cruz Cabral's doctoral dissertation on *Farm Journal* also contains a chapter on its absorption of *The Farmer's Wife.*

7. To minimize parenthetical references that could become intrusive, I will offer only those page numbers that are clearly indicated in the magazine itself (hence avoiding

excessive use of "n.p.") *and* that seem necessary (as when, for instance, a quotation is taken from a relatively small item that might be difficult to locate within a particular issue). Otherwise—particularly for major articles or stories—no page numbers will be indicated.

8. Quoted in Baker, *The Webb Company*, 52.

9. Wallace was directing editor from 1919 to 1935; he served originally as editor of *The Farmer*. According to the 1923 Country Life Proceedings, he believed in "a developed class consciousness" among farmers and defined the "task in hand" as "rais[ing] the general level of thought as to the rights of the farm family" (qtd. in Dean, "*The Farmer's Wife*"). His regular editorials in *TFW* clearly enact this goal.

10. Again, comparisons are helpful in suggesting that *TFW* was particularly dedicated to eliciting reader responses. According to Christopher Wilson, *Ladies' Home Journal* had "printed reams of letters from readers" in its earlier years (between 1890 and about 1910), a strategy that was "a Journal trademark" ("The Rhetoric of Consumption," 59). Yet Scanlon's study of *Ladies' Home Journal* between 1910 and 1930—when *TFW* was also circulating—reveals that its editorial policies regarding such contributions changed in significant ways. Scanlon points out that while *LHJ*, like *TFW*, offered small cash incentives to letter writers, this practice was mostly confined to the years between 1911 and 1920 (*Inarticulate Longings*, 61); moreover, "the changing structure of the magazine in the 1920s suggests that the *Journal* provided fewer direct responses to readers through [published or personal] letters and more indirect responses through the text of the magazine" (244). In contrast, *TFW*'s cash incentives for participation actually increased throughout its history and were occasionally quite substantial ($300 was the impressive top prize for one letter-writing contest in 1922); the typical number of pages per issue devoted to readers' contributions also increased. Hays reports that many editors of farm journals "gave prominent space to readers' letters" ("Introduction," xv) although, of course, *TFW*'s singularity as an all-woman's farm periodical ensured that it necessarily published more letters by women. Indeed, I have located only one *TFW* letter, published in October 1909, written by a man.

11. The working-class underpinnings of farm culture had much to do with this assumption, naturally. The assertion (or complaint) that farm women are constantly *busy* is a mainstay in *TFW*. On farm women's visions of themselves as diversified but underappreciated workers, see Jellison, *Entitled to Power*, especially chap. 2. Christopher Wilson argues that popular magazines of the period, by the very nature of their tone and design, "invited passivity and anomie" ("The Rhetoric of Consumption," 61). Even if this is true for *TFW* (and I will suggest later on that *TFW* does not quite fit with Wilson's model), Wilson's point does not speak to the self-perception of readers—which, of course, I am largely inferring from their contributions to the magazine itself.

12. The importance of the reflexivity established by this cover is suggested by its repeated use: the exact same cover image was used for the editions of May, June, July, and August 1907. This was not at all typical; indeed, I can find no other repeated cover images in the entire run of the magazine.

13. *TFW* reported on the activities of state and local clubs in nearly every issue, especially following its call in late 1914 for "Farm Clubs [to be] organized in every state of

the Union, that the farm woman . . . may attain such breadth of power as, through organized effort, her husband and his fellow farmers have reached" (Sept. 1915, 99). For more on rural clubs, see Holt's *Linoleum, Better Babies, and the Modern Farm Woman,* especially chap. 6.

14. The contest was announced in a full-page spread in the January issue. Prizewinning letters, all affirmative, were printed in May, June, and August. A two-page feature article in October summarized the negative responses. Eventually the contest results formed part of the data for a larger report, "The Advantages of Farm Life," by Emily Hoag of the USDA. According to Jellison, Hoag sought to locate and characterize "happy and forward-looking farm women" (*Entitled to Power,* 27), and her optimistic portrayal of the farmer's wife became the dominant depiction in agricultural reform literature. On Hoag's study, see also Neth, *Preserving the Family Farm,* 237. For a more specific discussion of the contest, see my "'This Is YOUR Magazine.'"

15. The text that sparked the controversy was written by Sally Sod, née Loretto [*sic*] Hughes Green, of Michigan. For a discussion of the ensuing debate, see my "'This Is YOUR Magazine.'"

16. Lears, "From Salvation to Self-Realization." See also Scanlon, *Inarticulate Longings,* and Garvey, *The Adman in the Parlor.*

17. Danbom, *The Resisted Revolution,* 22.

18. *TFW* Oct. 1927; ibid.; Oct. 1913, 143; Nov. 1916, 119; Nov. 1923.

19. Jan. 1910; March 1918, 236; Feb. 1919, 198; May 1908; Jan. 1910; April 1917, 255; June 1917, 8; July–Aug. 1921, 506; Jan. 1924, 294; Oct. 1925, 387; March 1927, 128; Feb. 1928, 24; March 1929, 7; June 1931, 7.

20. Such creeds and manifestos, generally separated from the text by enlarged print and/or special borders, were standard fare. See also, for instance, "A Country's Girl's Creed" (July 1915, 32) and "[Why] I Like to Live on the Farm" (May 1921, 459).

21. See Scanlon, *Inarticulate Longings,* especially 34–38, and Jellison, *Entitled to Power,* chap. 1.

22. Lears, "From Salvation to Self-Realization," 4.

23. This campaign was particularly compelling and, if we are to judge by its staying power, quite successful. Each version pictured another rosy, vigorous child in a rural setting, and the lead type (followed by a lengthy discussion of Cream of Wheat in smaller print) offered variations on the same basic idea: e.g., "You've Given Her the Biggest Thing of All! Be sure that she has, too, this one simple care that all children need" (Nov. 1930); "Lucky the Child Who Is Raised on a Farm! Yet with all the advantages that city children miss—your children must have this one important care" (Oct. 1931); "Little Farm Children Are Rich These Days. Every advantage for health is theirs . . . if mothers watch one simple care" (Oct. 1932).

24. Martin Pumphrey refers to this as the discourse of "self-surveillance." See his "The Flapper, the Housewife, and the Making of Modernity," which suggests how mainstream constructions of the housewife could erase farm women: "The modern Housewife is not bound to the past or tradition. . . . She is efficient, up-to-date, knowledgeable about domestic technology and an expert consumer" (191).

25. As Mary Neth puts it, "The city represented corruption, evil, and social disruption, but also adventure, progress, opportunity, and the future. The farm symbolized honesty, virtue, and social stability, but also stagnation, backwardness, decline, and an out-of-date past" (*Preserving the Family Farm*, 107).

26. Lears, "From Salvation to Self-Realization," 7.

27. Again, the single best (and most protracted) example is the Sally Sod controversy (1928). See my "'This Is YOUR Magazine.'"

28. Wilson, "The Rhetoric of Consumption," 44. Wilson notes that he uses the term "realism" to describe "a narrative mode [premised on] the illusion of veracity (persuasive narration, detail, the feeling of immediacy) to direct the reader's interaction with a text—in effect, to manage the 'reader's' responses" (219). I am suggesting, in contrast, that *TFW*'s "realism"—its relatively unmediated representation of the concerns and opinions of actual farm women—results from genuine inclusiveness.

29. Yet another contrast proves helpful. The *Progressive Farm Journal and Southern Ruralist,* the "most widely read farm journal in the South," appears to have offered in the 1930s only occasional "glimmer[s]" of farm women's negative attitudes toward farm life. See Tyler, "The Ideal Rural Southern Woman as Seen by *Progressive Farmer* in the 1930s." Katherine Jellison has argued that any negativity on the part of farm women regarding rural life was ignored or glossed over in the literature of agricultural reform movements (*Entitled to Power,* especially chap. 1). It is worth reiterating that women's perspectives were confined, in most agricultural journals, to a brief "woman's section," necessarily limiting their numbers and their impact.

30. Haraway, *Simians, Cyborgs, and Women,* 195.

31. Garvey, "Training the Reader's Attention: Advertising Contests," in *The Adman in the Parlor,* 51–79.

32. *TFW* May 1926, 268. The conference pamphlet was published as *The Farm Woman Answers the Question: What Do Farm Women Want?*

33. I am indebted to Patty Dean, formerly of the Minnesota Historical Society, for the information on Shaw. Chick Kircher, an editor of *TFW,* mentions Clara Sutter's poultry farm in his typescript reminiscences (Webb Company Records).

34. Scanlon discusses the dismissal of women's magazine fiction by scholars (*Inarticulate Longings,* 138). Of course, recent major studies of women and popular fiction—although not specifically of magazine fiction—by Janice Radway and Tania Modleski have offered new theoretical lenses through which to view women's magazine fiction. Radway is discussed below. See also Modleski, *Loving with a Vengeance.*

35. This is not to minimize the presence in *TFW* of romantic fiction with nonagrarian themes, of which there were multiple examples in every issue. See Scanlon for a useful discussion of such "mainstream" women's magazine stories, which, she argues, "promise happy lives through traditional means, but expose those means—and those ends—as less than satisfying for women" (*Inarticulate Longings,* 139).

36. By now this interactiveness is a given. For good discussions, see especially Ohmann (*The Politics of Letters,* chap. 10) and Scanlon (*Inarticulate Longings,* chap. 6).

Hays touches on this issue within the specific context of farm journals when he mentions, for instance, that advertisements for motor cars corresponded to the emergence of "the 'Ford on the Farm' theme" in "stories, articles, and columns" ("Introduction," xiv).

37. Radway, *Reading the Romance*, 8.

38. Radway, *Reading the Romance*, 192, 196–97, 198, 209. One farm woman, asked by *TFW* editors about the type of reading she enjoys, reportedly "flashed back: 'Something that will take me clear away from my work—only it must be clean!'" (Aug. 1925, 312). Sometimes the apparent "selfishness" of reading was justified as a means of renewing oneself for improved application to domestic labor, as in the case of Mrs. Maud Kannon, who insisted that reading for the purposes of "return[ing] to my work refreshed in mind and body" is a duty ("A Woman's Duty," March 1907).

39. Radway, *Reading the Romance*, 199.

40. The title of this story, apparently an allusion to the 1908 novel by Mary Wilkins Freeman in which an impoverished couple inherits a small farm (*The Shoulders of Atlas*), points to the relationships between farm magazines and popular writers of the period, especially those writers who used rural settings. Willa Cather's *O Pioneers*, for instance, was serialized in *Wallace's Farmer*. (See Hays ["Introduction," xxi–xxii], who includes a brief list of popular novels initially published in the farm press.) *TFW* occasionally reviewed farm novels for its readership; see, for example, "Farm Women in Fiction" (Aug. 1933).

41. For example, see Lott, *Love and Theft*.

42. Kolodny, *The Lay of the Land*, 150.

43. Symbolically, the farm woman is "at home" in the country because she *is* the home. Tableaux frequently positioned her between the house and the outdoors—the spiritual and psychic link between internal domestic spaces and external agrarian ones. In illustrations she is often depicted looking out from her doorway, or through a window, across the fields. A poem entitled "The Farmer's Wife" also captures this image; it begins, "Framed in the morning glories at her door/She stands to see the dawn break on the hill" (Aug. 1927, 422).

44. Radway, *Reading the Romance*, 203.

45. In "The Fads of Philancy's Friends," an unmarried woman invites several similarly situated acquaintances to accompany her for a summer as she tends to an unoccupied country house. Each woman is encouraged to follow her dream: one learns to play the cornet, another reads books all day long without interruption, and a third, confined to the city her whole life, tends a garden and raises chickens. (Although this last woman certainly embraces traditional roles, she also finds pleasure in relinquishing her corset.) In "A Country College," a young couple starts an alternative school on their small farm; after a period of success, the school expands to include a gymnasium, and even the girls of the town—over the objections of some citizens—are invited to use it.

46. According to Gerry Walter and Suzanne Wilson, "Farmer success stories—journalistic case studies that show actual farmers competently solving practical farming problems with new products and practices—have been a staple of American farm magazines since the early 1900s." For a discussion of this narrative tradition and its erasure

of women, albeit in a period somewhat beyond the scope of this book, see their "Silent Partners."

47. For example, in "A Close Squeak, by the Hired Man," the narrator announces his plan to burn his story as soon as he has written it down; by the end, though, he has decided to "dust it off" for "some editor," who may find it worth publishing. In "The Desert Shall Blossom," a rebellious wife is lured back to her rural home by her husband's essay, written for an agricultural paper, about the glories of their farm. And the title of a June 1917 story speaks for itself: "The Literary Lady: When Hearts Are Young and Glad, Returned Manuscripts May Not Be All Tragedy." Incidentally, the suggestion that "regular" folks could and should write for the farm press was constantly reiterated, in fiction and elsewhere, with obvious implications for *TFW* itself.

48. Examples taken from one year, 1921, help to illustrate this trend. A May nonfiction narrative entitled "We Three Women Kept the Farm" is illustrated by photographs, as is usual for such pieces. But a text stretching across the April and May issues—"How Ya Gonna Keep 'Em"—confuses the typical signifiers. Its title would seem to suggest an advice-oriented feature, and it, too, is accompanied by photographs, yet on closer inspection it becomes clear that this is a work of fiction. The caption under one photo, for instance, reads, "Phil had a home-picture *like this* in mind" (my emphasis). Adding to the mix, a one-page story in February entitled "Anne of the Country," and including a romantic drawing of a couple dancing, clearly suggests fiction; yet the fine print in the very last column reveals that this is a lengthy advertisement for dressmaking booklets published by the Woman's Institute of Scranton, Pennsylvania.

49. In April 1932, for instance, an autobiographical piece from "Happy of Texas" was published under the headline "I Glory in My Job!" An editorial blurb described it as a "radiant letter from [a woman] who finds nothing of hardship in her farm home-making, but only the God-given privilege of caring for loved ones." In response, "Happy of Maryland" published a letter in the June issue that began: "What are you giving us, fairy tales from Texas? Alice in Wonderland as a child was thrilling, but Alice grown up in 'Happy of Texas' is a problem."

50. Ohmann, *The Politics of Letters,* 171.

Chapter 3

1. This phrase, made famous in the film version, is an adaptation of Dorothy's original words. In the book, Dorothy "knocks her heels together" and directs her magic shoes to "Take [her] home to Aunt Em!" Baum, *The Wonderful Wizard of Oz,* 257–58.

2. "The Wizard of Oz, an American Fairy Tale" was on exhibit at the Library of Congress from 21 April to 23 Sept. 2000. See http://www.loc.gov/exhibits/oz/.

3. See Flynn, "Imitation Oz," and Swartz, *Oz before the Rainbow.* Ironically, the study of Oz has evolved into an intellectual market of sorts: the *MLA Bibliography* lists dozens of articles interpreting the cultural impact of Baum's books.

4. We might quibble here about the definition of a rural novel; Meyer, for instance, articulates strict criteria (including use of dialect and "accurate handling of the physical

details of farm life") for what he calls, more narrowly, farm fiction (*The Middle Western Farm Novel in the Twentieth Century,* 7). However, I am less interested in precise categories than in exploring the range of ruralities represented in modern literature and their relation to broad cultural trends. Hence the term "rural novel" will include texts, such as Willa Cather's *One of Ours,* that may contain substantial sections off the farm. For the record, all the rural novels mentioned in this chapter were considered as such by contemporaneous critics on the scene.

5. Macdonald, "Masscult and Midcult." For a more measured assessment of the perceived threat posed by middlebrow culture, see Rubin, *The Making of Middlebrow Culture,* and Radway, *A Feeling for Books.* The classic study of high modernism's reactionary response to mass culture is Huyssen, *After the Great Divide,* though his work has been challenged by recent critics.

6. Quoted in Mott, *Golden Multitudes,* 3.

7. Standard compilations of yearly "top ten" best-sellers, based on statistics gathered by *Publishers' Weekly,* are available in Korda, *Making the List,* and Hackett, *Fifty Years of Best Sellers.* However, such lists do not reveal actual volume of sales, as book reviewers of the time noted; in fact, the "problem" of defining the best-seller was widely discussed (see, for example, Strunsky, "About Books, More or Less," and "How 'Best Sellers' Are Made"). Frequently the term was used loosely to denote a popularity that was associated with mass audiences rather than elite literary readerships. For a stricter definition, see Mott's *Golden Multitudes,* which uses a formula based on sales relative to the percentage of the population. I have relied on statistics from *Publishers' Weekly* and *Bookman,* the standard sources for the period, in establishing popular status for the books discussed in this chapter.

8. Hicks, "Revolution and the Novel," 45; Aldrich, review of *A Lantern in Her Hand;* Kronenberger, "The Brighter Side of Farm Life." Incidentally, the Middle West was alleged to produce an excess of best-selling regionalist novels lacking in literary merit; see "Coteries and the Country Cousin."

9. The recent vigor of scholarly efforts to reclaim regional and popular literature, especially by women, suggests the proportional absence of these genres from previous literary considerations. For starters, see Inness and Royer, *Breaking Boundaries,* and Fetterley and Pryse, *Writing Out of Place.*

10. Crawford, "The American Farmer in Fact and Fiction."

11. "The Farm and the Novel"; Porterfield, "Reluctance of the American Novel to Enter the Barn."

12. Van Zile, "Our Barnyard School of Fiction"; Carter, "Back to the Farm and to Sanity."

13. Meredith, "Birth Control in Fiction." Stringer's books followed a pioneering farm family on the Canadian frontier.

14. According to James F. English, there were at least twenty-one American literary awards in 1929, and forty-eight by 1935, though these numbers probably underrepresent the actual count. See *The Economy of Prestige,* 326–27.

15. Radway, *A Feeling for Books,* chap. 6.

16. Looking back on the 1920s and 1930s, Macdonald commented contemptuously on both the Book-of-the-Month Club and the literary prize as classic midcult institutions. See "Masscult and Midcult," 594–96.

17. The Harper Prize Novel Contest was awarded biannually from 1924 to 1964 by Harper and Brothers (later Harper and Row) for an unpublished manuscript. See Kloman, "Pulitzer Prize Thumbnails Project." The quotation is from "Prize Novels."

18. Caroline Sherman, writing on the subject in 1938, considered the following Pulitzer Prize winners to be farm novels: Willa Cather, *One of Ours* (1923); Margaret Wilson, *The Able McLaughlins* (1924); Edna Ferber, *So Big* (1925); Louis Bromfield, *Early Autumn* (1927); Julia Peterkin, *Scarlet Sister Mary* (1929); Oliver LaFarge, *Laughing Boy* (1930); Pearl Buck, *The Good Earth* (1932); Caroline Miller, *Lamb in His Bosom* (1934); Josephine Johnson, *Now in November* (1935); H. L. Davis, *Honey in the Horn* (1936). Again, while we might quibble about some of her inclusions (note that Meyer's similar compilation is shorter [*The Middle Western Farm Novel in the Twentieth Century,* 4]), Sherman's list is useful precisely because it foregrounds a commonality among these texts that was more obvious at the time than it is today ("The Development of American Rural Fiction").

19. Chamberlain, "Books of the Times."

20. Lewis's letter was printed in the *New York Times* on 6 May 1926 ("Lewis Refuses Pulitzer Prize").

21. In his 1930 Nobel Prize acceptance speech, Lewis praised Willa Cather, among others. He persisted, however, in his complaints about the American literary scene generally, which, he felt, tended to reward novelists who assert "that all American men are tall, handsome, rich, honest, and powerful at golf; that all country towns are filled with neighbors who do nothing from day to day save go about being kind to one another; that although American girls may be wild, they change always into perfect wives and mothers." See Lewis, "The American Fear of Literature."

22. "Sends Lewis Hat, Size 207." The *Philadelphia Record* is quoted at length in "Sinclair Lewis's Hornet's Nest."

23. Mencken is quoted in "Sinclair Lewis's Hornet's Nest," 27; the editorial is "A Literary Main Street."

24. Sherman, "The Development of American Rural Fiction," 76.

25. "[T]he field of cultural production is the site of struggles in which what is at stake is the power to impose a dominant definition of a writer and therefore to delimit the population of those entitled to take part in the struggle to define the writer" (Bourdieu, *The Field of Cultural Production,* 42).

26. Korda, *Making the List,* 43. Sales's *The Specialist* was one of the top ten nonfiction best-sellers for 1929.

27. Meyer, *The Middle Western Farm Novel in the Twentieth Century,* 3.

28. As I discuss further on, for instance, Ferber's *So Big* first appeared in *Woman's Home Companion,* and Ostenso's *Wild Geese* was serialized in *Pictorial Review.* On the

assumption that best-sellers were written for and read by women, as well as on their tendency to appear first as serials, see Raub, *Yesterday's Stories*, xv. Raub dedicates one chapter of her study to best-selling farm and pioneer novels by women, although I disagree with her conclusion that these novels almost uniformly "privileged a conservative reading of women's roles and expectations" (75).

29. All excerpts can be found in the *Book Review Digest*.

30. Once again, Arthur Stringer was an easy target, as suggested by these reviews of *The Prairie Child*, quoted in the *Book Review Digest* for 1922: "A certain amount of sentimentality is inescapable in the particular type of story which Mr. Stringer is telling. The book was written first of all for serialization in a woman's magazine and despite the fact that the Pictorial Review has made several announcements that it had no desire to confine itself to the type of story definitely intended and designated as a woman's story, this tale of 'The Prairie Child' most emphatically belongs in that class" (D.L.M., *Boston Transcript* 17 May 1922); "Here is sentimentality a-plenty and the most distasteful of it is that it revolves about a mother's relation with her small son" (*Springfield Republican* 23 July 1922).

31. Raub, *Yesterday's Stories*, 61. On the value of conventional storytelling for marginalized groups, and the resulting challenge to poststructuralist claims that narrative represents the "tyranny of the symbolic order," see Friedman, *Mapping*, chap. 9, especially 228–30.

32. Rubin, *The Making of Middlebrow Culture;* Radway, *A Feeling for Books*. On the sentimental, see Tompkins, *Sensational Designs*, and Barnes, *States of Sympathy*.

33. The Botshon and Goldsmith quotations are on pp. 6 and 1, respectively; the Rubin quotation is found in *The Making of Middlebrow Culture, xviii.*

34. Korda, *Making the List*, 36. For these examples from the advertising campaign, see the *New York Times Book Review* 12 Oct. 1924: 29, and 25 Jan. 1925: 24.

35. On Ferber and her career, see Gilbert, *Ferber*, and, more briefly, the back matter included in the HarperCollins edition of *So Big*, to which all parenthetical page numbers refer.

36. "Briefer Mention," *Dial* 77 (Dec. 1924): 523; Riddell, *In the Worst Possible Taste*, 36, 33, 29; "Edna Ferber, Novelist, 82, Dies." On Ferber's predictions for *So Big*, see the HarperCollins text, p. 257.

37. Bromfield, "Edna Ferber," 10; Overton, "The Social Critic in Edna Ferber," 138, 143; White, "Edna Ferber," 36; Riddell, *In the Worst Possible Taste*, 30.

38. This was true of White in particular, who was a well-known journalist and, significantly, a member of the Pulitzer Prize Committee that chose *So Big* as the winner for 1924. Gilbert describes White's machinations as he urged the committee to vote for Ferber (*Ferber*, 385–88).

39. Rodgers, Introduction, xiii.

40. "So Big," *Times Literary Supplement*.

41. Rascoe, "So Big."

42. For the contest announcement see "Books and Authors." Review comments are from Lowrie, "A Prize Novel," 335; "Earth Hunger," 8; "Briefer Mention," *Dial* 80 (Jan. 1926): 68.

43. For a brief version of Ostenso's background, see Arnason, "Afterword." Ostenso apparently stated that *Wild Geese* was inspired by the lake district of Manitoba; see Overton, "A Novelist from Nowhere."

44. Hammill, "The Sensations of the 1920s." On Ostenso's possibly "international" aspirations, see Keahey, *Making It Home*, 15.

45. Hansen is quoted in "New Dodd, Mead Books." Brickell, "Clever First Novel"; Roedder, "Norse America in Fiction," 494; "Briefer Mention," *Dial* 80 (Jan. 1926): 68; Rich, review of *Wild Geese*. Vague references to Ostenso's northerly landscape are from Townsend, "The Book Table," and Lowrie, "A Prize Novel."

46. Hammill, "The Sensations of the 1920s."

47. Brickell, "Clever First Novel"; Lowrie, "A Prize Novel," 336; Douglas, "Sloth of the Soil."

48. See Hammill, "The Sensations of the 1920s," on critics' efforts to force *Wild Geese* into categories of romance or realism. A good argument for its naturalism can be found in Baum, "Martha Ostenso's *Wild Geese.*"

49. Page numbers refer to Ostenso, *Wild Geese*.

50. An important narrative thread concerns Caleb's religiosity. As a trustee of the local church, he prevents Anton, a Catholic, from being buried in the church cemetery, and his attitude of outraged morality concerning Amelia's illegitimate pregnancy and Judith's affair with Sven is particularly acute. For a provocative reading of Caleb's relation to empire, see Keahey, *Making It Home*.

51. Baum, "Martha Ostenso's *Wild Geese*," 118.

52. Overton, "A Novelist from Nowhere."

53. Viking Press advertisement, *New York Times Book Review* 29 Aug. 1926: 16; Book-of-the-Month Club notice, *New York Times Book Review* 7 Nov. 1926: 19. The revisionist historian is Gillman ("Regionalism and Naturalism," 101). In considering the critical climate of the mid-1920s, it is worth noting that William Faulkner, who would eventually lend legitimacy to rural regionalism, was not yet recognized as a major literary talent.

54. Walbridge, "The Book Table." For comparisons of Roberts to Woolf and Lawrence, see McDowell's preface in *Elizabeth Madox Roberts*, and Campbell and Foster, *Elizabeth Madox Roberts*, 112ff. On Ellen Chesser and the "elusiveness of expression," see Kramer, "Through Language to Self."

55. McDowell discusses in his preface the few book-length critical studies of Roberts, all of which appeared in the late 1950s and early 1960s. More recent efforts to revive her reputation include a special issue of the *Southern Review* (Fall 1984), wherein William Slavick, writing about the Roberts papers in the Library of Congress, states that "[a]lmost never is [Roberts's] regional identification defined in larger terms than Kentucky" ("Taken with a Long-Handled Spoon," 769). In the late 1990s an annual Roberts conference was established at Saint Catharine College, near Roberts's home in Springfield, Kentucky.

56. Again, see Inness and Royer, *Breaking Boundaries*, especially their introduction.

57. All page numbers refer to Roberts, *The Time of Man* (UP of Kentucky, 2000).

58. Walker, "The Autumn Novel Harvest."

59. From the private papers of Roberts, quoted in Slavick, "Taken with a Long-Handled Spoon," 768.

60. Quoted in Simpson, "The Sexuality of History," 790.

61. Warren, "Elizabeth Madox Roberts," xxvii. Roberts's comment is quoted in Lewis, "Elizabeth Madox Roberts, a Memoir," 814. Stuart, "Miss Roberts' Poignant Chronicle of the American Peasantry."

62. Quotations are from Davidson, "Yankee Yeomanry," and Matthews, "Novels, Stories, and Prophecies." For comments on the novel's allure for city dwellers, see Van Doren, "The Dispassionate Shepherds," and Springer, "The Seasons Come to Maine."

63. The advertisement appeared in the *New York Times Book Review* 23 July 1933: 20. Quotation is from Feld, "Man and the Seasons in Maine."

64. Follansbee, "Drama in the Fields."

65. Carroll created the folk play largely in reaction to the film, which she disliked intensely. The relations among the novel, the film, and the folk play are quite complex and beyond the scope of my purposes here, yet they suggest much about Carroll's struggle for aesthetic legitimacy and about the tensions and cross-fertilizations in these years between "serious" and "popular" narrative forms. In later years Carroll wrote a book about the folk play entitled *The Book That Came Alive.*

66. Matthews, "Novels, Stories, and Prophecies."

67. Letter to Greta Kerr, 26 July 1934, courtesy of the Gladys Hasty Carroll Collection, Maine Women Writers Collection, University of New England, Portland, Maine.

68. "As the Earth Turns," *Times Literary Supplement* 22 June 1933: 426.

69. Danbom, *The Resisted Revolution,* 10. Throughout chapter 1, Danbom discusses the ways that the myth of the farmer's individualism impeded his political progress and obscured the family and neighborly interreliance that was the hallmark of successful farm communities.

70. For example, in *States of Sympathy,* Elizabeth Barnes argues that, because sentimentalism involves the "conversion of the political into the personal" (2), melodramatic narratives involving seduction, betrayal, and even incest actively consolidate a vision of the American body politic that is based on a notion of mutual sympathy.

71. The former is the view of Meyer in *The Middle Western Farm Novel in the Twentieth Century,* 102.

Chapter 4

1. Corey was the author of the Mantz trilogy (*Three Miles Square* [1939]; *The Road Returns* [1940]; *County Seat* [1941]), a novelistic history of Iowa farm culture between the years 1910 and 1930. His works are of interest here because of their faithful rendering of agricultural labor and machinery and their indictment of city dwellers and industrialization.

2. Conlogue, *Working the Garden,* 66.

3. Denning, *The Cultural Front,* chap. 7.

4. Sinclair, "Farmers Made World Safe for Democracy, but—" (source unknown; newspaper clipping courtesy of the Selected Edith Summers Kelley Papers, Special

Collections Research Center, Morris Library, Southern Illinois University Carbondale). I have been unable to locate the Hicks review, but it is summarized in a letter of 4 February 1935 to Johnson from Louis Birnbaum (Josephine Winslow Johnson Collection, Special Collections, Washington University Library, St. Louis, Missouri).

5. Olsen, *Yonnondio,* 40. In this chapter of the text (chapter 4), Olsen narrates her protagonists' yearlong sojourn on a farm, where they at first revel in the pleasures of outdoor labor but eventually are defeated by the unfavorable economics of tenancy. When the family inevitably moves on so that the father can take yet another industrial job, this time at a slaughterhouse, the mother and children persist in recalling their months on the farm as a time of contentment and relative abundance—this despite the narrative's details, which stress the miseries of rural life, including the family's isolation, their vulnerability to the weather, and the excessive labor requirements of farming.

6. Kronenberger, "The Brighter Side of Farm Life."

7. The quotation is from Josephson, "The Frontier and Literature." For similar contemporaneous comments on Garland in particular and naturalistic agricultural fiction more generally, see "Coteries and the Country Cousin" and "Literary Iowa."

8. In *Keywords,* Raymond Williams offers a synopsis of naturalism's accumulated meanings, tracing its genesis to the deterministic science of Darwin and emphasizing its disregard for the supernatural (216–19).

9. See Brooks, *The Melodramatic Imagination.* The quotations are taken from pp. 9, 2, and ix, respectively.

10. Brooks, *The Melodramatic Imagination,* 15.

11. An essential aspect of Brooks's argument is that melodrama emerged at the historical moment when the concept of an absolute moral authority had lost its influence; melodrama responded to that loss by insisting on a transcendent realm of spiritual and ethical significance.

12. Gledhill, "The Melodramatic Field," especially 33–36.

13. Gledhill, "The Melodramatic Field," 31.

14. For Kelley's comments concerning the excision, see Goodman, "Afterword," 361. Alfred Harcourt wrote to Kelley that "the obstetrical incident . . . is what thousands of women go through, but—almost therefore—it is not peculiar to the story of Judith or the Tobacco country" (letter from Alfred Harcourt to Edith Summers Kelley, 6 April 1923, Selected Edith Summers Kelley Papers, Special Collections Research Center, Morris Library, Southern Illinois University Carbondale).

15. See Boynton, review of *Weeds;* review of *Weeds, Literary Digest;* Sherman, "Fresh Harvest."

16. Letters to Upton Sinclair, 2 April 1924 and 7 May [n.y.] (Kelley Papers, courtesy of the Lilly Library, Indiana University, Bloomington, Indiana). Sinclair had apparently arranged for Kelley to receive financing from the American Civil Liberties Union and later suggested that *Weeds* be included in a proposed radical library. The scenes excised from the novel, including those concerning a cooperative "Burley Society" (burley being

the type of tobacco cultivated in the novel's Kentucky locale), are available in the Kelley Papers of the Morris Library, Southern Illinois University Carbondale.

17. Both manuscripts are located in the Special Collections Research Center, Morris Library, Southern Illinois University Carbondale.

18. "We Went Back to the Land" (unpublished manuscript, Special Collections Research Center, Morris Library, Southern Illinois University Carbondale).

19. Page numbers refer to the 1996 Feminist Press edition of *Weeds.* On Kelley's serving as a model for female characters in Lewis's *More Miles* and *Arrowsmith,* see Matthew Bruccoli's introduction to the 1972 edition of *Weeds* (xi).

20. This is how Kelley described herself. See Bruccoli, "Introduction," vi, xi.

21. The excised scene, "Billy's Birth," is presented on pp. 335–51 in the cited edition. To avoid excessive citations, individual page references to this section are omitted.

22. Goodman, "Afterword," 361.

23. Letters from Alan Updegraff to Edith Summers Kelley, Special Collections Research Center, Morris Library, Southern Illinois University Carbondale.

24. Jabez plays a relatively minor role in the novel, but there is no question that his relation to Judith is crucial to our understanding of her character, as her response to his death—significantly, on the very last page of the text—suggests: "He had been the one real companion she had ever known. Now he was gone and she was alone. A weight like a great, cold stone settled itself upon her vitals; and as she gazed out over the darkening country it seemed to stretch endlessly, endlessly, like her future life, through a sad, dead level of unrelieved monotony" (333).

25. See the Updegraff letter headed "W.B., Sunday. [1912?]," opening with "Dear Edie" (Special Collections Research Center, Morris Library, Southern Illinois University Carbondale).

26. For an overview of traditional and contemporary considerations of the nature/culture divide, see Alaimo, *Undomesticated Ground,* 1–23.

27. Alaimo, *Undomesticated Ground,* 119. The quotation is from *Weeds,* 275.

28. Brooks, *The Melodramatic Imagination,* xi.

29. On this aspect of melodrama, see Brooks, especially chap. 1.

30. Daniels, "Mill Town"; Davis, "The Red Peril"; Cantwell, "Class-Conscious Fiction."

31. Cook, *From Tobacco Road to Route 66,* 107.

32. Alaimo, *Undomesticated Ground,* 117.

33. Daniels, "Mill Town."

34. See Shannon, "Biographical Afterword."

35. Shannon, "Biographical Afterword," 441.

36. Page numbers refer to the 1983 Feminist Press edition of *Call Home the Heart.*

37. Alaimo, *Undomesticated Ground,* 116–17. Elfenbein argues, further, that the scene exposes the limitations of Dargan herself, whose racist rhetoric here undermines her novel's efforts to dismantle racism ("A Forgotten Revolutionary Voice," 203–5). Cook, on the other hand, suggests that in writing this scene Dargan was more "intellectually honest"

than other novelists of the Gastonia strike (*From Tobacco Road to Route 66,* 453–54). For more on the novel's race issues, see Sowinska, "Writing across the Color Line."

38. Cheever, "While the Fields Burn."

39. Gledhill, "The Melodramatic Field," 33. Here Gledhill explains that melodrama traces an alternative route between realism, which tries to "possess the world by understanding it," and modernism and postmodernism, which perceive the "disillusion" of such an ambition: "Taking its stand in the material world of everyday reality and lived experience, and acknowledging the limitations of the conventions of language and representation, [melodrama] proceeds to force into aesthetic presence identity, value and plenitude of meaning."

40. Quotations from Rascoe, review of *Now in November,* and Walton, "A First Novel of Fine Distinction."

41. Walton, "A First Novel of Fine Distinction." Clifton Fadiman of Simon and Schuster also compared the novel to works by Roberts and Cather, and to Wharton's *Ethan Frome.* See his lengthy letter to Johnson dated 5 February 1934, Josephine Winslow Johnson Collection, Special Collections, Washington University Library, St. Louis, Missouri. Similarly, Lewis Gannett described Johnson's novel as "an *As the Earth Turns* with more of the strong vinegar of life in it; an *O Pioneers* of the life of Americans on the farm in 1934" ("Books and Things").

42. Quotation from a clipping of the *St. Louis Dispatch,* 17 May 1935, n.p. (Johnson Papers). On Johnson's life, see the edition of the *Kirkwood Historical Review* dedicated to Johnson (7 [Dec. 1968]); her autobiography, *Seven Houses;* and Hoffmann, "Afterword." Several articles by Johnson in this period are of particular interest regarding her political views, including "Cotton Share Croppers Facing 'War'" and "America's Domestic Problems" (publication venue of the latter is unknown; it is available as a clipping in the Johnson Papers at Washington University, St. Louis, Missouri).

43. Hoffmann, "Afterword," 243–49.

44. Parenthetical page numbers refer to the Feminist Press edition of 1991.

45. Walton, "Book Parade"; Hoffmann, "Afterword," 242.

46. Kocks, *Dream a Little,* 115.

47. The quotation is from Brooks, *The Melodramatic Imagination,* 6.

48. Johnson, "America's Domestic Problems."

Chapter 5

1. For an example of photography used for these purposes, see "A More Beautiful Home This Year" in the *Progressive Farmer and Southern Farm Gazette* and the following issues of *The Farmer's Wife:* Jan. 1912: n.p. (photograph with caption reading "An Attractive, Enjoyable Farm Home. . .") and Jan. 1919: 173. The latter photograph shows a woman pumping water at an outdoor pump, and the caption reads, "Here is a 'real' picture which conveys a very 'real' impression—not too pleasant an impression. The community spirit that is not mighty enough to make impossible such slavery of farm womanhood as we see illustrated here, sorely needs awakening by the voice of a live

and consecrated Neighborhood Club. . . . How much longer shall these cruelly hard inconveniences exist in our country?"

2. See McEuen's introduction to *Seeing America* for a discussion of women's changing roles and the emergence of photography, including the point about women not representing a threat to men in this field (3). Jane Gover also treats this issue substantially in *The Positive Image.*

3. Bernardin et al., "Introduction." The striking similarities between rural peoples and native peoples in terms of their physical and representational containments by a dominant culture are, unfortunately, beyond the scope of this project. As a preliminary indication, however, it is worth noting that a Field Matron Program, roughly corresponding to the rural extension programs for women, was sponsored by the U.S. Indian Service from 1890 to 1938. Its purpose was to bring "exemplars of white middle-class femininity" to native women in order to train them in "domestic arts" (Bernardin et al., "Introduction," 17).

4. Stange, *Symbols of Ideal Life,* 130.

5. Basic information on these women can be found in Rosenblum's *A History of Women Photographers.* A few have also received more extended critical attention: see Péladeau, *Chansonetta;* Robideau, *Flapjacks and Photographs;* Flynt, *The Allen Sisters;* Lucey, *Photographing Montana.* Emmons is also featured in Simpson, *The Way Life Was.*

6. Of course, while Bourke-White made her name in advertising, she also created a photographic record of Depression-era rurality, *You Have Seen Their Faces* (with text by Erskine Caldwell). However, her sensibility was and is frequently discussed—in contrast to Lange's—as ill suited for the task. For a discussion of Bourke-White's approach to rurality as compared with Lange's, see, for instance, McEuen's *Seeing America.*

7. In addition to Rosenblum, Gover, and Bernardin et al., see Davidov, *Women's Camera Work.*

8. Levine, "The Historian and the Icon," 28.

9. Bernardin et al. make this claim regarding photographs of Native Americans ("Introduction," 14–15). Others have argued the same regarding the FSA collection. Wendy Kozol, for instance, asserts that much FSA photography reproduced a division of male and female spheres and emphasized relatively small nuclear families, both of which were at odds with rural realities ("Madonnas of the Fields").

10. North, *Camera Works,* 40, 11; Agee and Evans, *Let Us Now Praise Famous Men,* 11.

11. In later years, Post actually used this word in reference to her FSA work. See Murray, "Q & A: Marion Post Wolcott," 86.

12. Levine, "The Historian and the Icon," 22.

13. Susan Fillin-Yeh refers to Ulmann as a "premodernist" in the introduction to Rosenblum and Fillin-Yeh, *Documenting a Myth.* The quotation is from Thornton, "Ulmann Forces a New Look at Pictorialism."

14. Ulmann, *The Faculty of the College of Physicians and Surgeons, Columbia University in the City of New York: Twenty-Four Portraits; A Book of Portraits of the Faculty of the Medical Department of the Johns Hopkins University, Baltimore; A Portrait Gallery of American Editors.*

15. In 1930, Dale Warren published an entertaining interview-narrative of some of Ulmann's more memorable experiences photographing the literati ("Doris Ulmann"). On the double signatures, see McEuen, *Seeing America,* 23; fig. 5.4 provides an example.

16. See Jacobs, *The Life and Photography of Doris Ulmann,* for the most complete discussion of Ulmann's biography. The quotations are taken from pp. 6 and 74.

17. McEuen, *Seeing America,* 13–17. Jacobs argues that those critics who have claimed a more personal connection between Hine and Ulmann are mistaken (*The Life and Photography of Doris Ulmann,* 269, n30).

18. See Jacobs, *The Life and Photography of Doris Ulmann,* 54, on this connection. Gilpin photographed Native Americans, and Sipprell interested herself in Mexican and Yugoslavian immigrants. Like Ulmann, both were pictorialists trained by Clarence H. White.

19. Letter from Ulmann to William J. Hutchins, qtd. in Jacobs, *The Life and Photography of Doris Ulmann,* 110; Eaton, "The Doris Ulmann Photograph Collection."

20. Most famously, Ulmann's photographs for *Roll, Jordan, Roll* (discussed further on) were heavily criticized, as the initial trade edition used halftone reproductions that failed to capture Ulmann's tonal subtlety. A second, deluxe edition featuring fine photogravure prints was more successful, but was also more expensive, and only 350 copies were produced.

21. Quoted in McEuen, *Seeing America,* 33. On Ulmann's equipment and its limitations, see McEuen, *Seeing America,* 30–31, and Jacobs, *The Life and Photography of Doris Ulmann,* 23–24. Ruth Banes suggests, however, that Ulmann's soft-focus lens was capable of some versatility ("Doris Ulmann and Her Mountain Folk," 38).

22. Jacobs offers the fullest treatment of Niles and his relations with Ulmann. Much of his information is drawn from Niles's unpublished notebooks and autobiography.

23. For instance, this champion of the marginalized kept house servants and a chauffeur.

24. Ulmann's will is discussed in McEuen, *Seeing America,* and Jacobs, *The Life and Photography of Doris Ulmann.* According to Banes, several of Ulmann's sitters, years after their encounters with Ulmann, continued to proclaim their affection for her ("Doris Ulmann and Her Mountain Folk," 40–41). Virtually all contemporary accounts testify to her congenial personality.

25. On gender symbols and images of the nuclear family in 1930s documentary photography, see Kozol, "Madonnas of the Fields." David Peeler makes similar points in *Hope among Us Yet,* 82, 94. The cultural currency of Madonna-like imagery in reference to destitute farmers perhaps explains why Ulmann's photograph of Bonnie Hensley and her baby son John (reprinted in Banes, "Doris Ulmann and Her Mountain Folk," and elsewhere), which departs from her typical singular portraits, is one of her most widely reproduced works.

26. Several of these are reprinted in Jacobs, *The Life and Photography of Doris Ulmann.*

27. McEuen, *Seeing America,* 58–60; see also Davidov, *Woman's Camera Work,* 186.

28. This was in addition to the gift, already noted, to John Jacob Niles. On Ulmann's devotion to Berea and Campbell, and on the details of her will (which was contested by her family), see Jacobs, *The Life and Photography of Doris Ulmann.* Brown and Sundell suggest that Ulmann considered the "recreations" of older agrarian cultures by those at settlement schools to be "interesting extensions of the cultures themselves" ("Stylizing the Folk," 343). More information on the settlement school movement and the mountain crafts revival can be found in Whisnant, *All That Is Native and Fine,* and Shapiro, *Appalachia on Our Mind.*

29. For a period example of a nativist perspective on Ulmann, see "The Mountain Breed."

30. Prominent examples include Lange and Taylor, *An American Exodus* (1939); Caldwell and Bourke-White, *You Have Seen Their Faces* (1937); Wright and Rosskam, *Twelve Million Black Voices* (1941); and Agee and Evans, *Let Us Now Praise Famous Men* (1941).

31. Peterkin and Ulmann, *Roll, Jordan, Roll,* 11–12.

32. See Jacobs, *The Life and Photography of Doris Ulmann,* 126 for a summary of period responses.

33. Natanson, *The Black Image in the New Deal,* 23–24; Brown and Sundell, "Stylizing the Folk," 342. On Ulmann's photographs as "artworks that function independently of the text," see also Lamunière, "*Roll, Jordan, Roll* and the Gullah Photographs of Doris Ulmann." Incidentally, Lamunière asserts that the entire idea for the book was Ulmann's.

34. Peterkin and Ulmann, *Roll, Jordan, Roll,* 166–67. The comment about the convicts is on p. 12.

35. Davidov, *Woman's Camera Work,* 190–93.

36. See especially Hendrickson, *Looking for the Light.* Jack Hurley is also interested in this question in his *Marion Post Wolcott* (note especially p. 147). Wolcott's insistence that his wife retroactively add her married name to all of her FSA images has provided much fodder for the notion that Post relinquished her identity upon marrying. Ironically, Ulmann did the opposite: when she divorced Charles Jaeger, she returned to her previous prints and wrote her newly reclaimed maiden name over her married one. (In this study I have chosen not to use Post's married name, since almost all the photographs under discussion were taken before her marriage.)

37. According to Levine, only about 28 percent of the photographs taken under the auspices of the FSA and its later incarnation, the Office of War Information, depict urban people or settings ("The Historian and the Icon," 28). The FSA began in 1935 as the Resettlement Administration, a New Deal agency designed to help the poorest of farm families. It was absorbed into the Department of Agriculture in 1937 and renamed the Farm Security Administration. Studies of the FSA and its photography are too numerous to be listed here, but one place to begin is Baldwin, *Poverty and Politics: The Rise and Decline of the Farm Security Administration.* Chapter 3 of Stange's *Symbols of Ideal Life* offers a usefully condensed overview of the FSA Photography Project. The classic study of 1930s documentary is Stott, *Documentary Expression and Thirties America.*

38. Melissa McEuen compares the two photographers' similar trips through Kentucky in "Doris Ulmann and Marion Post Wolcott."

39. According to McEuen, "Lange's personal vision and the [agency's] initial objectives dovetailed" (*Seeing America*, 105–6). Davidov argues similarly that Lange's *American Exodus* is an extension of the FSA project (*Women's Camera Work*, 260–61). On Lange's canny ability to create photos that presented the rural poor as "courageous, determined, and even a bit transcendent"—the goals of the RA/FSA—see Peeler, *Hope among Us Yet*, 65.

40. McEuen, *Seeing America*, 136. For details of Post's biography, see Hurley, *Marion Post Wolcott*, and Hendrickson, *Looking for the Light;* a usefully brief version is offered by Boddy ("Photographing Women").

41. The quotation is from Hurley, *Marion Post Wolcott*, 28. On Post's assignment to "fill in" the FSA file, see, in addition to the above-mentioned sources, Murray's interview with the photographer ("Q & A").

42. Quoted in Murray, "Q & A," 86. Similar comments by Post are included in Fisher, *Let Us Now Praise Famous Women*, 145.

43. That many of these houses are inhabited is made clear by Post's captions. Post also took photographs of prosperous homes, which, in the context of her FSA file as a whole, form an eloquent counterpoint to the ramshackle ones.

44. Many have discussed Lange's most famous photograph in this way. For an example, see Kozol, "Madonnas of the Fields."

45. Quoted in Snyder, "Marion Post Wolcott," 302. On Stryker's "Victorian" standards for Post and her responses to his strictures, see Snyder, "Marion Post Wolcott"; Hurley, *Marion Post Wolcott*, 53–58; and McEuen, *Seeing America* 146–47. Andrea Fisher addresses Lange's construction as documentary's "mother" and Post's role as its "girl" (*Let Us Now Praise Famous Women*, 144–51).

46. See Brownell, "Girl Photographer," and the "feature clip" on Post in the *New Orleans Times-Picayune* (June 1939) quoted at length in Hendrickson, *Looking for the Light*, 151.

47. See Hurley, *Marion Post Wolcott*, 36–38, where this charged exchange between Post and Stryker regarding Post's attire is quoted at length. It is also discussed in Snyder, "Marion Post Wolcott," 303, and McEuen, *Seeing America*, 146.

48. Qtd. in Hendrickson, *Looking for the Light*, 153.

49. On Post's generally positive assessment of Stryker as a boss, see McEuen, *Seeing America*, 156–57.

50. McEuen, *Seeing America*, 144. Hendrickson also mentions this image, asking, "Did she take it . . . to show the boss she wasn't afraid. . .?" (*Looking for the Light*, 71).

51. Library of Congress, Prints and Photographs Collection, image No. LC-USF34-050290-E.

52. For example, McEuen, *Seeing America*, 143.

53. For instance, one photograph shows a seemingly hearty white gas station attendant selling gas to a black man whose eyes are averted; Post's caption reads,

"Cherished customer." Another image is of the cramped interior space of a wooden shack, featuring two disheveled beds and a broken chair, and is labeled "Bedroom (and kitchen and living room) of former RR (Rural Rehabilitation) family." Library of Congress, Prints and Photographs Division, images No. LC-USF33–030391-M3 and No. LC-USF34–051436-D.

54. On minority representation in the FSA photography files, and on Stryker's lack of enthusiasm for such representation, see Natanson, *The Black Image in the New Deal,* chap. 2. Natanson asserts that Post, together with Lange, was "a vital force" in the collection of black imagery for the FSA (72).

55. Once photographic portraits became ubiquitous, consumable objects, writes Tagg, "It was no longer a privilege to be pictured but the burden of a new class of the surveilled" (*The Burden of Representation,* 59).

56. Qtd. in Snyder, "Marion Post Wolcott," 308.

Epilogue

1. Wood, *Revolt against the City.* Quotations can be found on pp. 16–19 and 33.

2. Williams, *The Country and the City,* 35–36.

3. Wood, *Revolt against the City,* 10.

4. For more on Wood's work, which was avowedly regionalist and largely agrarian, see Haven, *Going Back to Iowa.* It is no coincidence that Wood was known for wearing overalls in virtually every photograph taken of him.

5. Yaeger, *Dirt and Desire,* 98.

WORKS CITED

Agee, James, and Walker Evans. *Let Us Now Praise Famous Men.* 1941. Boston: Houghton Mifflin, 1988.

Alaimo, Stacy. *Undomesticated Ground: Recasting Nature as Feminist Space.* Ithaca, NY: Cornell UP, 2000.

Aldrich, Earl A. Rev. of *A Lantern in Her Hand,* by Bess Streeter Aldrich. *Saturday Review of Literature* 5 (17 Nov. 1928): 371.

Alexander, Ida M., M.D. "The Welfare of the Home." *The Farmer's Wife* April 1920: 372.

Altieri, Charles. "Can Modernism Have a Future?" *Modernism/Modernity* 7 (2000): 127–43.

Annals of the American Academy of Political and Social Science 40 (March 1912). [Special edition on Country Life.]

Ardis, Ann. *Modernism and Cultural Conflict,* 1880–1922. Cambridge: Cambridge UP, 2002.

Ardis, Ann, and Leslie W. Lewis, eds. *Women's Experience of Modernity,* 1875–1945. Baltimore: Johns Hopkins UP, 2003.

Arnason, David. "Afterword." Martha Ostenso, *Wild Geese.* 303–9.

Atkeson, Mary Meek. *The Woman on the Farm.* New York: Century, 1924.

Babbitt, Kathleen R. "The Productive Farm Woman and the Extension Home Economist in New York State, 1920–1940." *American Rural and Farm Women in Historical Perspective.* Ed. Joan M. Jensen and Nancy Grey Osterud. Washington, DC: Agricultural History Society, 1994. 83–101.

Bailey, Liberty Hyde. *The Country Life Movement in America.* New York: Macmillan, 1911.

Baker, Robert. *The Webb Company: The First Hundred Years.* St. Paul, MN: Webb, 1982.

Baldwin, Sidney. *Poverty and Politics: The Rise and Decline of the Farm Security Administration.* Chapel Hill: U of North Carolina P, 1968.

Banes, Ruth. "Doris Ulmann and Her Mountain Folk." *Journal of American Culture* 8 (Spring 1985): 29–42.

Barnes, Elizabeth. *States of Sympathy: Seduction and Democracy in the American Novel.* New York: Columbia UP, 1997.

Baum, L. Frank. *The Wonderful Wizard of Oz.* 1900. New York: William Morrow, 1987.

Baum, Rosalie Murphy. "Martha Ostenso's *Wild Geese:* More Insight into the Naturalistic Sensibility." *Journal of Canadian Culture* 1 (Fall 1984): 117–35.

Baym, Nina. "Melodramas of Beset Manhood: How Theories of American Fiction Exclude Women Authors." *Feminist Criticism: Essays on Women, Literature, and Theory.* Ed. Elaine Showalter. New York: Pantheon, 1985. 63–80.

Bederman, Gail. *Manliness and Civilization: A Cultural History of Gender and Race in the United States,* 1880–1917. Chicago: U of Chicago P, 1995.

Benson, Susan Porter. *Counter Cultures: Saleswomen, Managers, and Customers in American Department Stores,* 1890–1940. Urbana: U of Illinois P, 1986.

Bernardin, Susan, Melody Graulich, Lisa McFarlane, and Nicole Tonkovich. "Introduction: Empire of the Lens: Women, Indians, and Cameras." *Trading Gazes: Euro-American Women Photographers and Native North Americans,* 1880–1940. Ed. Susan Bernardin, Melody Graulich, Lisa McFarlane, and Nicole Tonkovich. New Brunswick, NJ: Rutgers UP, 2003. 1–31.

Bhaba, Homi K. "'Race,' Time, and the Revision of Modernity." *Oxford Literary Review* 13 (1991): 193–219.

Blair, Karen J. *The Clubwoman as Feminist: True Womanhood Redefined,* 1868–1914. New York: Holmes and Meier, 1980.

Boddy, Julie. "Photographing Women: The Farm Security Administration Work of Marion Post Wolcott." *Decades of Discontent: The Women's Movement,* 1920–1940. Ed. Lois Scharf and Joan M. Jensen. Westport, CT: Greenwood, 1983. 153–66.

"Books and Authors." *New York Times Book Review* 14 Oct. 1923: 10.

Boomhower, Ray E. *The Country Contributor: The Life and Times of Juliet V. Strauss.* Indianapolis: Guild P of Indiana, 1998.

Borsodi, Ralph. *This Ugly Civilization.* 1929. Philadelphia: Porcupine, 1975.

Botshon, Lisa, and Meredith Goldsmith. "Introduction." *Middlebrow Moderns: Popular American Women Writers of the* 1920s. Ed. Lisa Botshon and Meredith Goldsmith. Boston: Northeastern UP, 2003. 3–21.

Bourdieu, Pierre. *The Field of Cultural Production: Essays on Art and Literature.* New York: Columbia UP, 1993.

Bourke, Fielding [Olive Tilford Dargan]. *Call Home the Heart.* 1932. Old Westbury, NY: Westview, 1983.

Bowers, William L. *The Country Life Movement in America,* 1900–1920. Port Washington, NY: Kennikat, 1974.

Boynton, H. H. Review of *Weeds,* by Edith Summers Kelley. *Independent* 111 (8 Dec. 1923): 288–89.

Bradbury, Malcolm, and James McFarlane. "The Name and Nature of Modernism." *Modernism.* Ed. Malcolm Bradbury and James McFarlane. Sussex: Harvester, 1976. 19–55.

Brickell, Herschel. "Clever First Novel Nets Author Fame and—Money." *Literary Review* 6 (24 Oct. 1925): 2.

"Briefer Mention." [On Ferber, *So Big.*] *Dial* 77 (Dec. 1924): 523.

"Briefer Mention." [On Ostenso, *Wild Geese.*] *Dial* 80 (Jan. 1926): 68.
Bromfield, Louis. "Edna Ferber." *Saturday Review of Literature* 12 (15 June 1935): 10–12.
Brooks, Peter. *The Melodramatic Imagination: Balzac, Henry James, Melodrama, and the Mode of Excess.* 1976. New Haven, CT: Yale UP, 1995.
Brown, Anna L., M.D. "Laws of Sex Education and Country Girls." *Rural Manhood* 3 (Nov. 1912): 325–28.
Brown, Lorraine, and Michael G. Sundell. "Stylizing the Folk: Hall Johnson's *Run, Little Chillun* Photographed by Doris Ulmann." *Prospects* 7 (1982): 335–46.
Brown, Ruth. "Woman's Task." *Farm Journal* Feb. 1910: 107.
Brownell, Jean. "Girl Photographer for FSA Travels 50,000 Miles in Search for Pictures." *Washington Post* 19 Nov. 1940: 13.
Bruccoli, Matthew J. "Introduction." *Weeds,* by Edith Summers Kelley. 1923. Carbondale: Southern Illinois UP, 1972. v–xiii.
Butterfield, Kenyon. "The Outlook from the Farm Home." *Rural America* 4.3 (March 1926): 2.
———. "Rural Sociology as a College Discipline." *Annals of the American Academy of Political and Social Science* 40 (March 1912): 12–18.
Cabral, Nora Cruz. Farm Journal *and American Agriculture,* 1877–1965. Diss. U of Illinois, 1966.
Caldwell, Erskine, and Margaret Bourke-White. *You Have Seen Their Faces.* New York: Viking, 1937.
Campbell, Harry Modean, and Ruel E. Foster. *Elizabeth Madox Roberts: American Novelist.* Norman: U of Oklahoma P, 1956.
Cantwell, Robert. "Class-Conscious Fiction." Rev. of *Call Home the Heart,* by Olive Tilford Dargan. *Nation* 134 (25 May 1932): 606.
Carroll, Gladys Hasty. *As the Earth Turns.* New York: Macmillan, 1933.
———. *The Book That Came Alive.* Portland, ME: G. Gannett, 1979.
Carter, John. "Back to the Farm and to Sanity." *New York Times Book Review* 25 May 1924: 2.
Casey, Janet Galligani. "Farm Women, Letters to the Editor, and the Limits of Autobiography Theory." *Journal of Modern Literature* 28.1 (2004): 89–106.
———. "'This Is YOUR Magazine': Domesticity, Agrarianism, and *The Farmer's Wife.*" *American Periodicals* 14.2 (2004): 179–211.
Cather, Willa. *Not under Forty.* New York: Knopf, 1936.
Chamberlain, John. "Books of the Times." *New York Times* 8 May 1934: 21.
Cheever, Jon. "While the Fields Burn." Rev. of *Now in November,* by Josephine Johnson. *New Republic* 80 (26 Sept. 1934): 191.
Clark, T. J. *Farewell to an Idea: Episodes from a History of Modernism.* New Haven, CT: Yale UP, 1999.
Conlogue, William. *Working the Garden: American Writers and the Industrialization of Agriculture.* Chapel Hill: U of North Carolina P, 2001.
Cook, Sylvia Jenkins. *From Tobacco Road to Route 66: The Southern Poor White in Fiction.* Chapel Hill: U of North Carolina P, 1976.

Corey, Paul. *County Seat.* Indianapolis, IN: Bobbs-Merrill, 1941.
———. *The Road Returns.* Indianapolis, IN: Bobbs-Merrill, 1940.
———. *Three Miles Square.* Indianapolis, IN: Bobbs-Merrill, 1939.
"Coteries and the Country Cousin." *Nation* 110 (27 March 1920): 391.
Crawford, Nelson Antrim. "The American Farmer in Fact and Fiction." *Literary Digest International Book Review* Dec. 1925: 25–26+.
Crow, Martha Foote. *The American Country Girl.* New York: Stokes, 1915.
Danbom, David B. *The Resisted Revolution: Urban America and the Industrialization of Agriculture, 1900–1930.* Ames: Iowa State UP, 1979.
———. "Romantic Agrarianism in Twentieth-Century America." *Agricultural History* 65.4 (1991): 1–14.
Daniels, Jonathan. "Mill Town." Rev. of *Call Home the Heart,* by Olive Tilford Dargan. *Saturday Review of Literature* 8 (20 Feb. 1932): 537.
Davidov, Judith Fryer. *Woman's Camera Work: Self/Body/Other in American Visual Culture.* Durham, NC: Duke UP, 1998.
Davidson, Donald. "Yankee Yeomanry." Rev. of *As the Earth Turns,* by Gladys Hasty Carroll. *Saturday Review of Literature* 9 (6 May 1933): 573–74.
Davis, Elmer. "The Red Peril." Rev. of *Call Home the Heart,* by Olive Tilford Dargan. *Saturday Review of Literature* 8 (16 April 1932): 662–63.
Dawley, Alan. *Struggles for Justice: Social Responsibility and the Liberal State.* Cambridge, MA: Harvard UP, 1991.
Dean, Patty. "*The Farmer's Wife.*" Unpublished ms., n.d.
Denning, Michael. *The Cultural Front: The Laboring of American Culture in the Twentieth Century.* London: Verso, 1997.
Dettmar, Kevin J. H., and Stephen Watt, eds. *Marketing Modernisms: Self-Promotion, Canonization, Rereading.* Ann Arbor: U of Michigan P, 1996.
Douglas, Donald. "Sloth of the Soil." Rev. of *Wild Geese,* by Martha Ostenso. *Nation* 122 (6 Jan. 1926): 14–15.
Dyer, Thomas G. *Theodore Roosevelt and the Idea of Race.* Baton Rouge: U of Louisiana P, 1980.
"Earth Hunger." Rev. of *Wild Geese,* by Martha Ostenso. *New York Times* 18 Oct. 1925: 8.
Eaton, Allen. "The Doris Ulmann Photograph Collection." *Call Number* 19 (Spring 1958): 10–11.
"Edna Ferber, Novelist, 82, Dies." *New York Times* 17 April 1968: 1+.
Edwards, Rebecca. "Recent Literature on American Populism." <http://www.h-net.msu.edu/~shgape/bibs/populism.html>.
Elbert, Sarah. "Women and Farming: Changing Structures, Changing Roles." *Women and Farming: Changing Roles, Changing Structures.* Ed. Wava G. Haney and Jane B. Knowles. Boulder, CO: Westview, 245–64.
Elfenbein, Anna Shannon. "A Forgotten Revolutionary Voice: 'Woman's Place' and Race in Olive Tilford Dargan's *Call Home the Heart.*" *The Female Tradition in Southern Literature.* Ed. Carol S. Manning. Urbana: U of Illinois P, 1993. 193–208.

English, James F. *The Economy of Prestige: Prizes, Awards, and the Circulation of Cultural Value.* Cambridge, MA: Harvard UP, 2005.

Evans, James F., and Rodolfo N. Salcedo. *Communications in Agriculture: The American Farm Press.* Ames: Iowa State UP, 1974.

Fairbanks, Carol. *Prairie Women: Images in American and Canadian Fiction.* New Haven, CT: Yale UP, 1986.

"The Farm and the Novel." *Saturday Review of Literature* 6 (27 July 1929): 1+.

The Farm Woman Answers the Question: What Do Farm Women Want? St. Paul, MN: American Country Life Association and *The Farmer's Wife,* 1926.

"Farm Women Find Life Hard." *New York Times* 30 May 1915, sec. 5: 14–15.

The Farmer's Wife. St. Paul, MN: Webb, June 1906–April 1939. Housed at the Minnesota Historical Society, St. Paul, Minnesota.

F.E.B. "Mr. Borsodi's Way Out." *New Republic* 60 (28 Aug. 1929): 48–49.

Feld, Rose C. "Man and the Seasons in Maine." Rev. of *As the Earth Turns,* by Gladys Hasty Carroll. *New York Times Book Review* 7 May 1933: 6.

Felski, Rita. *The Gender of Modernity.* Cambridge, MA: Harvard UP, 1995.

"Feminism on the Farm." *Nation* 19 Oct. 1921: 440.

Ferber, Edna. *So Big.* 1924. New York: HarperCollins, 2000.

Fetterley, Judith, and Marjorie Pryse. *Writing Out of Place: Regionalism, Women, and American Literary Culture.* Urbana: U of Illinois P, 2002.

Fink, Deborah. *Agrarian Women: Wives and Mothers in Rural Nebraska,* 1880–1940. Chapel Hill: U of North Carolina P, 1992.

Fisher, Andrea. *Let Us Now Praise Famous Women: Women Photographers for the U.S. Government,* 1935 *to* 1944. London: Pandora, 1987.

Flynn, Richard. "Imitation Oz: The Sequel as Commodity." *The Lion and the Unicorn: A Critical Journal of Children's Literature* 20 (June 1996): 121–31.

Flynt, Suzanne L. *The Allen Sisters: Pictorial Photographers.* Lebanon, NH: UP of New England, 2002.

Follansbee, Clifton A. "Drama in the Fields." Rev. of *As the Earth Turns,* by Gladys Hasty Carroll. *New York Times* 7 Aug. 1938: 124.

Ford, James L. C. *Magazines for Millions: The Story of Specialized Publications.* Carbondale: Southern Illinois UP, 1969.

Fox, Richard Wightman, and T. J. Jackson Lears, eds. *The Culture of Consumption: Critical Essays in American History,* 1880–1980. New York: Pantheon, 1983.

Freeman, Mary Wilkins. *The Shoulders of Atlas.* New York: Harper and Brothers, 1908.

Friedman, Susan Stanford. *Mappings: Feminism and the Cultural Geographies of Encounter.* Princeton, NJ: Princeton UP, 1998.

Fry, John J. *The Farm Press, Reform, and Rural Change,* 1895–1920. New York: Routledge, 2005.

Galpin, Charles Josiah. *Rural Social Problems.* New York: Century, 1924.

Gannett, Lewis. "Books and Things." Rev. of *Now in November,* by Josephine Johnson. *New York Herald Tribune* 13 Sept. 1934: 17.

Garvey, Ellen Gruber. *The Adman in the Parlor: Magazines and the Gendering of Consumer Culture, 1880s to 1910s.* New York: Oxford UP, 1996.
Gilbert, Julie Goldsmith. *Ferber: A Biography.* Garden City, NY: Doubleday, 1978.
Gilbert, Sandra, and Susan Gubar. *No Man's Land: The Place of the Woman Writer in Twentieth Century Literature.* 3 vols. New Haven: Yale UP, 1988–1994.
Gillman, Susan. "Regionalism and Nationalism in Jewett's *Country of the Pointed Firs.*" *New Essays on "The Country of the Pointed Firs."* Ed. June Howard. Cambridge: Cambridge UP, 1994. 101–20.
Gilman, Charlotte Perkins. "Applepieville." *Independent* 103 (25 Sept. 1920): 365, 393–95.
———. "That Rural Home Inquiry: Why Are There No Women on the President's Commission?" *Good Housekeeping* 48 (Jan. 1909): 120–22.
Gilroy, Paul. *The Black Atlantic: Modernity and Double Consciousness.* Cambridge, MA: Harvard UP, 1993.
Gledhill, Christine. "The Melodramatic Field: An Investigation." *Home Is Where the Heart Is: Studies in Melodrama and the Woman's Film.* Ed. Christine Gledhill. London: BFI Publishing, 1987. 5–39.
Goodman, Charlotte Margolis. "Afterword." *Weeds,* by Edith Summers Kelley. 1923. New York: Feminist Press, 1996.
Goodwyn, Lawrence. *Democratic Promise: The Populist Moment in America.* New York: Oxford UP, 1976.
Gover, C. Jane. *The Positive Image: Women Photographers in Turn of the Century America.* Albany: State U of New York P, 1988.
Grosz, Elizabeth. *Volatile Bodies: Toward a Corporeal Feminism.* Bloomington: Indiana UP, 1994.
Groves, Ernest R. "Suggestion and City-Drift." *Rural Manhood* 7.2 (April 1916): 47–52.
Hackett, Alice Payne. *Fifty Years of Best Sellers, 1895–1945.* New York: Bowker, 1945.
Hagood, Margaret Jarman. *Mothers of the South: Portraiture of the White Tenant Farmwoman.* Chapel Hill: U of North Carolina P, 1939.
Hammill, Faye. "The Sensations of the 1920s: Martha Ostenso's *Wild Geese* and Mazo de la Roche's *Jalna.*" *Studies in Canadian Literature* 28.2 (2004): 66–89.
Haraway, Donna J. *Simians, Cyborgs, and Women: The Reinvention of Nature.* New York: Routledge, 1991.
Harding, Desmond. *Writing the City: Urban Visions and Literary Modernism.* New York: Routledge, 2003.
Harrison, Elizabeth Jane. *Female Pastoral: Women Writers Revisioning the American South.* Knoxville: U of Tennessee P, 1991.
Haven, Janet. *Going Back to Iowa: The World of Grant Wood.* <http://xroads.virginia.edu/~ma98/haven/wood/home.html>.
Hays, Robert. "Introduction: Rural America and Its Magazines." *Early Stories from the Land: Short-Story Fiction from American Rural Magazines.* Ed. Robert Hays. Ames: Iowa State UP, 1995. xi–xxii.

Heath, Mrs. Julian. "The New Kind of Housekeeping: Why and How It is Different from the Old." *Ladies' Home Journal* 32 (Jan. 1915): 2.

Hendrickson, Paul. *Looking for the Light: The Hidden Life and Art of Marion Post Wolcott.* New York: Knopf, 1992.

Hicks, Granville. "Revolution and the Novel." 1934. *Granville Hicks in the* New Masses. Ed. Jack Alan Robbins. Port Washington, NY: Kennikat, 1974. 17–66.

Hicks, John Donald. *The Populist Revolt: A History of the Farmers' Alliance and the People's Party.* Minneapolis: U of Minnesota P, 1955.

Hilton, Kathleen C. "'Both in the Field, Each with a Plow': Race and Gender in USDA Policy, 1907–1929." *Hidden Histories of Women in the New South.* Ed. Virginia Bernhard. Columbia: U of Missouri P, 1994. 114–33.

Hoffmann, Nancy. "Afterword." *Now in November,* by Josephine Johnson. 1934. Old Westbury, NY: Feminist P, 1991. 235–74.

Holt, Marilyn Irvin. *Linoleum, Better Babies, and the Modern Farm Woman.* Albuquerque: U of New Mexico P, 1995.

"How 'Best Sellers' Are Made." *Literary Digest* 88 (9 Jan. 1926): 66–7.

Howe, Irving. "The Idea of the Modern." *Literary Modernism.* Ed. Irving Howe. Greenwich, CT: Fawcett, 1967. 11–40.

Hurley, Jack. *Marion Post Wolcott: A Photographic Journey.* Albuquerque: U of New Mexico P, 1989.

Huyssen, Andreas. *After the Great Divide: Modernism, Mass Culture, Postmodernism.* Bloomington: Indiana UP, 1986.

I'll Take My Stand: The South and the Agrarian Tradition, by Twelve Southerners. New York: Harper, 1930.

Inness, Sherrie A., and Diana Royer. *Breaking Boundaries: New Perspectives on Women's Regional Writing.* Iowa City: U of Iowa P, 1997.

"Is This the Trouble with the Farmer's Wife?" *Ladies' Home Journal* 26 (Feb. 1909): 5.

Jacobs, Philip Walker. *The Life and Photography of Doris Ulmann.* Lexington: UP of Kentucky, 2001.

Jardine, Alice A. *Gynesis: Configurations of Woman and Modernity.* Ithaca, NY: Cornell UP, 1985.

Jellison, Katherine. *Entitled to Power: Farm Women and Technology,* 1913–1963. Chapel Hill: U of North Carolina P, 1993.

Johnson, Josephine. "Cotton Share Croppers Facing 'War.'" *Illinois Magazine, East St. Louis Journal* 5 July 1936: 1+.

———. *Now in November.*1934. Old Westbury, NY: Feminist P, 1991.

———. *Seven Houses.* New York: Simon and Schuster, 1973.

Johnson, Katie N. *Sisters in Sin: Brothel Dramas in America,* 1900–1920. New York: Cambridge UP, 2006.

Josephson, Matthew. "The Frontier and Literature." *New Republic* 68 (2 Sept. 1931): 77–78.

Juster, Norton. *So Sweet to Labor: Rural Women in America,* 1865–1895. New York: Viking, 1979.

Kaplan, Amy. *The Social Construction of American Realism.* Chicago: U of Chicago P, 1988.
Keahey, Deborah. *Making It Home: Place in Canadian Prairie Literature.* Winnipeg: U of Manitoba P, 1998.
Kelley, Edith Summers. *Weeds.* 1923. Westport, NY: Feminist P, 1996.
Kline, Ronald R. *Consumers in the Country: Technology and Social Change in Rural America.* Baltimore: Johns Hopkins UP, 2000.
Kline, Wendy. *Building a Better Race: Gender, Sexuality and Eugenics from the Turn of the Century to the Baby Boom.* Berkeley: U California P, 2001.
Kloman, Harvey. "Pulitzer Prize Thumbnails Project." <http://www.pitt.edu/~kloman/thumbframe.html>.
Knowles, Jane B. "'It's Our Turn Now': Rural Women Speak Out, 1900–1920." *Women and Farming.* Ed. Wava G. Haney and Jane B. Knowles. Boulder, CO: Westview, 303–18.
Kocks, Dorothee. *Dream a Little: Land and Social Justice in Modern America.* Berkeley: U of California P, 2000.
Kolodny, Annette. *The Lay of the Land: Metaphor as Experience and History in American Life and Letters.* Chapel Hill: U of North Carolina P, 1975.
Korda, Michael. *Making the List: A Cultural History of the American Bestseller,* 1909–1999. New York: Barnes and Noble, 2001.
Kozol, Wendy. "Madonnas of the Fields: Photography, Gender, and 1930s Farm Relief." *Genders* 2 (Summer 1988): 1–23.
Kramer, Victor A. "Through Language to Self: Ellen's Journey in *The Time of Man.*" *Southern Review* 20 (1984): 774–84.
Kronenberger, Louis. "The Brighter Side of Farm Life." Rev. of *State Fair,* by Phil Strong. *New York Times Book Review* 8 May 1932: 6.
Lamunière, Michelle C. "*Roll, Jordan, Roll* and the Gullah Photographs of Doris Ulmann." *History of Photography* 21 (1997): 294–302.
Lange, Dorothea, and Paul Schuster Taylor. *An American Exodus; A Record of Human Erosion in the Thirties.* New York: Reynal and Hitchcock, 1939.
Lears, T. J. Jackson. "From Salvation to Self-Realization: Advertising and the Therapeutic Roots of the Consumer Culture, 1880–1930." *The Culture of Consumption.* Ed. Richard Wightman Fox and T. J. Jackson Lears. New York: Pantheon, 1983. 1–38.
———. *No Place of Grace: Antimodernism and the Transformation of American Culture,* 1880–1920. New York: Pantheon, 1981.
Levine, Lawrence. "The Historian and the Icon: Photography and the History of the American People in the 1930s and 1940s." *Documenting America.* Ed. Carl Fleischhauer and Beverly W. Brannan. Berkeley: U of California P, 1988. 15–42.
Lewis, Janet. "Elizabeth Madox Roberts, a Memoir." *Southern Review* 20 (1984): 803–16.
Lewis, Sinclair. "The American Fear of Literature." [Nobel Prize acceptance speech.] <http://nobelprize.org/nobel_prizes/literature/laureates/1930/lewis-lecture.html>.
"Lewis Refuses Pulitzer Prize." *New York Times* 6 May 1926: 1+.
Lind, Robert Staughton, and Helen Merrell Lind. *Middletown: A Study in Contemporary American Culture.* New York: Harcourt, Brace, 1929.

"Literary Iowa." *New York Times* 26 Feb. 1930: 24.
"A Literary Main Street." *Nation* 122 (19 May 1926): 546.
Lott, Eric. *Love and Theft: Blackface Minstrelsy and the American Working Class.* New York: Oxford UP, 1993.
Lovett, Laura. *Conceiving the Future: Pronatalism, Reproduction, and the Family in the United States,* 1890–1938. Chapel Hill: U of North Carolina P, 2007.
Lowrie, Rebecca. "A Prize Novel." Rev. of *Wild Geese,* by Martha Ostenso. *Saturday Review of Literature* 2 (28 Nov. 1925): 335–36.
Lucey, Donna M. *Photographing Montana,* 1894–1928*: The Life and Work of Evelyn Cameron.* New York: Knopf, 1991.
Macdonald, Dwight. "Masscult and Midcult." *Partisan Review* 27 (Spring 1960): 203–33; 27 (Fall 1960): 589–631.
Manchester, Harland. "The Farm Magazines." *Scribner's* 104 (Oct. 1938): 25–29, 58–59.
Manning, Carol S., ed. *The Female Tradition in Southern Literature.* Urbana: U of Illinois P, 1993.
Marti, Donald B. *Women of the Grange: Mutuality and Sisterhood in Rural America,* 1866–1920. New York: Greenwood, 1991.
Marx, Leo. *The Machine in the Garden: Technology and the Pastoral Idea in America.* New York: Oxford UP, 1964.
Matt, Susan. "Frocks, Finery, and Feelings: Rural and Urban Women's Envy, 1890–1930." *An Emotional History of the United States.* Ed. Peter N. Stearns and Jan Lewis. New York: New York UP, 1998. 377–95.
Matthews, T. S. "Novels, Stories, and Prophecies." Rev. of *As the Earth Turns,* by Gladys Hasty Carroll. *New Republic* 75 (7 June 1933): 106–7.
McDowell, Frederick P. W. *Elizabeth Madox Roberts.* New York: Twayne, 1963.
McEuen, Melissa A. "Doris Ulmann and Marion Post Wolcott: The Appalachian South." *History of Photography* 19 (Spring 1995): 4–12.
——. *Seeing America: Women Photographers between the Wars.* Lexington: UP of Kentucky, 2000.
McMath, Robert C. *American Populism: A Social History,* 1877–1898. New York: Noonday, 1993.
McNeill, John Charles. "The White South." *Progressive Farmer and Southern Farm Gazette* 25 June 1910: 8.
Melosh, Barbara. *Engendering Culture: Manhood and Womanhood in New Deal Public Art and Theater.* Washington, DC: Smithsonian Institution P, 1991.
Meredith, Lucile. "Birth Control in Fiction." *New Republic* 32 (27 Sept. 1932): 121–23.
Meyer, Roy W. *The Middle Western Farm Novel in the Twentieth Century.* Lincoln: U of Nebraska P, 1965.
Miller, Perry. *Nature's Nation.* Cambridge, MA: Harvard UP, 1967.
Modleski, Tania. *Loving with a Vengeance: Mass-Produced Fantasies for Women.* New York: Routledge, 1984.
"A More Beautiful Home This Year." *Progressive Farmer and Southern Farm Gazette* 5 Feb. 1910: 103.

Mott, Frank Luther. *Golden Multitudes: The Story of Best Sellers in the United States.* New York: Macmillan, 1947.
———. *A History of American Magazines.* Vol. 4. Cambridge, MA: Harvard UP, 1957.
"The Mountain Breed." [Commentary on Doris Ulmann.] *New York Times* 2 June 1928: 16.
Murphy, Paul V. *The Rebuke of History: The Southern Agrarians and American Conservative Thought.* Chapel Hill: U of North Carolina P, 2001.
Murray, Joan. "Q & A: Marion Post Wolcott." *American Photographer* March 1980: 86–93.
"My Everyday Problems." [Selected letters from readers.] *Woman's Home Companion* July 1923: 25–26, 29.
Nash, Roderick. *Wilderness and the American Mind.* New Haven, CT: Yale UP, 1967.
Natanson, Nicholas. *The Black Image in the New Deal: The Politics of FSA Photography.* Knoxville: U of Tennessee P, 1992.
Nelson, Lowry. *Rural Sociology: Its Origin and Growth in the United States.* 1969. Westport, CT: Greenwood, 1980.
Neth, Mary. *Preserving the Family Farm: Women, Community, and the Foundations of Agribusiness in the Midwest,* 1900–1940. Baltimore: Johns Hopkins UP, 1995.
"New Dodd, Mead Books." *New York Times Book Review* 8 Nov. 1925: 11.
Newman, Louise Michele, ed. *Men's Ideas/Women's Realities:* Popular Science, 1870–1915. New York: Pergamon, 1985.
North, Michael. *Camera Works: Photography and the Twentieth-Century Word.* Oxford: Oxford UP, 2005.
———. *Reading* 1922*: A Return to the Scene of the Modern.* New York: Oxford UP, 1999.
Norwood, Vera. *Made from This Earth: American Women and Nature.* Chapel Hill: U of North Carolina P, 1993.
N. W. Ayer and Son's Directory of Newspapers and Periodicals, 1930–1969. Philadelphia: N. W. Ayer and Son.
Ohmann, Richard. *The Politics of Letters.* Middletown, CT: Wesleyan UP, 1987.
Olsen, Tillie. *Yonnondio: From the Thirties.* New York: Dell, 1974.
Ostenso, Martha. *Wild Geese.* 1925. Toronto: New Canadian Library, 1989.
Overton, Grant. "A Novelist from Nowhere." *Mentor* 15 (June 1927): 57.
———. "The Social Critic in Edna Ferber." *Bookman* 64 (Oct. 1926): 138–43.
Passet, Joanne E. *Sex Radicals and the Quest for Women's Equality.* Urbana: U of Illinois P, 2003.
Peeler, David. *Hope among Us Yet: Social Criticism and Social Solace in Depression America.* Athens: U of Georgia P, 1987.
Péladeau, Marius B. *Chansonetta: The Life and Photographs of Chansonetta Stanley Emmons,* 1858–1937. Waldoboro, ME: Maine Antique Digest, 1977.
Peterkin, Julia, and Doris Ulmann. *Roll, Jordan, Roll.* New York: Ballou, 1933.
Porterfield, Allen W. "Reluctance of the American Novel to Enter the Barn." *New York Times Book Review* 11 Feb. 1923: 2.
"Prize Novels." *Saturday Review of Literature* 4 (11 Feb. 1928): 585.

Pumphrey, Martin. "The Flapper, the Housewife, and the Making of Modernity." *Cultural Studies* 1.2 (1987): 179–94.

Quick, Herbert. "Women on the Farms." *Readings in Rural Sociology.* Ed. John Phelan. New York: Macmillan, 1920. 313–19.

Rabinowitz, Paula. *Labor and Desire: Women's Revolutionary Fiction in Depression America.* Chapel Hill: U of North Carolina P, 1991.

Rado, Lisa, ed. *Modernism, Gender, and Culture: A Cultural Studies Approach.* New York: Garland, 1997.

Radway, Janice. *A Feeling for Books: The Book-of-the-Month Club, Literary Taste, and Middle-Class Desire.* Chapel Hill: U of North Carolina P, 1997.

———. *Reading the Romance: Women, Patriarchy, and Popular Literature.* Chapel Hill: U of North Carolina P, 1991.

Rainey, Lawrence. *Institutions of Modernism: Literary Elites and Public Culture.* New Haven, CT: Yale UP, 1998.

Ransom, John Crowe. "Reconstructed but Unregenerate." *I'll Take My Stand: The South and the Agrarian Tradition, by Twelve Southerners.* New York: Harper and Brothers, 1930. 1–27.

Rasco, Burton. Rev. of *Now in November,* by Josephine Johnson. *Books* 23 Sept. 1934: 3.

———. "So Big." Rev. of *So Big,* by Edna Ferber. *New York Tribune* 16 March 1924: 19.

Raub, Patricia. *Yesterday's Stories: Popular Women's Novels of the Twenties and Thirties.* Westport, CT: Greenwood, 1994.

Reed, James. *From Public Vice to Private Virtue: The Birth Control Movement and American Society since* 1830. New York: Basic, 1978.

Report of the Commission on Country Life. New York: Sturgis and Walton, 1911.

Review of *Weeds,* by Edith Summers Kelley. *Literary Digest International Book Review* Dec. 1923: 74.

Rich, S. L. Rev. of *Wild Geese,* by Martha Ostenso. *Boston Transcript* 31 Oct. 1925: 3.

Riddell, John. *In the Worst Possible Taste.* [With illustrations by Miguel Covarrubias.] London: Scribner's, 1932.

Roberts, Elizabeth Madox. *The Time of Man.* 1926. Lexington: UP of Kentucky, 2000.

Roberts, Nora Ruth. *Three Radical Women Writers: Meridel Le Sueur, Tillie Olsen, and Josephine Herbst.* New York: Garland, 1996.

Robideau, Henri. *Flapjacks and Photographs: The Life Story of the Famous Camp Cook and Photographer Mattie Gunterman.* Vancouver, BC: Polestar, 1995.

Rodgers, Lawrence R. Introduction. *Roast Beef, Medium: The Business Adventures of Emma McChesney.* By Edna Ferber. Urbana: U of Illinois P, 2001. ix–xxvii.

Roedder, Karsten. "Norse America in Fiction." *Bookman* 62 (Dec. 1925): 493–95.

Roediger, David. *The Wages of Whiteness: Race and the Making of the American Working Class.* London: Verso, 1991.

Roosevelt, Theodore. Introduction. *Report of the Commission on Country Life.* New York: Sturgis and Walton, 1911.

———. "On American Motherhood." [Speech.] Washington, DC: 13 March 1905. <http://www.nationalcenter.org/TRooseveltMotherhood.html>.

Rose, Phyllis. "Modernism: The Case of Willa Cather." *Modernism Reconsidered.* Ed. Robert Kiely. Cambridge, MA: Harvard UP, 1983. 123–45.

Rosenberg, Rosalind. *Divided Lives: American Women in the Twentieth Century.* New York: Hill and Wang, 1992.

Rosenblum, Naomi. *A History of Women Photographers.* New York: Abbeville, 1994.

Rosenblum, Naomi, and Susan Fillin-Yeh. *Documenting a Myth: The South as Seen by Three Women Photographers, Chansonetta Stanley Emmons, Doris Ulmann, Bayard Wooten,* 1910–1940. Portland, OR: Douglas F. Cooley Memorial Art Gallery, 1998.

Rosenfeld, Rachel Ann. *Farm Women: Work, Farm, and Family in the United States.* Chapel Hill: U of North Carolina P, 1985.

Ross, Edward A. "The Causes of Race Superiority." *Annals of the American Academy of Political and Social Science* 19 (July 1901): 67–89.

Rothman, Sheila M. *Woman's Proper Place: A History of Changing Ideals and Practices,* 1870 *to the Present.* New York: Basic, 1978.

Rubin, Joan Shelley. *The Making of Middlebrow Culture.* Chapel Hill: U of North Carolina P, 1992.

Rutherford, Janice Williams. *Selling Mrs. Consumer: Christine Frederick and the Rise of Household Efficiency.* Athens: U of Georgia P, 2003.

Rydell, Robert W. *World of Fairs: The Century-of-Progress Expositions.* Chicago: U of Chicago P, 1993.

Sachs, Carolyn E. *Gendered Fields: Rural Women, Agriculture, and Environment.* Boulder, CO: Westview, 1996.

Santmyer, Helen. "A Pageant of Sisterhood." *Rural Manhood* 6.9 (Nov. 1915): 333–37.

Scanlon, Jennifer. *Inarticulate Longings: The* Ladies' Home Journal, *Gender, and the Promises of Consumer Culture.* New York: Routledge, 1995.

"Sends Lewis Hat, Size 207." *New York Times* 15 May 1926: 8.

Shannon, Anna W. "Biographical Afterword." *Call Home the Heart,* by Olive Tilford Dargan. 1932. Old Westbury, NY: Feminist P, 1983. 433–46.

Shapiro, Henry D. *Appalachia on Our Mind: The Southern Mountains and Mountaineers in the American Consciousness,* 1870–1920. Chapel Hill: U of North Carolina P, 1978.

Sherman, Caroline. "The Development of American Rural Fiction." *Agricultural History* 12.1 (1938): 67–76.

Sherman, Stuart P. "Fresh Harvest." Rev. of *Weeds,* by Edith Summers Kelley. *Literary Review* 15 Dec. 1923: 363.

Shi, David E. *The Simple Life: Plain Living and High Thinking in American Culture.* New York: Oxford UP, 1985.

A Short History of the Ladies' Home Journal. Philadelphia: Curtis, 1953.

Shortridge, James R. *The Middle West: Its Meaning in American Culture.* Lawrence: UP of Kansas, 1989.

Shulman, Stuart W. "The Progressive Era Farm Press: A Primer on a Neglected Source of Journalism History." *Journalism History* 25.1 (1999): 26–35.

"Silas Lapham's Wife and Mother." *Progressive Farmer and Southern Farm Gazette* 2 Feb. 1913: 17.

Simpson, Jeffrey. *The Way Life Was: A Photographic Treasury from the American Past.* New York: Praeger, 1974.

Simpson, Lewis P. "The Sexuality of History." *Southern Review* 20 (1984): 785–802.

"Sinclair Lewis's Hornet's Nest." *Literary Digest* 89 (29 May 1926): 27–28.

Slavick, William H. "Taken with a Long-Handled Spoon: The Roberts Papers and Letters." *Southern Review* 20 (1984): 752–73.

Slotkin, Richard. *Regeneration through Violence: The Myth of the American Frontier, 1600–1800.* Middletown, CT: Wesleyan UP, 1973.

Smith, Henry Nash. *Virgin Land: The American West as Symbol and Myth.* Cambridge, MA: Harvard UP, 1950.

Snyder, Robert E. "Marion Post Wolcott: Photographing FSA Cheesecake." *Developing Dixie: Modernization in a Traditional Society.* Ed. Winifred B. Moore, Joseph F. Tripp, and Lyon G. Tyler. New York: Greenwood, 1988. 299–309.

"So Big." Rev. of *So Big,* by Edna Ferber. *Times Literary Supplement* 13 March 1924: 158.

Sowinska, Suzanne. "Writing across the Color Line: White Women Writers and the 'Negro Question' in the Gastonia Novels." *Radical Revisions: Rereading 1930s Culture.* Ed. Bill Mullen and Sherry Lee Linkon. Urbana: U of Illinois P, 1996. 120–43.

Springer, Gertrude. "The Seasons Come to Maine." Rev. of *As the Earth Turns,* by Gladys Hasty Carroll. *Survey Graphic* 22 (July 1933): 381.

Stage, Sarah, and Virginia Bramble Vincenti, eds. *Rethinking Home Economics: Women and the History of a Profession.* Ithaca, NY: Cornell UP, 1997.

Stange, Maren. *Symbols of Ideal Life: Social Documentary Photography in America, 1890–1950.* Cambridge: Cambridge UP, 1989.

Stein, Rachel. *Shifting the Ground: American Women Writers' Revisions of Nature, Gender, and Race.* Charlottesville: UP of Virginia, 1997.

Steinbeck, John. *The Grapes of Wrath.* New York: Viking, 1939.

Steinberg, Salme Harju. *Reformer in the Marketplace: Edward W. Bok and the* Ladies' Home Journal. Baton Rouge: Louisiana State UP, 1979.

Stott, William. *Documentary Expression and Thirties America.* New York: Oxford UP, 1973.

Strauss, Juliet Virginia [The Country Contributor]. "Ideas of a Plain Country Woman." *Ladies' Home Journal* 22–35 (1905–1918).

———. *The Ideas of a Plain Country Woman.* New York: Doubleday, 1908.

Strunsky, Simeon. "About Books, More or Less: As to Best Sellers." *New York Times Book Review* 11 Dec. 1927: 4.

Strychacz, Thomas. *Modernism, Mass Culture, and Professionalism.* Cambridge: Cambridge UP, 1993.

Stuart, Henry Longan. "Miss Roberts' Poignant Chronicle of the American Peasantry." *New York Times* 22 Aug. 1926: 7.

Swartz, Mark Evan. *Oz before the Rainbow: L. Frank Baum's* The Wonderful Wizard of Oz *on Stage and Screen to* 1939. Baltimore: Johns Hopkins UP, 2002.

Szalay, Michael. *New Deal Modernism: American Literature and the Invention of the Welfare State.* Durham, NC: Duke UP, 2000.

Tagg, John. *The Burden of Representation: Essays on Photographies and Histories.* Minneapolis: U of Minnesota P, 1988.

Thompson, Stephanie Lewis. *Influencing America's Tastes: Realism in the Works of Wharton, Cather, and Hurst.* Gainesville: UP of Florida, 2002.

Thornton, Gene. "Ulmann Forces a New Look at Pictorialism." *New York Times* 12 Jan. 1975: 121.

Tompkins, Jane. *Sensational Designs: The Cultural Work of American Fiction, 1790–1860.* New York: Oxford UP, 1985.

Townsend, R. D. "The Book Table." Rev. of *Wild Geese,* by Martha Ostenso. *Outlook* 141 (25 Nov. 1929): 485.

Tugwell, Rexford Guy. "The Woman in the Sunbonnet." *Nation* 120 (21 Jan. 1925): 73–74.

Tyler, Pamela. "The Ideal Rural Southern Woman as Seen by *Progressive Farmer* in the 1930s." *Southern Studies* 20 (1981): 278–96.

Ulmann, Doris. *A Book of Portraits of the Faculty of the Medical Department of the Johns Hopkins University, Baltimore.* Baltimore: Johns Hopkins P, 1922.

———. *The Faculty of the College of Physicians and Surgeons, Columbia University in the City of New York: Twenty-four Portraits.* New York: Hoeber, 1919.

———. *A Portrait Gallery of American Editors.* New York: Rudge, 1925.

Van Doren, Dorothy. "The Dispassionate Shepherds." Rev. of *As the Earth Turns,* by Gladys Hasty Carroll. *Nation* 136 (21 June 1933): 704.

Van Zile, Edward S. "Our Barnyard School of Fiction." *New York Times Book Review* 4 May 1924: 2.

Walbridge, Earle F. "The Book Table: Four New Novels." *Outlook* 144 (8 Sept. 1926): 57.

Walker, Charles R. "The Autumn Novel Harvest." Rev. of *The Time of Man,* by Elizabeth Madox Roberts *Independent* 117 (6 Nov. 1926): 535.

Walker, Melissa. *All We Knew Was to Farm: Rural Women in the Upcountry South, 1919–1941.* Baltimore: Johns Hopkins UP, 2000.

Walter, Gerry, and Suzanne Wilson. "Silent Partners: Women in Farm Magazine Success Stories, 1934–1991." *Rural Sociology* 61 (1996): 227–48.

Walton, Edith H. "Book Parade." Rev. of *Now in November,* by Josephine Johnson. *Forum and Century* 92 (Nov. 1934): iv.

———. "A First Novel of Fine Distinction." Rev. of *Now in November,* by Josephine Johnson. *New York Times* 16 Sept. 1934: 6.

Warren, Dale. "Doris Ulmann: Photographer-in-Waiting." *Bookman* 72 (Oct. 1930): 129–44.

Warren, Robert Penn. "Elizabeth Madox Roberts: Life Is from Within." Roberts, *The Time of Man.* xvii–xxix.

Watts, Sarah. *Rough Rider in the White House: Theodore Roosevelt and the Politics of Desire.* Chicago: U Chicago P, 2003.

Webb Company Records. Minnesota Historical Society. St. Paul, Minnesota.
"What May Happen Here After the War." [Photomontage with text.] *Ladies' Home Journal* Jan. 1917: 3.
Whisnant, David E. *All That Is Native and Fine: The Politics of Culture in an American Region.* Chapel Hill: U of North Carolina P, 1983.
White, William Allen. "Edna Ferber." *World's Work* 59 (June 1930): 36–38.
Williams, Raymond. *The Country and the City.* New York: Oxford UP, 1973.
———. *Keywords: A Vocabulary of Culture and Society.* New York: Oxford UP, 1983.
———. *The Politics of Modernism: Against the New Conformists.* London: Verso, 1989.
Wilson, Christopher P. "The Rhetoric of Consumption: Mass-Market Magazines and the Demise of the Gentle Reader, 1880–1920." *The Culture of Consumption* Ed. Richard Wightman Fox and T. J. Jackson Lears. New York: Pantheon, 1983. 39–64.
Wilson, Warren H. "Social Life in the Country." *Annals of the American Academy of Political and Social Science* 40 (March 1912): 119–30.
Winter, Alice Ames. "They Starve for Beauty." *Ladies' Home Journal* 42 (March 1925): 35+.
Wood, Grant. *Revolt against the City.* Iowa City, IA: Clio, 1935.
Wood, James Playsted. *Magazines in the United States.* New York: Ronald Press, 1970.
Wright, Richard, and Edwin Rosskam. *Twelve Million Black Voices: A Folk History of the Negro in the United States.* New York: Viking, 1941.
Yablon, Nick. "The Metropolitan Life in Ruins." *American Quarterly* 56 (2004): 309–47.
Yaeger, Patricia. *Dirt and Desire: Reconstructing Southern Women's Writing, 1930–1990.* Chicago: U of Chicago P, 1990.

INDEX